Microcomputers in
African Development

Microcomputers in African Development

Critical Perspectives

EDITED BY

**Suzanne Grant Lewis
and Joel Samoff**

Westview Press
BOULDER • SAN FRANCISCO • OXFORD

Permission to reprint revised versions of various portions of text from Bennetta Jules-Rosette, *Terminal Signs: Computers and Social Change in Africa* (Berlin: Mouton Gruyter Publishers, 1990), pp. 288–310, in Chapter 4 is gratefully acknowledged.

This Westview softcover edition is printed on acid-free paper and bound in library-quality, coated covers that carry the highest rating of the National Association of State Textbook Administrators, in consultation with the Association of American Publishers and the Book Manufacturers' Institute.

Published in 1992 in the United States of America by Westview Press, Inc., 5500 Central Avenue, Boulder, Colorado 80301-2847, and in the United Kingdom by Westview Press, 36 Lonsdale Road, Summertown, Oxford OX2 7EW

Library of Congress Cataloging-in-Publication Data
Microcomputers in African development : critical perspectives /
   edited by Suzanne Grant Lewis and Joel Samoff.
      p. cm.
   Includes bibliographical references (p.) and index.
   ISBN 0-8133-7934-2
   1. Microcomputers—Social aspects—Africa. I. Lewis, Suzanne
Grant. II. Samoff, Joel.
QA76.M532 1992
303.48′34′096—dc20   91-2047
                                                                              CIP

Printed and bound in the United States of America

⊚ The paper used in this publication meets the requirements
    of the American National Standard for Permanence of Paper
    for Printed Library Materials Z39.48-1984.

10   9   8   7   6   5   4   3   2   1

To

Paul

and

Rachel

Contents

Tables and Figures

About the Editors
and Contributors

Bruce J. Berman is professor of political studies at Queen's University in Kingston, Ontario, and has published on computers and political aspects of science and technology in *Science as Culture, Artificial Intelligence and Society,* and *World Futures.* He is the author of *Control and Crisis in Colonial Kenya* (1990).

Craig Calhoun is professor of sociology and director of international programs at the University of North Carolina at Chapel Hill. His recent work includes a book on the 1989 Chinese student movement and numerous articles concerning nationalism and social movements.

John A. Daly is acting director of USAID's Office of Research. He has spent twenty years in development assistance after ten years of employment in the computer industry.

Pamela F. DeLargy is a research associate at the Carolina Population Center, University of North Carolina, whose recent work has focused on politics in population and health issues in the Horn of Africa. She is currently working on a USAID population project in Yemen.

Suzanne Grant Lewis is a Science, Engineering, and Diplomacy Fellow of the American Association for the Advancement of Science. She is assigned to the Bureau for Africa in USAID where she conducts analyses on the social and political aspects of education assistance programs, with particular attention to gender issues.

Kedmon N. Hungwe is a lecturer in the Faculty of Education, University of Zimbabwe, where he teaches courses in curriculum theory as well as media and technology. He has published several articles on media and technology.

Bennetta Jules-Rosette is professor of sociology at the University of California, San Diego. Her research interests include semiotic studies of tourism, tourist art, religious discourse, and new technologies in Africa. Her most recent book is *Terminal Signs: Computers and Social Change in Africa* (1990).

Joel Samoff is a visiting scholar at the Center for African Studies, Stanford University, and a consultant to the ILO-UNESCO Interagency Task Force on Austerity, Adjustment, and Human Resources. He is also a consultant to the Swedish International Development Authority on development, education, and microcomputers. His most recent book is *Education and Social Transition in the Third World* (1990), with Martin Carnoy.

Mohammed Sheya is director of technology development and policy at the Tanzania Commission for Science and Technology (COSTECH). He served on the Faculty of Engineering at the University of Dar es Salaam, prior to joining COSTECH.

1

Introduction

Suzanne Grant Lewis and Joel Samoff

The arrival of microcomputers in Africa is both a trivial, technical process and a profound, political event. It is trivial in that the microcomputer is just another tool in a large set of tools imported from the North Atlantic. The large and small problems accompanying this new tool are to a great extent the same as for other imported tools. It is profoundly political in that the importation of microcomputers has become a central component in the external direction of African economies and of African affairs more generally. Even more, the *process* of introducing microcomputers is an integral part of the specification of the constructs, the language, and thus meanings in the development discourse.

Our concern here is to explore that introduction process. For that, we shall rely primarily on empirical studies of the arrival and dispersion of microcomputers[1] in particular African settings. To do so is not to advocate a raw and uncritical empiricism, but rather to acknowledge the limited development of relevant theory in this arena, to reject the commonly asserted disjunction between what is theoretical and what is empirical, and to insist that drawing inferences and elaborating theory require integrating the concrete and the abstract.

The Setting

The context for the importation of microcomputers into Africa is of course the contemporary underdevelopment of Africa, including both moments of apparent economic progress and times of economic crisis, increasing debt, and stagnating or declining production. Hence, although reviewing the underdevelopment process and its literature is beyond the scope of this book, it is essential to understand that in examining African experiences with microcomputers, we are dealing with dependent states conditioned by the broader global system.

The late 1980s and 1990s are a time of widespread economic difficulty throughout the continent. It is striking that this economic distress is so pervasive, crossing not only national boundaries but also very different political orientations and development strategies. Many, perhaps most Africans are experiencing stagnating or declining standards of living, countries are incurring an increasing and for many a stifling debt burden, and the forces of indirect external intervention have been restored to an earlier level of power and influence. This crisis situation has both extended and entrenched the role of microcomputers in contemporary Africa.

Africa averaged a decline of 2.2 percent in annual GNP per capita growth rate from 1980 through 1988. While the region of Latin America and the Caribbean also recorded a decline in annual per capita GNP, it was only -0.4 percent for that region (UNDP 1991:169). Already low per capita incomes have declined in those same years. There is widespread concern over the social costs of the crisis and the measures taken to address it. In most countries per capita expenditures for health and education have declined. The year 2000 may find Africa with a greater proportion of its population ill and illiterate than at any time since the end of European rule.

The 32 African countries classified as low income by the World Bank (1991) have continued to suffer since the 1970s from poor terms of trade. The commodity wholesale price index for Africa has declined from 100 in 1980 to just 54.2 by the end of 1988 (Lone 1989:3).

Sub-Saharan Africa's debt has grown faster than that of other Third World regions. From $6 billion in 1970, the continent's debt stood at $130 billion in 1987, a 21-fold increase (Jaycox 1989: 36). An extraordinary increase took place between 1985 and 1990. The long-term debt grew in 1990 alone at a rate of 10.7 percent (World Bank 1991:190). The debt service ratio tripled during the 1980s with the service obligation rising to 47% of export revenues in 1988. In response to this untenable level, 25 sub-Saharan African countries rescheduled their debts 105 times between 1980 and 1988 (World Bank 1989c:21).

Economic Reorganization

Since 1980, 34 African countries have been involved in structural adjustment of some sort at a financing level of US$29.9 billion (Wolgin 1990:5). The introduction of micro-computers into government ministries and parastatals in Africa must be understood in terms of these efforts to restructure the public sector on the continent because these efforts define the context to a great extent. Public sector institutions are the primary microcomputer users in all sub-Saharan African countries. The reorganization of African economies at the macroeconomic, sectoral, and institutional levels is of direct interest to understanding the role microcomputers have and might play in furthering African development.

External agencies play a dominant role in formulating, designing, implementing, and monitoring structural adjust-ment programs, resulting in what the African Alternative Framework report characterized as "the gradual erosion of sovereignty" (United Nations Economic Commission for Africa 1989). The goals of structural adjustment, the accompanying emphasis on measuring productivity, and the influence of foreign assistance agencies in the planning and implementing functions of the country help explain the assumptions and rationale behind much of the foreign financed microcomputer acquisitions. The DeLargy and Calhoun case study of the Sudan illustrates this point. At the macroeconomic level alone, the information requirements for monitoring structural adjustment efforts and documenting compliance with loan conditions are immense. Since structural adjustment programs have become a requirement of many bilateral agencies for countries seeking financial assistance, it is important to address, albeit briefly, both structural adjustment and the broader roles of the international financing institutions.

Structural adjustment has in recent years become the generic term used to refer to a more or less extensive economic reorganization stimulated by severe economic problems of varying causes.[2] Although the specific mix of policies varies from one setting to another, this economic reorganization generally includes currency devaluation, reduced public expenditures, reduced subsidies (especially to consumers, intended both to reduce government expenditures and to modify production incentives to favor goods to be exported), reduction or elimination of price controls (intended to bring domestic prices closer to world market prices), revised trade policies intended to encourage exports, revised fiscal, especially tax, policies intended to increase government revenue, new or increased user charges for public services, privatization of both enterprises and social services, and institutional reforms required to implement these policies.

As we have noted, *structural adjustment* also refers to the cluster of policies recommended by the World Bank, the International Monetary Fund (IMF), and other organizations and more or less explicitly required for the provision of external assistance.[3] Although the World Bank differentiates among stabilization, structural adjustment, and adjustment policies, it acknowledges that the general use of these terms "is often imprecise and inconsistent" (World Bank, Africa Region 1990:21).

Structural adjustment is in practice generally a two-stage process of macro-economic reform, primarily financed through the IMF and the World Bank. Initial stabilization programs are designed as short run means of addressing substantial balance of payment deficits and foreign exchange shortages by reducing the government deficit (through increased tax revenues or decreased expenditures) and shifting demand from foreign products to domestically-produced products, usually through a currency devaluation. Subsequent measures are aimed at increasing supply over the medium term. Those measures may include policy reforms in virtually any macro-economic area, including trade policy, public sector management, fiscal policy, financial sector management, and deregulation. External agencies commonly require additional devaluations, changes in the allocation of foreign exchange, parastatal divestiture, reduction in import tariffs, elimination of price controls, new and increased user fees for government provided services, and the privatization of agricultural marketing and other functions. While some of these measures are intended to affect the economy broadly, others are limited to particular sectors and supported by sectoral (rather than structural) adjustment loans.

Operationally, the loan funds are commonly disbursed in periodic partial payments upon IMF/World Bank agreement that the government has met specified conditions negotiated at the start of the program. Stabilization and structural/ sectoral adjustment programs involve comprehensive external access to a country's monetary and fiscal plans and records to an unprecedented extent. It is now common practice for the World Bank to conduct a public expenditures review, an in-depth examination of all accounts and budgetary procedures of the central and local governments. Such a review often suggests specific policy changes required as conditions for additional financing.

The correspondence of economic reorganization with increased diffusion of microcomputers becomes clearer when one examines the extent of foreign assistance agency involvement in information technology (IT) procurement and application. A review of World Bank lending activities in information management and technology applications in all developing countries made two important points.

> First, World Bank financing and assistance in information technology has become quite pervasive and diffused and has not been adequately acknowledged and studied so far. A recent survey of IT components in Bank lending

for fiscal year 1989 showed that significant IT components are present in about 90 percent of all lending
operations. In addition, and perhaps more significantly,
the volume of Bank lending has been growing since 1981
at an average annual rate of nearly 30 percent.

Second, IT components in the Bank's development
assistance are becoming more and more critical to the
success of projects. In many lending operations, the
information management system components constitute
the primary means for addressing the institutional
development and managerial improvement objectives for
whole sectors, programs, and institutions. Often they are
a critical tool for managing and monitoring structural
adjustment programs, for building local capacity for
policy reforms and debt management, and for strength-
ening public sector financial management and account-
ability. Frequently, these components proved to be
significantly attractive to borrowers who were otherwise
reluctant to accept the overall institutional reforms or
technical assistance measures deemed necessary under a
lending operation (Hanna and Schware 1990:255).

The authors' second point deserves reiteration: not only is
loan-financed IT essential for the success of structural adjustment, it is frequently used to sell the structural adjustment
program.

The international financial institutions are not alone in
insisting on policy reform. Bilateral assistance agencies are
also financing structural adjustment programs in Africa. The
U.S. Agency for International Development (USAID) funded
42 separate policy reform programs in 22 African countries
between 1984 and 1989 for a total commitment of US$760
million (Wolgin 1990:39). USAID finances sectoral adjustment
programs which call for policy reforms in a particular economic sector such as agriculture. These stress improvements in
sector productivity, efficiency, and equity. USAID's sectoral
adjustment support is usually associated directly or indirectly
with World Bank programs.

Efforts to build consensus among foreign assistance
agencies on needed policy reforms have been energetic. From
the perspective of the assistance agencies, the goal is to
enhance the impact of one agency's funds by linking that

support to another agency's program. The Special Program Assistance (SPA) of the World Bank promotes coordination among transnational and national assistance agencies through the pooling of funds and through agreement on the general orientation and specific terms of adjustment programs in individual countries as well as procurement and disbursement procedures. This coordinated effort at restructuring African economies is considered by most agencies a positive, efficient strategy. One senior economist in USAID's Bureau for Africa goes so far as to proclaim it a revolution empowering the masses and takes responsibility and considerable credit when he proudly claims that it is

> a revolution imposed from without, by a group of do-
> nors and international institutions who supported the
> establishment of elite rule in the first place, and now,
> amid the ashes of the models on which regimes were
> built, have reversed ground, and are dismantling these
> regimes piece by piece, parastatal by parastatal, regula-
> tion by regulation (Wolgin 1990:1).

From the African perspective, those links among foreign assistance agencies often seem more collusion than cooperation, intended at least in part to preclude African attempts to constrain or avoid the conditions imposed by one agency through the support provided by another agency. With reference to the dismantling of elite structures, both foreign assistance agencies and international computer vendors are depending on, and sometime aggressively building, national elites to implement structural adjustment programs. At the same time African governments are also relying on national elites to assert at least some sovereignty in the face of increased foreign penetration. Reliance on a local elite in the informational/computational sphere may be perceived as a necessary but temporary stage. The dynamic roles of local computer elites in the Tanzanian context is explored in Chapter 3. The possibilities for changing the role of international and bilateral agencies in the introduction of microcomputers is explored by Daly in the chapter, "Foreign Assistance

Agencies as Advocates and Innovators." Unfortunately, his prognosis is not hopeful.

Microcomputers as a Technical and Trivial Development

Microcomputers are the latest development fad, one in a long line of such technological fads. The technology is exciting because outsiders and those Africans best connected with the outside find microcomputers exciting and seductive and justify their introduction in terms of improved management through the more systematic control of information flows and storage, all at reduced costs. Often, this general faith in the use of microcomputers to manage information is not accompanied by specific attention to exactly what information is flowing and in which direction, as Berman points out in the chapter, "The State, Computers, and African Development: The Information Non-Revolution." Consequently, although clearly microcomputers are capable of facilitating the management of information, they may prove to be quite unsuitable for managing the particular information that is most important to those who acquire the microcomputers. Similarly, in the absence of specific attention to the directions and pathways of the flow of information, microcomputers may in practice render more, not less, difficult the control of the information flows deemed most important and may indeed institutionalize particular transfers of information that are quite inconsistent with the goals of those who acquire the microcomputers.

Technical developments in microcomputer design have increased enthusiasm for their use throughout the developing world, including Africa. First, the size and cost of microcomputers in relation to larger systems make them attractive. Government and university computers in Africa in the 1970s and 1980s were generally large and old and often suffered from lengthy backlogs. Microcomputers offer newer and faster technology in a smaller, seemingly less expensive package.[4]

Second, the staffs of organizations requiring large computer processing must travel to the centralized installation to conduct work and pay for most computing services. Having in-house microcomputers is more convenient and more secure than using a large computer in the capital city or sending the data overseas for processing. Third, computational power and memory capacity continue to increase as cost decreases, making microcomputers appropriate for a wider range of uses, including scientific applications, than was previously possible. Fourth, many of the environmental problems that troubled early microcomputer use have been solved through improved ruggedness of the machines and their peripherals. Battery- and solar-powered options make use in rural areas of Africa feasible. Fifth, the installation, repair, and maintenance of microcomputer systems can now be routinely performed within some countries as local microcomputer expertise and technical capabilities have developed. A review of the trade magazine, *Computers in Africa,* suggests that at least 24 countries in sub-Saharan Africa have microcomputer vendors offering maintenance.

A sixth technical feature that makes microcomputers attractive for Africa is the increased friendliness of human-machine interfaces, rendering microcomputers relatively easy for non-specialists to use. Seventh, since a wide range of applications is available commercially, little or no programming expertise is necessary for many uses.

These recent developments that have made microcomputers more accessible to non-specialists have made more manageable the special problems of adopting and mastering an unfamiliar approach to information in settings where few people have had prior experience with advanced technology or automation in general. Software can be adapted to a local institution's needs through a process that is often understood as fundamentally technical in character. That is, by defining the task as one of learning a new technology (rather than developing a new sense of what information is and of the links between information and power) a largely technical strategy is plausible: use the new technology itself to modify its form to be less forbidding and alienating. This eminently flexible technology makes computing power more accessible to more organizations and to a greater range of individuals within those organizations.

In short, it is possible to address the arrival of microcomputers in Africa in the same way that individuals and organizations have addressed the arrival of improved seed strains, or solar-powered pumps, or photocopiers. The new technology is understood as a new instrument or tool. Its own content and its inherent ability to influence not only the process and direction of communications but also their substance can be largely ignored. Contributors to this book reject this approach. For example, Jules-Rosette's discussion of the Nairobi Handicraft Cooperative's experience argues that the process, direction, and substance of communication may indeed change with the application of microcomputer technology (see "Fragile and Progressive Computer Contracts in Kenya and Ivory Coast: New Social Forms in the Workplace").

It is important to note that even within the above narrow understanding of the dispersion of microcomputers in Africa, many of the problematic characteristics of computing that are ostensibly technical persist. The diffusion of new information technologies in Africa has been "sporadic and generally confined to large urban centres" (UNESCO 1989:89). Notwithstanding their reduced cost, greater ruggedness, and more accessible software, microcomputers often remain the domain of a specialized elite. That elite maintains the mystique of computing, enhancing its own authority, status, and remuneration. The chapter "Microcomputer Adoption in Tanzania and the Rise of a Professional Elite" documents this phenomenon in the Tanzanian context. Computing remains heavily dependent on external expertise and equipment, and thus a costly enterprise that increases rather than reduces the demand for scarce foreign exchange. This continued reliance on external expertise, established within a generally dependent political economy, tends to entrench, even rigidify, both hardware and software incompatibilities, further undermining the local ability to set goals and priorities for the uses of the new technology. That in turn makes it even more difficult to develop a local capability to modify the technology to suit local needs and to participate in the development of successor technology.

Microcomputerization as a Profound, Political Process

The deep-seated, sociopolitical aspects of microcomputer introduction are less obvious and scarcely resemble the original naïve, enthusiastic predictions of the information revolution. In an exploration of how computers exacerbate the "information gap" along geographical, gender, occupational, and even generational lines, contributors to the special issue of the *Journal of Communication* (Siefert, Gerbner, and Fisher 1989) reveal the invisibility of the socially constructed information poverty in North America. Numerous authors argue that the designs of the information technology, as well as the meanings which the user brings to the machines, serve to reproduce old patterns of power and privilege. A design may determine what meanings and uses can be accommodated more readily than others (Curry Jensen 1989). Bowers (1990) also explores the less than obvious biases of computers, arguing that they help reinforce a mindset—a Cartesian epistemology—that has made a considerable negative contribution to the ecological crisis.

Likewise, the arrival of microcomputers in Africa carries profound political implications precisely because the technology has to do with processing information, because the technology is highly regarded by the outsiders most influential in Africa, and because access to and use of it is limited to a select few.

Far beyond its use in monitoring development projects and reducing the reliance on larger computers, this technology has the potential to play a dramatic role in contemporary Africa by affecting the world view, conditioning the interactions between Africa and the world outside, specifying the language and symbols of both local and local-global discourse, advantaging particular groups while disadvantaging others, and entrenching (rather than transforming) economic, social, and political relations. These themes are explored in this book through analyses of specific contexts which, we hope, serve to highlight the complexity of the issues.

Microcomputers in Africa

Microcomputers have been entering Africa since the early 1980s. Their entry routes have been numerous, some routes more important than others. Thus far, foreign assistance agencies have been the primary source of finance for this process, both directly and indirectly.

As we have noted, many externally assisted projects incorporate the acquisition of microcomputers. In some projects microcomputers have played a direct role (for example, in aiding management of foreign debts, enhancing demographic data collection, or assisting instruction). Other projects have required microcomputers to record, store, and manipulate data and to monitor progress toward short- and long-term objectives. A less direct entry route that was especially important in the early phases of the arrival process was through externally assisted project personnel. Even when projects did not specifically require microcomputers, often the foreign staff, accustomed to using microcomputers in their home setting, brought microcomputers with them. Aware that microcomputers carried status as well as utility, some, perhaps many, expatriates left their hardware and software when they returned home. They left as well an important set of symbols and a new social meaning. To have a microcomputer was to be among the highest status experts. For the African partici-pants in these projects came the expectation that it was normal, ordinary, unexceptional for project staff to own (or rather, have control over) a microcomputer. Subsequent project proposals assumed the provision of additional micro-computers.

African governments established a second set of entry routes for microcomputers. In some settings the new equip-ment was acquired to reduce the reliance on larger and aging computers. There has also been replacement on a smaller scale, as where microcomputers have replaced accounting machines in banks and parastatal firms. Governments have also acquired microcomputers for particular specialized uses, both within and outside externally assisted projects. Less commonly, governments have purchased microcomputers for use in educational institutions, though far more to teach computing and programming than to play a major role in instruction.

As the barriers to microcomputer importation have been reduced, both private firms and individuals have acquired them for a wide range of uses. Individuals who have traveled overseas—especially those enrolled for advanced degrees in settings where microcomputers have become standard tools for their fellow students—now frequently return with microcomputers.

Initially, most microcomputers that arrived in Africa were purchased from overseas vendors, even where there were local sources of supply. That, of course, reflected the foreign initiative in and funding of microcomputer acquisitions and the tendency and often legal requirement for countries receiving assistance to purchase equipment from suppliers in the country financing their purchase. A major consequence of this process was a proliferation of manufacturers, types, and models that were generally incompatible with each other and that had little if any local service or technical support.

It has not been uncommon for microcomputers to be acquired in the pattern more common elsewhere for larger computers: as a complete package of hardware, software, service, and perhaps support. While that practice may have facilitated particular uses of the new technology, in general it vitiated many of the advantages of smaller over larger computers. The acquired packages (both hardware and software) were likely to become the exclusive domain of a very small set of computer experts. Like the installation and local adaptation of the hardware, the software—generally special-purpose programs developed for a particular institution and a particular set of uses—required rather advanced expertise to modify. That in turn maintained the mystical and forbidding character of computing and certainly discouraged, often directly prohibited, individual experimentation and innovation in microcomputer use.

More recently, both public and private purchasers of microcomputers have turned to local suppliers, generally the agents of overseas vendors.) These are only sometimes the hardware manufacturers. For example Lotus uses a London firm to distribute and support its software products in Africa. That firm appoints a network of authorized dealers.) While local acquisition provides the funds to build capacity in service and technical support, it also tends to limit the range of both the hardware and software that are easily available. All too frequently, it seems, the particular models offered to the African market are either outdated or not well suited to local needs or both. Technical support and training for local vendor staff is infrequent and inadequate: a Tanzanian vendor was selling local area network technology a year before the firm had any familiarity with data communications or with the particular technology being sold; the Olivetti M40 microcomputer line continued to be sold in Tanzania long after the manufacturer ceased production.

Acquisition from both foreign and local sources in the early 1980s, was at high, often very high, prices. Neither channel facilitated price competition among manufacturers and vendors, and there were few Africans with experience and skill in negotiating discounted prices directly with the original suppliers. The experience of the Tanzania Housing Bank (THB) provides an example of misrepresentation at exorbitant cost. In 1984 THB purchased four microcomputers, for approximately $32,439. each, on the incorrect understanding that the machines were compatible, cheaper, and more powerful than the auditing machines they were to replace (Grant Lewis 1988a:216-223).

The arrival of microcomputers is a recent process everywhere in Africa. It is impossible to provide precise data on the number of microcomputers in most African countries, or on particular firms' shares of the African market. Publicly available information on computer usage is not available. Government and industry statistics are limited in supply and accuracy, as Schware found to be the case in the global software industry in industrialized and developing countries (Schware 1989:5). It is still more difficult in African countries with comparatively small and less documented industrial records. The Tanzania national inventory reported in the Appendix to Chapter 3 is a rarity and is included in part to make such work part of the published history of computing in Africa. Even the annual country surveys by the trade journal *Computers in Africa* rely on stories of individual firms or government departments rather than providing a national overview. Nevertheless, some illustrations may help the reader. A 1982 survey found just 37 microcomputers in use in Africa in projects funded by USAID (Berge and Ingle 1982). In 1986 Grant Lewis and Sheya found nearly that many in USAID projects in Tanzania alone (See the Appendix to Chapter 3). It is estimated that in 1981, Botswana had six personal computers. In 1990, there were at least 300 Apple II computers, 500 Apple Macintosh sites, and 45 Novell local area networks (LANs), varying in size from four to 70 machines (*Computers in Africa* 1989 3(5):36; 1990 4(9):26). The country has more than 30 computer dealers. In Zimbabwe *Computers in Africa* estimated that investment in new computer equipment for 1989 was US$16.4 million (Z$40 million), for new software US$7.4 million (Z$18 million), and maintenance contracts US$4.1 million (Z$10 million) (*Computers in Africa*, August 1990:19). The survey by Price Waterhouse (1986) in Kenya highlighted the rapid growth in the first half of the 1980s in Kenya's computer industry, particularly the microcomputer end of the market. Sixteen vendors were operating in 1986, seven of them having opened since 1984. Such expansion is uneven across the continent, however, as coverage in *Computers in Africa* suggests.[5] Sahelian and Central African countries are noticeably absent from the news. The growth seems to be concentrated in eastern, southern and parts of west Africa.

The Technology of the Information Revolution

The late 1970s and early 1980s saw a profusion of studies of computers and projections of their impact on industrialized society. These writings were in part a response to Daniel Bell's predictions of profound social changes in *The Coming of Post-Industrial Society* (1973). In post-industrial society, he argued, "knowledge and information become strategic and

transforming resources of the society, just as capital and labor
have been . . . of the industrial society" (Bell 1979:23). "Information Age," "microelectronics revolution," and similar
phrases became the stock of the social commentators.

With time, students of microcomputers came to puzzle over
what it all meant for the poor countries at the periphery of the
world system. Early assessments were optimistic: authors
spoke enthusiastically of the promise of the microelectronics
revolution to bring about a New World Order. Strategies for
Third World participation were proposed. Expanded use of
microcomputers was seen as part of this transformation
strategy, delivering the revolutionary promise of the new
technology in a package deemed both technologically and
economically appropriate, and compatible with the "small is
beautiful" philosophy of which Schumacher wrote (1973).

Many promises are attributed to the technology in the
microcomputer literature, which follows one of two directions.
One views microcomputers as tools of liberation with the
power to transform society. Microcomputers are purported to
offer liberation from underdevelopment, from centralized
hierarchical structures, and from individual repression. A
second approach stresses their potential as management tools
that can streamline and improve the decision making process
and lead to greater organizational efficiency and substantial
economic benefits.

Tools of Liberation

Microcomputers are seen by some as the perfect tools for
bridging the information gap between North and South by
offering easy and universal access to information at low cost
(Bell 1979). People speak earnestly of introducing microcomputers into villages in a manner similar to the introduction of
radios (James 1982). The journal *Development Forum* entitled its
tenth anniversary colloquium "A Speculation on the Barefoot
Microchip—Communications for development at the village
level" and published a special issue.

Microcomputers have been touted as populist tools with
the potential to democratize the workplace and society in both

the industrialized and developing world (Garrett and Wright 1981). By allowing widespread access to information through microcomputer networks, communication would be stream-lined, society would benefit from enriched discourse, and all workers could participate in decision making. According to this argument, the microcomputer is democratic by nature since it does not discriminate by nationality, race, gender, or age but rather places the same potential in everyone's hands. With computer skills and equipment available to all, comput-ers would be demystified and illegitimate authority exposed. People could take control of their lives by participating in all decisions affecting them.

Microcomputers also promise to improve the quality of work by eliminating the drudgery. Record keeping, tabula-tions, and analyses previously done by hand can be done more swiftly and accurately by the microcomputer. With the touch of a key, records can be retrieved, accounts can be updated, and analyses extended to include new factors. The power of the worker is enhanced at the same time that work conditions are improved.

This enthusiasm has been tempered by more critical observers such as McAnany, who wrote that "the implication that a home computer in every farm house in the Third World will be the answer to what are both political and social problems of long standing is a disturbing continuation of technocratic ideology" (McAnany 1983:24).

Unfortunately, much of the writing about the potential of microcomputers to transform the Third World is just that—proclamations about possibilities with little attention to concrete experiences or to the political and social contexts into which the new technology is being inserted, and assessments of experiences with microcomputers that have at times confused potential with realized contribution (Janssens 1986).

Some African governments have embraced the notion that computers, or information technologies more generally, provide their countries the means to leapfrog ahead and help close the gap between the North and South. Jules-Rosette's exploration of the Ivory Coast government's disposition provides a fine example of this. The populist theme of enhanced quality of life for workers is less frequently embraced. For example in Tanzania, a case examined within this volume, the policies surrounding microcomputer importation and distribution were never articulated in socialist terms. While a product of an ethos of centralized planning, in which the right of the government to make decisions regarding importation was never challenged, the policy in fact led to unplanned microcomputer distribution and use with no attention to developing a national technological capacity.

Tools for Improved Management

The second orientation in this literature focuses on microcomputers as management tools. This perspective has become the dominant one,[6] which is not surprising given the frequency with which the major constraint to development is diagnosed by foreign assistance agencies as weak management skills, the professional background of those making such diagnoses, and the role of these agencies in promoting microcomputer use.

A number of arguments are advanced in the "microcomputers for improved management" approach, all asserting that microcomputers can lead to improved decision making. First, microcomputers are promoted as tools for developing analytical skills among Third World managers. Microcomputers give managers direct access to both information and computing power while eliminating the programming and administrative intermediaries required by large computer installations (Mann 1983:16). With quick and easy access to information and the ability to explore what-if questions, managers can make more realistic and effective decisions.

Second, microcomputer use improves the quality of information used in decision making and in turn makes decision making more efficient and rational. By freeing staff from tedious data management and manual calculations, microcomputers give them more time to work with more information and to examine it more extensively and more critically. The use of analytic rather than merely descriptive information as inputs into decision making improves the process (Schware and Trembour 1980:16). The resulting information is said to be more focused, timely, accurate and flexible (Pinckney, Cohen, and Leonard 1983). In short, greater productivity and efficiency result.

A third claimed benefit of microcomputer use is an improvement in the way information is handled and perceived within the organization. According to this line of argument, the enhanced role for information improves the quality of decision making (Leonard, Cohen, and Pinckney 1983:19). While a number of authors have acknowledged the need for exploring the impact of microcomputers on the quality of decision making (for example Brodman 1985:135,150-4), discussion remains at the level of "difficult to assess."

These themes are certainly taken up by vendors operating in Africa, whose advertisements make productivity claims and link their wares to modern management and rational business decisions. African governments, however, seldom couch their positions in these terms, as Jules-Rosette's discussion of Kenya makes clear. In the case of Tanzania, where one might expect the government to espouse such an approach in recognition of the role the technology might play in enhancing state control, we find that rather than coming out as a proponent of computerization of the government bureaucracy, the policy frequently obstructed such efforts.

Technical-Administrative Evaluations

For the most part, evaluations of the experiences with microcomputers in Africa have focused primarily on improving the way microcomputers are introduced in order to ensure "success." These assessments have been largely concerned with development projects, often commissioned and supported by USAID and other agencies, and conducted by expatriate consultants.[7] Their approach is commonly that of the outsider looking into a very restricted, task-specific domain of microcomputer use. The unit of analysis in such work is the organization, and the emphasis is on planning and evaluating the technological intervention. The principal queries revolve around what government has and has not done.

Although many of the documented experiences are of
African development projects, there are few African voices in
these writings. That these evaluations are commissioned by
external agencies, that those agencies are inclined to rely on
consultants with whom they are familiar, and that the assessments are prepared in a very specialized language and style
leaves little opportunity for Africans to become credible
participants in these discussions or to develop the expertise
needed to undertake and legitimize their own research.

The evaluations usually attempt to generalize beyond the
specific context, offering advice on how best to introduce
microcomputers (for example, Gotsch's typology of
microcomputing environments, Pinckney, Cohen, and
Leonard's "lessons learned," Westcott's "Principles in Introducing Microcomputers" (Ruth and Mann 1987), and Ingle's
"Do's and Don'ts of Acquisition, Installation, and Use" (Ingle,
Berge, and Teisan 1986).

An Externalized World View

We recognize that these writings reflect the nascent state of
the literature, the recency of microcomputer introduction, and
the interests of parties funding such writings. While it is of
course important to have these experiences documented, we
find much about this literature troublesome. The writings
seem to assume that expatriates are and will be making the
decisions as to where, when, and for what purposes microcomputers are to be introduced. Has this really been the case
so far? If this is the situation, then surely it is time to address
that situation critically and to direct the discussion of microcomputers in Africa to a broader audience that reaches beyond
the foreign assistance agencies to include both African governmental and non-governmental organizations and individuals.
Second, the common recourse to a checklist of concerns and
steps to be taken (or avoided) suggests a technician's approach
to the adoption of new technology and emphasizes implementation to the exclusion of larger issues. That inattention to

history, to context, and to politics precludes the development of a solid foundation for understanding the arrival of micro-computers in Africa, their dispersion, and their uses.

Third, the assumptions behind the specification of appro-priate uses of microcomputers remain largely concealed and unchallenged. Surely it is essential to consider critically alternatives to the development assistance agency's measures of appropriateness, success, and failure. Fourth, most of this literature is concerned with how governments and official agencies, both foreign and African, deal with microcomputers. Yet it is apparent that there is a good deal of private initiative, both individual and organizational, in the arrival of microcom-puters in Africa. What is happening in organizations where there is not a long-term team of expatriates advocating microcomputer use? In this dimension, too, we need to broaden the focus and the audience of the discussion.

Finally, although this literature asserts the importance of integrated local participation in setting up microcomputer applications if efforts are to be sustained, it is generally silent on the roles Africans have played and are to play in decisions prior to delivery and installation. There has been little effort to explore how decisions are made on where microcomputers are introduced, into which public and private organizations, for which departments, for what types of workers, and for what tasks. Nor does the literature address systematically the ways in which the structure of the decision-making process (both formal and informal) facilitates or alternatively discour-ages, even precludes local participation. Consequently, it is difficult to know how to interpret even the well-documented "success" stories. Take for example the Kenya Ministry of Agriculture and Livestock Development experience which was evaluated on management grounds on the three stages of introduction, use and institutionalization by Brodman (1985) and for individual productivity gains by Westcott (1985) but which involved heavy expatriate influence for the entire time assessed.

A Rejoinder to "Breathless Naïveté"

This collection developed as a rejoinder to this literature on microcomputers and development—both as a challenge to what Berman calls the "breathlessly naive coverage" (Berman 1987:16) that promises liberation through the microchip, and as an alternative to the management advice and recipes that focus on optimal strategies for introducing microcomputers. Both approaches ignore what appear to be crucial issues: where the technology goes, how it gets there, and what social changes result from the interaction of the technology and the specific context. The management perspective starts with the placement of the technology as a given. The liberation approach fails to recognize that the realization of the potential of microcomputers to decentralize authority and empower workers depends to a very large extent on who gets hold of the technology and by what process.

It is equally important to avoid painting Africa as silent victim to Western imperialism. The case studies presented here highlight the active role of the state, and occasionally non-governmental organizations, individuals, and firms, in the adoption of computer technology and the vested interests of different segments of society in its expanded use.

Thus, our orientation is self-consciously revisionist and critical. Our strategy is to examine microcomputerization in context, attentive to each situation's unique economic, political, and social characteristics. We regard the process of computerization as far more political than technical. On the international stage that process plays an important role in the continuing (under)development of Africa, posing particular challenges for self-reliant and locally-directed development.

Notes

1. In an era in which computers are continually becoming both smaller and more powerful, commentators have offered numerous and not entirely consistent definitions of *microcomputer*. Here, we are concerned with those computers that are small enough to be assigned, managed, and operated by individuals, that are relatively easily moved from one location to another, and that function effectively without special power sources,

climate controls, and highly trained specialized operators. We consider large (often termed "mainframe") computers those that cannot easily be relocated, that do require extensive power and climate controls, that are normally operated by trained specialists rather than the individuals who actually use their output, and that are generally physically distant from the individuals who rely on them to organize and manipulate information. Although there are areas of overlap between these categories, their boundaries--which have remained discernable through several generations of computer development--distinguish between different sorts of computer use.

2. Note that the terminology itself is misleading. While *adjustment* suggests a relatively minor and limited reorientation of economic policies, what is often required is a fundamental economic transformation.

3. World Bank publications on structural adjustment are numerous. A useful summary is provided in Chapter 1 of World Bank, Africa Region, SDA Unit (1990), *Structural Adjustment and Poverty* (Washington, DC: The World Bank). Structural adjustment has become an increasingly popular focus for academic research. A search in a major university library in May, 1990, yielded more than sixty relevant book titles (that is, not including articles, agency reports, and the like). For critiques of structural adjustment policies and conditions, see, among others, Mahjoub 1990 and United Nations Economic Commission for Africa 1989.

4. As Chapter 3 documents, microcomputers are not necessarily low cost in Africa and can be as costly as minicomputers.

5. There are now multiple publications covering computing developments in Africa. The *East African Computer News* did not survive but it was the earliest such periodical published in Africa, starting in May 1985. The *Computer Forum* was published for the first time in 1990 by the Computing in Southern Africa Foundation (CISNA), a regional organization with chapters in Malawi, Botswana, Namibia, Zimbabwe, Lesotho, and South Africa. Publications published outside the continent include *Computers in Africa*, a monthly started in September 1987 and now published by Information Technology Publishing Co. Ltd of the UK, and *African Telecommunications Report*, a monthly newsletter published by AFCOM International Inc. of Washington, DC. The latest arrival is *Africa Communications*, a bimonthly published since late 1990 also by AFCOM International, Inc. and covering the telecommunication, computer, and broadcasting industries.

6. For examples of the literature, see Ingle 1983, Brodman 1985, Smith and Sensenig 1986, Ingle, Berge, and Teisan 1986 and Ruth and Mann 1987.

7. For examples see *Microcomputers and Their Applications for Developing Countries* (Boulder: Westview Press for the Board on Science and Technology for International Development, National Research Council, 1986) and the articles by Westcott on Kenya, Brodman on Kenya and Indonesia, and Pinckney, Cohen, and Leonard on Kenya in *Microcomputers in Public Policy: Applications for Developing Countries*, ed. Stephen R. Ruth and Charles K.

Mann (Boulder: Westview Press for the American Association for the Advancement of Science, 1987).

2

Computerization, Aid-Dependency, and Administrative Capacity: A Sudanese Case Study

Craig Calhoun and Pamela F. DeLargy

Introduction

From 1983 through 1985 the Sudan was reeling from an influx of nearly a million refugees, having the misfortune to share borders with several of Africa's most unstable states. Its economy was in shambles, having deteriorated fairly steadily since the early 1970s when the OPEC oil bonanza (from which much of the rest of the Arab world benefitted) shot the fertilizer and fuel prices of this agrarian country sky high. Agriculture itself entered a further calamitous decline as the result of one of the modern era's worst droughts, bringing famine to much of the country. Jaafar Numeiri, the Sudan's authoritarian military ruler, was growing increasingly eccentric and unpopular, and sought (ultimately unsuccessfully) to rescue his failing regime by imposing a strict, if poorly thought-out version of Shari'a law. This proved the last straw for Southerners who had been chafing under the gradual retraction of the concessions they had been granted when civil war was brought to an end a decade before; they resumed fighting in an all-out military struggle.

Why, in the midst of all this, did the Government of Sudan contract with USAID for a series of major computerization projects? Was this another glaring instance of inappropriate development aid, a counterproductive response to the glamour of high technology? We would hardly defend the proposition that computers were what the Sudan needed most, nor do we want to wrestle here with the question of what priority they should be given vis-à-vis other potentially useful goods. We do, however, want to suggest that even under these extraordinary circumstances, the Sudan did (and does) need the information management capacity which computers have to offer. Moreover, and perhaps more importantly, we want to suggest that any adequate understanding of the process of computerization (and on that basis, any really adequate advice for those involved in such a process) must take into account the impact of a range of background factors well beyond those generally addressed in computer manuals or classes on systems analysis.

In a sense, then, we construe our task of examining the relationship between microcomputers and social change in the Sudan as calling for a kind of "deep background" to the concrete process of design and implementation of computer systems. Put another way, while computerization may cause or shape a variety of social changes, it is not the prime mover in any such process. The factors that lead to computerization, the conditions under which it takes place and the specific design decisions of those who implement it are the crucial determinants of its effects. And while our concern is in part with giving advice to those who may design such systems, we would stress that the voluntary decisions of designers are much less influential than the background factors and context.

Computers were and are needed in Sudan primarily because of the information management demands of state administration and economic development. These demands are imposed largely by the structure of the world political economic system—including the capacity of other actors to produce and in turn require massive flows of information. Sudan is in a position to ignore these demands only at very great cost. It does not exaggerate, indeed, to say that the cost may include an element of national sovereignty. The Sudan is host to a bewildering array of international aid agencies, multilateral and bilateral donors, lenders and operative agencies. In the early to mid-1980s, over 100 foreign or international organizations were involved in refugee relief and famine assistance efforts alone. Without major reforms, the Sudanese government lacked the capacity to monitor the activities of these various actors. This meant, thus, that the government not only risked losing some of the aid donors and lenders offered by failing to comply with their informational demands, but risked losing its own capacity to bring order to both temporary aid efforts and long-term development plans. This is not to say that all foreign actors were inclined to let the Sudanese government exercise full autonomy. Nonetheless, it is significant that even if all foreign and international actors had attempted fully to respect Sudanese decision making, the government lacked the capacity to manage the situation. And beyond management of the various foreign actors working in the Sudan, there was the question of how the government might deal with such challenges as the influx of refugees or the growth and redistribution of its own population. These were (and remain) equally potent challenges to the administrative capacity of the government. Dealing with them also posed massive needs for new capacity to gather, manage and analyze information, and to present it effectively to policy makers.

In the following pages, we will first defend the initial proposition that computerization (financed by foreign aid) can be of value. Then we will describe something of the challenge of information management in the Sudan, focusing on the problems of aid dependency and development planning. From this background, we will turn to issues more closely related to the practical side of computerization efforts, considering some specific challenges of the Sudanese context and offering a number of suggestions for system development in similar settings.

A Bad Idea from the Start?

This chapter is based on our experiences as technical advisors to the Government of Sudan on two USAID-funded projects in which computerization played a major role. One (receiving greater discussion here) involved the design and implementation of systems for financial accounting, developmental budgeting, project monitoring, commodity assistance tracking and donor coordination for the Sudanese Ministry of Finance and Economic Planning. The other involved support for the Sudanese National Population Committee in a program of research, policy formulation and education.[1] The two projects delivered and installed several microcomputers, developed specialized software (as well as supplying off-the-shelf software) and trained users. The systems installed were used for a range of functions from word processing in both Arabic and English through data base management to formal simulation modeling.

A variety of objections may be raised to work of this sort. It is done on behalf of aid agencies whose agendas may not coincide with those of domestic policy makers or be based on any independent verification of the interests of the citizens of the host country. It involves the transplantation of a foreign technology, and the transplant may, moreover, work to enhance the position of indigenous elites or of the state at the expense of subalterns and/or democracy. There are inevitably power relations in all technology transfers, involving not only asymmetries between rich and poor countries but also between international consultants and indigenous users. All these are valid concerns, and each should be borne in mind by those doing this sort of work. Yet none, in our view, invalidates it. For the Sudan to do without computer technology would mean simply for it to be even less able to chart a desirable course in the contemporary world system. Increasingly, it is as unreasonably abstract to ask whether computers are "good" for a country as to ask whether roads or telephones are. All are indispensable parts of the infrastructural basis for economic vitality and effective government. That both of these will be defined in terms of an exploitative international economy or a system of states of unequal power and arbitrarily imposed boundaries may be unfortunate, even tragic. It is, however, inescapably the way the world is, and even changing the world demands starting where it is.[2]

This said, it should not be thought that our projects went any great way toward reversing the Sudan's long economic decline, ending its civil war, feeding its hungry or otherwise addressing its immediate ills. Moreover, even within their specific scopes, the projects suffered from flaws which we do not propose to minimize. We write not simply to extol their virtues, but to improve work of broadly similar genres and to provide an account of it which can be integrated into more general understandings of both technology and social change and what it means to be among the least "developed" countries of the world.

Though we do not challenge the utility of computers or even the value of many of the projects for which they are used, we do want to challenge the naive view of microcomputer technology as either neutral or automatically beneficial. Such technology always has a politics, as Langdon Winner (1985) has stressed, if for no other reason than that it represents a deployment of resources and is an occasion for struggle over alternative futures. The machines as such determine little, however. Nearly every significant outcome depends on how computer applications, and information systems generally, are designed, implemented and used, not on intrinsic characteristics of the machines. Accordingly, our suggestions will be aimed mainly at the process of system development and implementation. Power relations, larger strategies and highly specific local contexts stand behind and shape each system and its use. This political dimension to "technical assistance" is usually ignored, especially by the staffs of funding agencies and the consultants who make their living by guiding implementations. Ignoring the political and organizational biases and sensitivity of any computerization effort, however, both masks troubling side effects which deserve our attention, and makes for instrumentally less effective implementations.

Implicit in our account is the suggestion that the difficulties of computer use in less developed countries are not due simply to low educational levels or other failings of indigenous users. While a variety of problems stem simply from the lack of support for machines—a shortage of local parts suppliers, for instance, or undependable electrical current—others have to do with the conditions of international domination and self-interested domestic government. Even apparently "purely technical" difficulties often cannot be dealt with effectively unless they are viewed within this political-economic context.

Recognizing this fact necessitates breaking with the notion that the problems of Third World countries are simply a series of "absences" or "underdevelopments" of conditions or goods present in more "advanced" countries. It has been one of the unfortunate features of Western "orientalist" ideology to treat the rest of the world as essentially similar insofar as it was/is non-Western (or non-rich or non-powerful). This point is driven home to those who work in Africa and read development studies texts based on Latin America, or advice to computer consultants based on Southeast Asia. It is crucial to grasp the specificities of any context, of course, but the issue is especially acute in Africa because so much of the literature—even the critical and sensitive literature—on the Third World is rooted in other experiences. So is most of the lore of professional consultants and officials of international agencies. Even within Africa, differences are enormous. In fact, differences are in many ways greater among the less developed societies precisely because their conditions have not been recast in the common mold of the modern world system.

Information Management as a Problem in Developing Countries

Information management is a crucial issue for developing countries. Faced with both domestic and international demands for statistics and record-keeping, many governments find themselves stretched to the limits of their resources. This is especially true of those which attempt any form of central planning and/or monitoring of development activities. Whether the aims are improved service delivery, economic growth, or more effective monitoring of climatic variation, management of a large volume of information is essential. Trained personnel are at a premium; material facilities are minimal and funds for their improvement usually slight.

Despite the importance and difficulty of information management, the transfer of advanced technology to assist in it has been, until recently, only slight. This is so largely because most versions of this technology prior to about 1980 were (a) expensive both to purchase and to operate, (b) dependent on highly trained personnel, and (c) unreliable in the inescapably harsh operating conditions of many less developed countries. This was particularly true of mainframe computing.

Microcomputers (and in some cases related new communications technologies) offer new potential. They are relatively inexpensive, and moreover can be introduced incrementally so that a whole system need not be procured "up front." Though they require trained operators the number of specialists and the extent of training required is vastly less than on even moderately powered mainframes of a generation ago. Crucially, microcomputers also demand less in the way of environmental control. They do not require air conditioned rooms, for example (though our experience on the edge of the Sahara desert still suggests that air conditioning is advisable, if more for keeping dust out than for keeping machines cool).

As a result, microcomputers have been purchased for a wide variety of uses in Third World countries and prescribed for even more. They are tools which may, we think, improve many services and even support national autonomy. One of the best ways to see the potential usefulness of computers is to examine the information management demands placed on those charged with national economic planning and financial management in the Sudan.[3]

There is an international mandate for Third World countries to engage in national economic development planning and concomitant maintenance of national accounts. It is implicit in the activities of the World Bank and IMF. Evidence of development planning is sought by both private and public donors—even by the United States, despite the fact that it is one of the few countries in the world to lack its own domestic planning agency. Scholars hold up successful cases of planned development as models for other countries, and their words are backed up by the ability of agencies to deliver billions of dollars in aid. But most economists and government officials in the Third World are already convinced of the merits of planning and national accounts, even where they reject the specific proposals of the IMF and other international agencies. They are graduates of the same university programs as the IMF officials, and they have been trained to believe in development planning. Yet this pursuit of planned development and effective national accounting runs up against severe limits of both political will and bureaucratic capacity (Rondinelli 1983; Robertson 1984), as both serious planning efforts and superficial attempts to meet the requirements of international donors require the management of an enormous range and complexity of information.

The various domestic and international actors who demand development planning (a) may have very little sense of the complexities of data management, (b) may have no intention of doing actual analysis on the data collected, and therefore (c) are often mandating not actual planned development but conformity to a myth concerning the role of planning and centralized monitoring (Robertson 1984). The demands for development plans, ironically, may even be at their most extreme in those cases where they are least likely to be effective--the poorest countries of the world.

In the Sudan, during the drought of the mid-1980s, foreign aid and related activities accounted for the absolute majority of macro-economic activity. Without it, we might reasonably say, there would have been no national-level economy but only local subsistence economies. The Sudan is thus a paradigmatic, even extreme, case of what Abu-Lughod (1984) has provocatively but accurately termed the "charity-economies." Even in the few good years since 1973, formal sector domestic production has been relatively small in relation to international borrowing and aid. In such a setting, the ideals of centralized planning and monitoring face the realities of seemingly intractable economic problems, the absence of a transportation and communications infrastructure to knit the country together, and an organizationally weak government. In the Sudan, it should be stressed, the governmental bureaucracy was not always weak, but rather was one of Africa's most efficient. A severe brain drain, increasing political interference with the civil service and dramatic deterioration in educational institutions, as well as simple lack of resources, all contributed to its decline. Moreover, the various external actors (such as USAID and other bilateral donors, the World Bank, UN agencies) which may call for effective central government nonetheless help in many ways to undermine it. Their agents demand constant attention from senior government officials, distracting the latter from their domestic duties.[4] Each international organization imposes its own set of rules and procedures and demands information in its own format; too many also shift constantly from one to another currently fashionable strategy for economic development (Morss 1984). The number of donors and the extent of dependence on them have increased dramatically in the last several years.

These challenges, and the need for solutions which underlie them, were (and are) particularly great in the Sudan. One of the world's poorest countries, the Sudan is nonetheless involved in a wide range of publicly financed development activities. It is the recipient of an enormous volume of foreign aid--a volume recently multiplied in an (only partly successful) effort to cope with Sudan's influx of refugees from Ethiopia and other troubled neighboring states, and its own domestic drought.[5] Sudan's British colonial rulers started a tradition of very large-scale development projects--the most well known of these being the Gezira scheme, a mechanized farming venture focused largely on cotton. After independence, Sudan continued on the same path, hoping (with a good deal of international support) to become "the breadbasket of the Arab world." New agricultural schemes were set up and old ones enlarged; industrial facilities were planned; housing was built to house migrants; shipping facilities were improved.

Ventures of this sort placed increasing demands on the central government's ability to plan and monitor dispersed activities (as well as to finance them). Like most of the countries of the world, the Sudan chose to engage in centralized planning for economic development. A Planning Ministry was created, though later merged with the Ministry of Finance, of which it is now the Planning Section. The planners were charged with (a) planning, but also (b) monitoring activities, and (c) maintaining liaison with foreign and multilateral lenders and donors. The last of these responsibilities became, in a sense, the tail which wagged the dog. The scale of activities involved was not the only major issue. Government officials were also working in a very large country (Africa's largest, about the size of the U.S. east of the Mississippi) with a minimal transportation and communications infrastructure.

There were, however, problems in the Ministry as well. First and foremost, there was a lack of effective record-keeping.[6] Though quite a few accountants were employed, procedures were minimal and primitive. No running balance was maintained, for example, of the outstanding lines of credit the country had open with various foreign lenders. No domestic bookkeeping allowed the accounts of foreign donors to be checked; indeed, in most cases the requests for payment from individual contractors were approved without any attempt to verify their claims. To the extent that record-keeping was carried on, it was in a system oriented far more to storage than to retrieval. Though ledgers and binders were filled with numbers and forms, senior officials could not get answers to their requests for information. The Ministry had little ability to use data analytically. Each year's Development Budget, for example, was prepared without knowledge of how much of the previous year's had in fact been spent. Linking past records with future plans was impossible (and alas, we cannot claim that our system has entirely eliminated this problem).

To these internal difficulties foreign donors added a great deal. They demanded frequent reports, drawing on the time and attention of Ministry staff members. Perhaps more problematically and less necessarily, nearly every foreign and multilateral aid organization and lender insisted—and still insists—upon its own distinctive procedures for recording and reporting data.

The Context of Computerization:
A System-Poor Environment

Even in the world's richest, most technologically advanced countries, computer use is still expanding into new applications and new organizational settings. New users can draw, however, on a rich background of experience, training institutions, support organizations and, in general, technological infrastructure. This is of enormous importance in even small applications, but even more so in relatively larger ones. As Kling and Scacchi (1982a) suggest, computer use involves a whole web of activities, relationships and technologies. No one application can well be understood in isolation. This holds a particular import for those countries of the world where computerization is still very limited. These are mostly to be found among the least developed countries. There computerization efforts cannot build on strong foundations from prior computer use, on strong support systems, physical infrastructure, technological familiarity or even, in many cases, a common linguistic basis. Not only foreign exchange and spare parts but such basics as electricity may be in short supply.

In such settings, computing environments are unstable and underdeveloped. Yet computerization makes significant demands on environments. Unfortunately, the planning of many systems presumes settings like the United States, Western Europe or Japan, where a high level of environmental support can be taken for granted. Failure to think through the special challenges of early applications in a "system-poor" environment is an important cause of failure and/or under-utilization. Moreover, it is important that early applications foster wherever possible the development of a stronger computing (and, more generally, information management) environment. Early computerization efforts, thus, ought to be judged in part on whether they make later ones easier. In countries like the Sudan, however, there are serious limits to this. Computers represent a technology which cannot in the foreseeable future be fully "acquired" by the Sudan. While specific machines may be put in place, in other words, the overall process of technology transfer is truncated because the Sudan is not in a position to become a self-sustaining producer as well as a consumer of computer systems (and thus is in a very different situation even from such other less-developed countries as Brazil, Indonesia, China or the Philippines).

It is important also to note the difference between simply introducing computers, and introducing information management with computers as the medium. In planning for computerization in the Sudanese Ministry of Finance we faced, as mentioned above, the problem that no very satisfactory system of paper accounts was in place. The task was not to computerize an existing system, but to create a management information system anew. The computer, we thought (following the work of Pinckney, Cohen, and Leonard in Kenya, 1983), might be something of a catalyst. The glamour attached to new technology might persuade some people to interest themselves in data management who otherwise would not do so.

A variety of other factors also represented barriers to effective system development. The Sudan suffers from an extraordinary brain drain. Until the recent collapse of oil prices, the oil-rich Arab states employed some 45% of Sudan's professionally educated workforce. Any Ministry staff members whom we trained in computer use would become prime candidates for employment abroad or in the Sudanese private sector. In addition, the Government of the Sudan is able to pay its employees--once perhaps the best trained and best organized civil service in Africa--little more than a pittance. Beyond the issue of staff stability, the physical environment posed a problem. Dust is a constant presence, even without the occasional dust storms--haboobs--which sweep over Khartoum from the desert. Few buildings are sealed against the dust; after all the warm, dry climate makes for little need to protect humans (if not computers) from the elements. Temperatures reach over 130 degrees Fahrenheit. The Ministry did provide a closed and air conditioned room (which, however, encouraged an apparent over-centralization of access to the computers, though a few were dispersed to other offices despite inclement conditions). Electricity was another matter. Supplies are subject to frequent interruption and to wide fluctuation. "Brown-outs" are common, especially during the summer, and black-outs may last for days. Beyond the usual reserve power supplies and line filters, of course, there was little to be done about this.

What was to be done about this range of challenges to any computer system, we thought, was to take an incremental approach. Computerization should proceed through the creation of several more or less self-contained systems rather than one large, centralized one. If some failed, others would continue to function. Moreover, a gradual process of computerization seemed in order. Design, system construction, training and implementation could not be four separate processes in a strict linear arrangement. Rather, each would have to take place simultaneously, at least in part, and influence the others. A "turnkey" system seemed guaranteed to fail in practice whatever its technical merits. An incremental approach would not only allow a high degree of tailoring of the system to the specifications of its actual users and the specifics of its actual situation. It would also allow us to build up the necessary flow of documents, the familiarity and confidence of a wide range of interested and/or essential staff, and the support of senior administrators not just for a system, in the abstract, but for the concrete system being implemented. An incremental approach allowed us to incorporate several layers of administrators in the actual design process, thus simultaneously (a) improving the system, (b) increasing support for it, and (c) giving administrators a clearer idea of what could and could not reasonably be expected from it. If anything, in retrospect, we underestimated the advantages of incrementalism, and overestimated the extent to which "a way could always be found" to implement any technically sound feature of the system.

Microcomputers are a technology particularly well suited to an incremental approach. The unit cost is low, yet systems can be expanded almost indefinitely. Relative levels of centralization or decentralization can be shifted in the field. Computers initially deployed as discrete machines (though linked by common software and transferability of data by disk) can later be linked in a network. New technology (or newly affordable technology) can be added piecemeal; indeed the whole system can gradually be changed over from one brand of computers, say, to another. This is particularly important in a developing country that is dependent on foreign donors for its computer equipment. Donors are fickle; those interested in supporting an MIS system this year may have other priorities next year. A new donor may have a commitment to a different hardware supplier, perhaps because its aid is tied to its own national business interests (as is most US aid). Where a mainframe computer system could become instantly obsolete in the absence of a continuing source of support, and where it may be hard to find new donors willing to cough up the cost of an entire new system, a microcomputer-based system would, we thought, more likely survive the vicissitudes of aid dependence. In a sense, microcomputers are closer to the sort of smaller-scale technology often advocated under the label "appropriate technology."

The Finance Ministry Management Information System

Our system was planned in response to several specific issues and concrete tasks within the Ministry. The first was a need to keep track of expenditures and activities involved in the implementation of foreign loans and grants. This was of interest not only to the Planning Section of the Ministry, which had little ability to monitor physical implementation or plan for fiscal needs, though it bore responsibility for both, but also to the various foreign donors. Assembled as a group in the Joint Monitoring Committee, they recognized (at least gave lip service to) a need for donor coordination and data about each other's activities. It would be helpful, for example, for two donors offering road-building assistance each to know what the other had in the pipeline. The Project Directory sub-system was designed with this purpose in mind.

Secondly, it developed very quickly in our work that despite the presence of a substantial "official" accounting apparatus, the Ministry had no good financial records system, still less one which could make current data easily available to those charged with establishing and monitoring foreign loan and grant arrangements. A Financial Accounting System became the highest priority for the Ministry, if not for the outside donors.

Thirdly, and at the lowest level of technological sophistication, we worked on spreadsheets to help the Commodity Assistance Committee keep track of the flow of physical imports. Requests from various implementing agencies in both private and public sectors have to be coordinated, and referred to potential donors. Lines of credit must be opened against foreign loan or grant agreements; tenders of goods must be received and approved; shipments monitored, payments made, and delivery vouched for. Time lags may enter at any point and may prove critical (as for example when trucks are not available to move necessary food, which rots at the docks). At the time we began work, only partial paper records were maintained of this chain of activity; the primary data were in the head of the Director of the Committee, and to a lesser extent, the heads of his staff (see Adkins 1988:38 on similar problems in monitoring the even more complex commodity flows of Tanzania). Yet analysis of where delays arise is one of the main means for improving the efficacy of the entire foreign aid operation.

At least in principle, all three of these sets of activities (and the MIS sub-systems tracking them) should contribute to effective budgeting. In fact, budgeting is carried on largely as a separate activity with no systematic relationship to the monitoring of either expenditures or physical implementation, and with no established flow of data about either. As we mentioned earlier, the Development Budget is prepared each year in nearly complete ignorance of the actual expenditures made the year before, let alone of whether those expenditures were translated into appropriate physical outcomes. We provided computer support for the Development Budget process, though top Ministry officials and USAID staff alike regarded this as a luxury. Regrettably, the budget process remains largely disconnected from the other activities. It appears to lack the political backing to take the central organizational role one might expect (on the other hand, as of 1990, the computerized budget system was the only component of the project still being consistently used). The failure to connect planning to disbursement was not an anomaly, but an indication of a general state of affairs at the Ministry. Indeed, in the absence of a clear relationship of the monitoring and record-keeping activities of the Ministry to its disbursement and planning activities, we felt a lack of organizational sense of purpose on the part of many, at least in the Planning Section of the Ministry. Indeed, staff come into the Ministry with backgrounds wildly unsuited or unrelated to the specific jobs they will hold. Economic planners, for example, may hold degrees in chemical engineering (as did one of the best computer-trainees to pass through our Management Information Systems Unit). Nothing in the organizational structure or the lines of power relations, and nothing in the job descriptions under which individuals work, really suggests very forcefully that planning (or the monitoring of physical implementation) is the central function of the Planning Section. And, in fact, it may not be. As Robertson (1984) suggests, planning is largely a ritual activity, undertaken for the benefit of various domestic and international audiences. In the Sudan, at least, the core function of the Planning Section of the Ministry of Finance seemed to be placating donors. Beyond planning, record-keeping was also apparently largely a matter of ritual, as it involved filing various documents with no attention to the possible purposes for which they might be retrieved, and entering financial transactions chronologically with no effort to reconcile income and expenditure or even to sum columns. There was little notion that data need to be gathered for use in analysis, rather than as mere records. But that is another story.[7]

The main thrust of our approach, and the main insights of our experience, can be revealed through a look at one of the subsystems in the larger management information system we helped to develop. This is the Project Directory of Foreign Loans and Grants.

The Project Directory subsystem was planned to meet two goals. First, it was to provide a database for the use of the Government of Sudan and the foreign donor community in achieving greater coordination of donor activities. Second, it was to enable the Sudanese Ministry of Finance and Economic Planning to maintain its own accounts with regard to foreign loans and grants, rather than depending entirely on the accounts of the donors themselves. The former goal was of interest primarily to donors, including especially the USAID which paid for the project; the latter goal was of much more interest to the Sudanese officials in the Ministry. In both cases, the need was for information on plans themselves, on actual agreements, and on physical implementation. A separate system was developed for financial accounting (see Whittington, Calhoun, and Drummond 1986).

Previous efforts had been made to gather this sort of information; some of it was collated in the course of routine work in various "sectoral" (for example transport, energy, agriculture) offices within the Planning Section of the Ministry. There was, however, no systematic effort to ensure that records existed for every project. Indeed, there was no one who could list all foreign-financed projects underway in the Sudan--even with the aid of a file cabinet of his or her choosing. As a result, project planning was not based on explicit records of past experience--and, given the very high rate of turnover in Sudanese and especially foreign staff, such planning often was not based on any form of experience.

An attempt to enhance collective memory was one of the central reasons why the foreign donors wanted a project directory. Foreign donors, however, tended to see this as primarily a Sudanese problem. An ineffectual Secretariat for the Joint Monitoring Committee had been established; one early view of our project was as an effort to "beef it up." The Ministry tended to proliferate units aimed at improving administration, but not to attend to the underlying problems. Shortly before our MIS project spawned an MIS Unit, for example, a "Follow-Up Section" had been created to follow-up on the undone data collection work of the other units (perhaps needless to say, it did not do so). While the Ministry was able to offer precious little information management capacity, it has to be said that few donors could do much better. Most information was shared by informal word of mouth, or more formal announcements at meetings of a Joint Monitoring Committee. The UN Development Program office in Khartoum appended a summary of those projects of all donors from whom it could gather data to its annual reports. This was the only real effort to gather data across donors, and it was not only inadequate in contents, it was almost always too late to affect project planning and development. Even within the missions of individual donors, record-keeping was generally conceived of as a necessary evil and was undertaken only to placate the home office, not to aid in planning, analysis, or transfer of responsibilities among the ever-changing field staff.

Given this situation, several kinds of data seemed to us potentially useful. In the first place, it would be helpful simply to know what each donor was doing, so that their activities might be coordinated—at least to the level of avoiding duplication (or, though this was less often mentioned, to avoid leaving gaps when all donors rushed to follow the latest fad in development aid). It was important that such data be current and reflect the actual state of implementation efforts, not merely the existence of an agreement. The political volatility of the Sudan, together with other problems, meant that only a fraction of development projects approved in the early 1980s actually reached completion. Secondly, systematic data on the course of implementation of each project might provide the basis for learning what roadblocks were characteristic and beginning to remove them. A concern for trying to speed the movement of aid was voiced by nearly every donor. Thirdly, data on both Sudanese and expatriate contractors and other personnel might allow for more intelligent choice among candidates for future contracts. Fourthly, it was thought by the government and foreign assistance agencies that the Project Directory might provide a ready index to all reports or other publications resulting from projects or their evaluations.

We developed the Project Directory as a database using dBASE III software.[a] The design of the database was actually fairly straightforward.[8] Our problems—and these were considerable—arose in implementation.

First, there was the question of designing a form on which to solicit information. Administrators at nearly every level of the Ministry, together with some expatriate advisors, insisted upon putting their own stamp on the form and content of the questionnaire. Many of their suggestions were helpful; the problem was that over a period of more than a year, no end could ever be brought to this process of revision. We never succeeded in persuading the senior officials involved that each revision of the form might mean a considerable delay because it sent us back to redesign the database structure. Waiting for the perfect form, moreover, seemed an excuse for not getting on with data collection.

This raises the second main problem: a difficulty in translating interest in the computer as machine and status symbol into a willingness to do the information gathering work which is the true basis of an effective MIS. Indeed, constant tinkering with forms was only one way in which senior officials coped with the problems that (a) no one in the Ministry wanted to do data collection, and (b) at least unconsciously, many people must have known there was precious little good data to be had. With regard to the first problem, we found that those who were sufficiently senior to be chosen to work with us regarded mere data collection as a form of clerical work and beneath them (this was somewhat less true of women). Moreover, the staff of the Management Information Systems Unit saw themselves as technically trained computer specialists, not researchers or fillers-out of forms. We tried in vain to convince them that the computers could not do the work without good data, that computerization was

---

[a] dBase is a trademark of Ashton Tate.

merely the introduction of a tool into an effort which was really about information.

The third difficulty with the Project Directory may hold a less obvious lesson. This is the importance of a relatively transparent system. We chose dBASE III as a powerful tool with which to accomplish the ends listed above, and in technical terms it performs admirably. In practice, however, almost any dBASE III program works as a black box into which ordinary users feed data and from which they receive reports. While the most complicated spreadsheet is at least partly transparent, the simplest data base is usually not. The issue is not just one of training users to a high enough standard that at least some can make innovations in the system. That, indeed, would have been very difficult in the circumstances, but the Financial Accounts System developed in LOTUS 1-2-3 is not easily altered by users of moderate training either. The crucial issue is that it is very hard to show anyone how the database system works. The interest must be in the output, and so the potential role of computer as "catalyst" is reduced. This aggravates the second set of difficulties discussed above. Anyone chosen for such an honorable (and potentially remunerative) job as working with a computer in a very poor country is likely to feel "above" and bored by clerical tasks such as entering data into and requesting reports from a database. One of the best typists we encountered was a young "gaffir"—a sort of porter, almost literally a go-fer in the Ministry. He was personable, would have loved to enter data, and was considered ineligible because he did not have a university degree. It was suggested, by contrast, that we train economists and engineers with master's degrees to do data entry.[9]

All of these problems internal to the Management Information Systems Unit and the Ministry pale before the fourth. Despite their initial support for this effort, voiced officially through the Joint Monitoring Committee, the donors— especially the major Western and multilateral donors— failed to respond to requests for data. We had expected some problems getting data from those donors not active in the Joint Monitoring Committee, such as the Arab donors and the

African Development Bank. On the contrary, these replied promptly and generally quite thoroughly to our requests. It was the World Bank, France, Great Britain, and the EEC which failed to complete our forms, and failed even to respond to follow-up letters from the Under-Secretary of the Ministry (the highest civil service rank in the Sudanese Government and in this case a dynamic and powerful figure, who later was promoted to Minister of Finance). USAID, the agency which funded the project, responded but only after considerable nagging on the part of the project's supporters, including the Chief of Mission, and direct intervention on our part to supervise completion of the forms. It seems worthwhile at least to pose some hypotheses as to why the donors may not have responded. Each of the following is probably true in part for at least some of the donors.

First, there are possible reasons which have to do with the internal affairs of various donor organizations. Then, there are also several likely reasons having to do with donor-representatives' perceptions of the situation outside their own organization.

Internal

1. Data may be in a central office, not in Khartoum. This was voiced as an excuse, and at least some of those voicing it had definitely requested the data from their headquarters. The failure of headquarters staffs to respond presumably has a variety of bases with the common denominators that records are not readily ordered in this fashion there and doing the work to so order them is not a high priority for anyone back in Washington, New York, Geneva or Paris.

2. Donors (and/or their representatives) may simply not care; they may have no interest in donor coordination. Indeed, the latter does seem to be something which everyone claims to want--but with the unvoiced condition that no one else be allowed to coordinate them! Among the hundred-odd organizations trying to alleviate the refugee and drought crises in Sudan, at least half a dozen—from the U.N. High Commissioner for Refugees to Grassroots International and Bob

Geldoff's Live Aid--claimed that their role is to coordinate the others, or at least information about the others.

3. It is likely that even where senior officials gave verbal commitments to participate in this effort (as nearly all did, repeatedly) they did not translate these into incentives for anyone in particular in their organizations to do the work involved. Aid missions are chronically over-worked (and poorly administered); in the absence of a strong inducement to do otherwise, many staffers would let a mere request for information by the host government gather dust. The extreme and urgent problems facing the Sudan even give such decisions a moral cast: "how can I fill out these forms when people are starving?" Of course, the same people who make such statements find time to go on innumerable, generally useless, "familiarization visits" to the scene of hardship. The latter give them a sense of activity which effective administration does not.

External

4. Many donors may have reasoned that others would fail to do their part, and so decided not to waste their own time or energy. This "others won't so why should we?" reasoning is a sort of free-rider problem in reverse (as well as a self-fulfilling prophecy). We think it was an important factor.

5. Many donors seem to have perceived the Ministry of Finance (or at least its Planning Section) as either irrelevant or incompetent or both. They simply chose on that basis not to support its efforts, anticipating that they would amount to nothing.

6. Some donors may have felt quite the same way about the MIS technical advisors—us—or at least the system we appeared to be developing. A number certainly seemed to feel that the MIS system would not work, either because it was impossible to get the Ministry that organized or because they thought a computerized MIS was not a good way to go about it.

7. Privately, at least one donor voiced what may have been a more common sentiment—that this project was too closely

tied to USAID for their tastes. Rivalries among donors are intense, and the multilateral donor whose agent made the above remark had previously unsuccessfully proposed another approach to many of the same issues. In any case, USAID appeared to some other donors to be encroaching on their turf—in part because it seemed to want to take the active role in promoting (doing) donor coordination.

Whatever the reasons, the non-compliance of the donors with this major effort by the Sudanese Ministry of Finance and Economic Planning to get its records in order must call into question their willingness to support the development of effective government administration in the Sudan. It should be said that we responded not only by expressing our disappointment, but by gaining direct access wherever we could to the files of the donors so that we could gather at least baseline information for the system. It would appear, however, that for the future the Sudan would be well advised to depend on donors for as little information as possible, and to ensure that adequate procedures are developed for its own record keeping and information management. Our efforts can only count as a step or two in that direction.

Simpler Applications

The introduction of microcomputers at the National Population Committee (NPC, part of the National Research Council) involved some other interesting dynamics--partly due to the different functions of the computers, and partly to the very different nature of the organization itself. Computerization at the NPC was part of a larger program of technical assistance in the development of a national population policy. The program (USAID-funded "OPTION for Population Policy") included support for task force research on major population and health issues, preparation of a national conference, development of policy constituencies through educational campaigns and regional seminars, and assistance to sectoral ministries in planning and awareness raising. Initially, one microcomputer and existing software were used to prepare graphic presentations of population projections. Fairly senior staff were trained on the software. However, quite soon the secretarial staff began to use the computer for word processing of Committee documents and correspondence (in part because of lack of typewriters). Upon the request of the NPC, OPTIONS added more computers and training in word processing in English (Wordstar) and then in Arabic (Multilingual Scholar). At this point, the microcomputers became critical to the function of the office and played a large role in the institutionalization of the organization. The NPC grew from basically a one-person activity to a full-fledged government institution with its own building and staff and with greatly expanded credibility within the government.

As the project went on, the staff (mainly the secretaries) themselves pressed for training in DOS, Lotus, and dBASE; as professional staff came and went, the senior secretary became the office expert in the demographic software as well. This obviously affected office dynamics. Senior staff were keen to maintain status differences (some, by purposely not learning to use the microcomputers), but became dependent on the few lower-level staff for all applications. This led to considerable wrangling over salaries as the computer-expert staff improved their bargaining positions and as their many job offers from the private sector increased their awareness of the economic value of their skills. After a year, it became clear to the leadership that mid-level staff should be developed, and two young economists were trained and placed in charge of the demographic software. The resentment this fostered in the senior secretary was predictable. The economists have since gone on to graduate school; the secretary remains.

The placement and authorization for use of the computers at the NPC were very different from those at the Finance Ministry. Computers were in the open center of the building, accessible to all staff and visitors. The informal tone of the NPC allowed everyone to have a turn on the computers.

A number of graphics programs also were installed for use in creating color graphics for presentation with the population projections. Some staff members were trained to use the application Storyboard, but many others taught themselves through trial and error. The more entertaining aspects of creating color graphics using a mouse and a system which required little English reading attracted almost all of the staff, from the media officer right down to the tea maker. The senior analysts still remain quite isolated from the actual use of the microcomputers, partially due to lack of time to learn the programs. They are clearly aware of what the microcomputers (and staff) can do, however, and they guide their work.

Computers at the NPC (all Compaqs) were initially chosen for their portability and durability and have lived very hard lives--traveling by plane, train, jeep and truck all over the country for use in regional seminars. Considering their heavy use and the dusty environment, the Compaqs held up fairly well, but there were constant maintenance problems which cost both the project and the NPC considerable energy and money. In fact, the OPTIONS project was plagued by debates over who had responsibility for the maintenance of the machines. Some felt that the project had done its part by providing all of the hardware, software and training, and that the Sudanese government (the NPC) should show its commitment by at least keeping the machines in working order. Others felt that the project should have this responsibility, since the NPC had no budget for such things at the time and there were no spare parts to be had in the local market. Generally, the project provided parts and the NPC paid for the repairs (until USAID pulled out). This presented serious problems, however. The NPC was completely dependent on OPTIONS for hardware and software for almost three years. As the environment for the computers (and printers and other peripherals) was harsh, parts frequently had to be replaced. Whole computers were sometimes brought back to the U.S. for repair or just replaced outright. All support materials had to be shipped as excess baggage with consultants on trips. At $100 per box for shipping alone, one box of computer paper became extraordinarily expensive. Printer ribbons, fuses, electronic parts and diskettes all had to travel with technical assistance team members from the U.S. to Khartoum, due to a freight embargo by airlines (even before this, shipments would often not arrive at all or would be detained without

notice by customs authorities). During a five month hiatus in
1988 when USAID forbade project staff to travel to Sudan for
security reasons after a terrorist bombing, some NPC work
came to a halt due to lack of printer ribbons (which were not
available on the local market). When USAID pulled out of
Sudan for political reasons in December 1989, NPC was left to
its own devices to keep things functioning. The financial costs
to the organization are astounding. In December 1989, a
printer ribbon cost the equivalent of $10, a box of diskettes
$50—about the same as the annual salary of an office assistant.
Paper was unavailable. To complicate the situation, even
when the NPC can find these items in the market and has
money in the budget to purchase them, it cannot maintain
proper accounting procedures because merchants will not
provide invoices. Why? Because severe import restrictions
(encouraged, even demanded, by the IMF, USAID and others)
do not allow for use of hard currency to import these
"non-essential" items. Consequently, all computerized projects
and offices which need these items have had to develop
creative ways to obtain them; often, the items are smuggled in
by personnel who travel abroad. So, although the computerization of institutions may be useful, or even necessary, to
effective functioning, if it is supported by donors which are
unreliable suppliers it may actually result in draining the
institution of scarce resources. Until another source is found
for hardware and software support, the NPC must use a major
part of its finances and staff time just to keep the system
working.

As the NPC expanded its activities, got its own building
and became institutionalized (and recognized how dependent
it was on foreign consultants to bring parts for the Compaqs),
there was increasing interest in having more easily serviced
but non-portable IBMs for office use. The NPC has recently
built a separate, small, air-conditioned, dust-free room for the
computers, which will undoubtedly cut down on maintenance
problems but which limits access to the machines. In many
ways, this is unfortunate, as the computers attracted quite a bit
of attention and experimentation from staff and visitors when
they were physically more accessible.

An interesting and unexpected result of computerization at the NPC came from the installation of a word-processing program in the indigenous language, Arabic. This was done initially so that conference papers could be produced in both English and Arabic (a "first" in the country), but the Arabic facility created a demand from sectoral ministries all over Khartoum for assistance in their work. This helped the NPC to establish important relationships with other government agencies and made it a meeting place for numbers of other project directors and ministry personnel. It placed great strain on NPC secretarial staff and sometimes delayed the NPC's own work, but it was critical to the development of key relationships. As more and more of NPC's work began to be done in Arabic, eventually the English was used only for reports to USAID or for materials to be presented to an international audience. In order better to reach audiences outside Khartoum, OPTIONs staff also created an Arabic version of the demographic software and graphics programs. (This was only possible because the programmer on the OPTIONs team was also fluent in Arabic.) As far as we know, this project is the only donor-supported project in Sudan to work in both English and Arabic; this was a result of the determination of the OPTIONs staff (even more than our Sudanese counterparts) to work in Arabic whenever possible.[10] We see working in the local language as very important, especially in projects, such as the NPC's, which involve public (or even bureaucratic) awareness raising. But this is very difficult, even impossible in some cases. Luckily, some Arabic word-processing software existed and we knew where to find it, but transforming other software into Arabic was time-consuming and required very specialized skills. Other languages may be even more difficult. Sometimes English (or French or Spanish) may be the common language in business or government, and so computerization will occur in that language by default. The implications of this include limited institutionalization of computing facilities, restriction of computer access to elites, and often dependence on international suppliers (see discussions of these in the chapter on Tanzania).

After three years of support and intermittent training from the OPTIONs project, NPC staff are able to carry on with all the activities originally envisioned for the microcomputers, and they have added new ones. In fact, we believe that a strength of the project was that instead of establishing a set system and training program, it was flexible enough to respond to the needs and interests of the NPC staff who, in time, became enthusiastic and creative users, constantly finding new functions for the computers. The whole project became a common learning experience. We believe that the success of computerization at the NPC (despite sustainability questions) is partly a result of microcomputers filling a real need—in this case for demographic projections, word processing and graphics representations—which was felt by indigenous staff. In addition, the NPC's own organizational style and structure was loose enough to encourage everyone to get involved in the process. Last but not least, the uses at the NPC did not involve the sort of demands for new and continuous data collection which the Finance Ministry systems did.

Suggestions

Our suggestions, based on our experiences in Sudan, can be summarized as follows:

Equipment: Keep It Simple

Reliability is more important than "state-of-the-art" in hardware. The number of unanticipated problems is multiplied in a physically hostile environment. Of course, in a country like Sudan, with an unreliable electricity supply, alternate power supplies are absolutely necessary. Repair services in the Sudan were extremely limited not only in absolute terms but in the kinds of problems they could solve. This stems from the country's poverty, from the low level of previous computer and other technological system use, and even from its dependence on foreign aid. The last skews equipment choice to those products manufactured in donor countries, and may introduce problems (for example the availability of hard currency or stable direct relationships with vendors) in securing a ready supply of parts. The issue is not just that technology must be imported from industrial countries—already a problem—but that many donors will give funds only for the purchase of goods manufactured in their own countries. Such conditions impede any rational and coordinated equipment purchasing policy in the governments of aid-dependent countries. Hence, point #2:

Buy locally if you can. U.S. government procurement policy systematically undercuts computer vendors in poor, low-technology economies not only by requiring purchases to be made from U.S. manufacturers, but by following lowest bid price rules which eliminate local vendors. Aid is tied to purchases in donor countries in order to ensure that government spending on foreign aid boosts the donor's own economy and (in the case of capitalist countries) the private interests of the donor's manufacturers. Lowest bid price rules simply represent an attempt to manage costs and combat corruption. Unfortunately, keeping initial prices down in this way does not always keep long-term costs down. Moreover, undercutting the position of local vendors is both antithetical to the professed goal of development and damaging to the immediate task of computerization, to the extent that it minimizes the development of support systems. Even where local purchases may be precluded, local maintenance contracts would be helpful; foreign donors characteristically do not make any provision for later maintenance of the goods they provide. Despite our requests, USAID was unwilling to deal with the fledgling computer stores of Khartoum, except for emergency service (and service, moreover, was considered the financial responsibility of the Sudanese government, not being covered in contract arrangements). This is also an argument in favor of "brand name" purchases, insofar as they provide not merely prestige but a much better chance of service in remote settings.

An easy-to-maintain, simple system is better than an easy-to-use but more complex system. In the U.S., software development has moved toward increasing internal complexity in an effort to achieve "user-friendliness". User-friendliness is of course a desirable goal anywhere, but an extremely unstable computing environment (like that in the Sudan) makes flexibility more important. Difficulties in training and retaining employees mean that any system will have to be easily learned. Few highly skilled people will be available to "maintain" or modify extremely complex software. Users will not be able easily to buy a new system or hire new technical advisors as applications change. Turnkey systems which work fine at the start will tend to fail because of lack of software maintenance or a changed organizational environment. Simple applications are also often overlooked by microcomputer advisors who have little real familiarity with the institution they are advising, its staff capabilities, or its needs. For example in the NPC project, microcomputers were originally introduced to facilitate population modeling; but the greatest impact they had on the organization and its work turned out to be in English and Arabic word processing, which allowed for the development of improved record keeping, journal publication, correspondence, etc. In this case, it was important that advisors were familiar with Arabic software in order to select the best system and to provide training.

Observable, interactive, visually-oriented systems stand a better chance of succeeding than "black box" or batch systems. The interactive friendliness and visual appeal of microcomputers is an important virtue to be maximized—even at the cost of system power. Shared goals and boss's orders are often insufficient motivations for learning to use a system. We found an ability to see the program do its work to be important not only in teaching new users, but in explaining the workings of our systems to the senior decision makers in both Sudanese government and donor bureaucracies. In the Finance Ministry project, no one ever paid much attention to, really understood or even wished to understand the system based on dBASE III; it will probably not be used very much. Those based on Lotus 1-2-3 caught the attention of all sorts of people during demonstrations and generated an interest that will probably translate into more effective use. The simulation package on population projections—"RAPID"—provided an initial source of high-level interest in computers, which then made possible a range of other uses.

Systems with modular, decentralized component parts will be more likely to survive. Highly integrated systems have undeniable advantages, but not as first (or early) computer implementations in very unstable, poorly developed computing environments. It is important to remember that systems will always fail. In a modular system, the failure of one sub-system will not cripple the whole. Not only are technological reasons not entirely controllable, but there are political/organizational reasons for failure. In the Sudan, the Presidential Palace for a time overruled the Ministry of Finance's authority to enforce development budget allocations. If work on the budget itself (the ultimate unifying system of our project) had to stop, the other information management functions could proceed separately. Moreover, implementing one module at a time allows for an iterative feedback process to inform the whole effort (see #12 below).

People: Training and Organization Are Key

The success of any computer application will be determined largely by its effect on the career paths (and remuneration) of individuals. One serious difficulty both projects faced was providing career tracks for the computer personnel we trained. USAID and the Sudanese managers were unable to establish a fair method of additional pay to people who could dramatically increase their salaries by leaving the Ministry of Finance as soon as they were trained. One of our better pupils secured a part-time position paying ten times her government salary. Three years after completion of the project, only a handful of the nearly thirty trainees remained with the Ministry. Such problems could become one of the greatest barriers to further introduction of computer technology within any specific unit, though of course the departed personnel will help to provide a better computing environment for the country as a whole, so long as they do not leave to market their skills abroad.

Training a few people to very high levels will not be as effective as training many people to lower levels. The highly trained specialists will, in the absence of very expensive inducements, probably leave. It might make more sense, anyway, for such experts to be trained through the usual educational channels. Only spreading training widely will help the organization as a whole to become a hospitable environment for computer applications. It will make computer training less of a scarce "property" to be controlled by individuals (or their supervisors) for personal advantage, and will encourage many more employees to feel an investment in the new systems rather than a hostility toward them.

Training must include senior decision makers as well as junior staff specializing in using a particular system. Senior officials cannot be expected to make good policy decisions regarding computerization efforts without a general knowledge of the equipment and systems in question. Moreover, they will shy away from discussing the crucial questions if they think that junior staff under them will discover them to be ignorant. Special kinds of training are needed for senior officials who need to understand a system but are not expected to use it hands-on. First, the senior officials will very likely consider it "inappropriate" to receive training side by side with the junior staff (even the middle-range managers for whom we designed one course failed to come after the Undersecretary decided that several very junior staff should also attend). In the National Population Committee case, the secretary whose duties initially were filing and occasional typing is now an indispensable part of the organization. Despite the importance of the computer in the committee's daily activities, no higher level staff have become familiar enough with the software to carry on in the secretary's absence.

Prior technical training and/or use of machines is an important predisposition to success in computer training. In the advanced economies nearly everyone deals with a sufficient range, variety, and complexity of mechanical and electro-mechanical appliances to be at least superficially familiar with how any specific device, such as a microcomputer, works. All manner of general information we may take to be obvious is not common currency in a system-poor environment. In a very poor country, even fairly well-educated people may find it hard to grasp the basic, essential information in an orientation to the machine. For example, in the Ministry of Finance and Planning, many people were totally unfamiliar with an English keyboard and lacked typing skills in general. This proved a major obstacle for some individuals. The same problem may occur separately from direct machine use. Progress on our project directory was continually delayed as a series of committees redesigned forms for data gathering. We had failed to communicate both that a database structure need not be precisely a copy of the visual appearance of data on a form, and that changing kinds or definitions of data for various fields would necessitate restructuring the database. As Kaplinsky has noted:

> the recognition of the systemic nature of technology is not something that can be left to common sense. It requires a specific recognition in the structure of training programs, right across the skill spectrum (Kaplinsky 1985:435).

People with engineering backgrounds tended to do better in our course than those who studied mathematics or economics. That, however, raises another problem: such people often had little interest in economic planning or financial management and only worked in the Ministry of Finance for lack of a job more appropriate to their training. In the NPC, most staff had already had some exposure to computers or at least an interest in what they could do.

Technique: Developing the Computing Environment

Technical efficiency in itself is seldom a sufficient reason for adoption of an innovation. The gains from such efficiency may be spread very thinly through the organization as collective goods not of sufficient benefit to anyone for him or her to sponsor the innovation; may be offset by a loss in personal power on the part of an important decision-maker;

may not be accompanied by a corollary improvement in personal situation in the organization. Generally, every application, no matter how self-evident its benefits may seem, requires an enthusiastic and powerful sponsor within the organization (compare Moris 1977:127). One subsystem that we proposed in the Ministry of Finance and Planning, for example, offered a fairly obvious gain in efficiency. Budget preparation—a task on which half a dozen staff members work for several months each year, and in which burdensome and repetitive clerical and arithmetical work overwhelms policy analysis—was computerized in 50 man-hours, including both system design and data entry. Revisions that previously had necessitated lengthy and error-ridden human re-computing were rendered routine. But the computer system was not fully or enthusiastically implemented, as best we can make out, because no one saw a direct gain. It would probably have cut the staff of an important section head; at the same time (against our advice) the physical computer (the potential reward) would have been located in the centralized MIS Unit, rather than in the section whose work would be computerized.

Any system which requires a new information flow, however reasonable or efficiently designed, will be more likely to fail than one which does not. Systems should be designed to make maximum use of existing information flows in order to make data collection as simple as possible. It proved much easier for us to develop software systems than to get the data collection organized to make the systems worthwhile. One should not underestimate the sheer shortage of reliable data, or the difficulty of getting government officials to do research to find data. Indeed, those who possess new computer skills seem particularly prone to feel that they are above searching for or checking data. While professionals may see computers as worthy of their attention, they think of dealing with data as a mere clerical matter (even when, as in our case, clerical assistants able to do this work are not available). Consultants need to build a substantial plan for implementing data collecting and management processes, rather than assuming that these will follow easily from good system design.

Applications should be computerized incrementally to allow the implementation experience to influence the design and to increase organizational fit and commitment. Implementation of this principle may run counter to the prevailing emphasis on top-down programming, but as Simon has suggested, ". . . complex systems will evolve from simple systems much more rapidly if there are stable intermediate forms than if there are not" (Simon 1969:209). Within the Ministry of Finance we found little appreciation of the need for accurate paper records. Ministry personnel did not themselves understand the flow of information from donors and within the Ministry. At the beginning of the system development process, virtually no one understood what was being computerized. As a result, it was necessary to design a simple system prototype, partially implement it to show how it worked, then gain the benefit of comments from Ministry staff who began to better understand what was going on and what the range of possibilities were.[11] Verbal explanations are no substitute for seeing the systems at work. Any system which is designed completely in advance will tend to be less well suited to user needs and less accurately understood by users. It is also easier to keep the systems simple when they are developed modularly.

Implementations should be planned to promote rather than subvert development of a country's support-systems for computing. Both within a particular organization and in a country as a whole, we think it likely that the biggest gains from early computerization efforts will be contributions to the creation of a stable, supportive computing environment which will allow future implementations to be made at higher and higher levels of sophistication and efficacy. One of the strengths of microcomputer technology as opposed to mainframe computing, of course, is the lower level of infrastructural support it requires. Nonetheless it requires a fair amount, and much of that may be lacking in developing countries. At present, applications tend to undercut the growth of better computing environments by failing to buy from local suppliers, use and support local computer specialists and institutions (such as University computer science departments or computer centers), and to provide as much training and infrastructural development as they might. Any turnkey system, for example, that is designed to be run by very low-skilled locals with high-skilled contributions coming only from foreigners will make little or no contribution to developing a better local computing environment.

Conclusion

Computers may in important ways influence or even cause social change. The spread of computers may reshape job markets, for example, and redefine specific jobs. Computerization generally reinforces the power of those bringing the new technology into organizations (Danziger 1985; King and Kraemer 1985), but they may also pose threats to established fiefdoms. Computer implementations may be occasions for needed bureaucratic reorganizations. It is our hope, not least of all, that microcomputers may help to give weak Third World governments the administrative capacity to chart something of their own courses of development even in the face of aid-dependency. Nonetheless, the primary causal arrow runs not from microcomputers to social change, but the other way around.

The basic social changes that have created the need for microcomputer technology in the Sudan and that continue to shape the course of implementations include the creation of a world full of international organizations and the formation of bilateral dependencies, each with their own demands for and challenges to information management capacity. Behind this lies the Sudan's dependence on big-project aid, and the long-standing predilection of the international aid community for such mega-projects (despite frequent exhortations to the contrary). Computerization in Sudan reflects also the influence of an internationalization of culture in which computers are attractively portrayed through the media, in which Sudanese elites receiving education abroad learn of their desirability, and in which various international agencies operate throughout the world as exemplars.

Microcomputers are not, as some of their boosters have proclaimed, a panacea for Third World development, a magic way to overcome the asymmetries of wealth and power which shape world affairs. On the contrary, it is largely those asymmetries that make computerization essential, not optional, as a part of the effort to maintain government administrative capacity in the Third World. This may serve government elites most of all, but weak states in Africa have not really served anyone very well.

There can be little doubt that microcomputers will continue to spread through much of the Third World in the coming years (the symposium in *South*, July 1987). They will do so in large part simply because they are becoming a part of standard operations in an enormous range of organizations and professional activities. The poorest of Third World countries—many of them in Africa—are apt to lag behind this process of computerization, to their considerable disadvantage. This is all the more unfortunate, given the special needs for informational management capacity which aid-dependency forces on them.

In this chapter, we have tried to suggest something of this need. Perhaps more importantly, we have offered a variety of suggestions for how to improve efforts to meet it by computerization in countries like the Sudan. These are based on project experience, not systematic research. No doubt they could be improved upon. But as the brief description of one aspect of one of the projects shows, the problems, the needs, and the challenges they reflect are not altogether idiosyncratic. There are many other settings in which microcomputers are being introduced into bureaucracies with very inadequate paper record-keeping systems. There are many other settings where general infrastructural support for computing is weak. Perhaps the single most distinguishing factor of the Sudanese case is one that it shares with other aid-dependent countries and that is the flip side of their considerable special need for technical support in administration: This is the distortion and difficulty imposed on processes of computer implementation by the preponderance of external pressures in the push for computerization and the decision-making about actual system

forms. This distortion is a reflection of the lack of organizational control and independence from domestic political elites
and especially from international and foreign actors, a lack that
the computers ought to help overcome yet cannot without the
assertion of local initiative by the organization's staff.

In short, in using computers to enhance administration, as
well as for other areas of national struggle, countries like the
Sudan are apt to encounter a "catch-22." Despite that, struggle
will go on, and computerization will play a part in efforts to
achieve the state administrative capacity essential to empowering countries in the contemporary world system.

Notes

1. Calhoun was co-director (with Dale Whittington) of the first project,
lasting from 1984 to 1986; from 1986 to 1990, DeLargy worked on and later
directed the second (on behalf of The Futures Group and the Carolina
Population Center). We learned a great deal from our colleagues, and
thank them and the staff members of the USAID mission in Khartoum and
of the Ministry of Finance and Economic Planning and the National
Population Committee, without whom none of this work would have been
done. Needless to say, they bear no responsibility for the present paper
which reflects our views alone.

2. Sudan is certainly in no position to opt out of the world system and
attempt to follow an autochthonous development strategy by closing its
borders, as did China thirty years ago.

3. A more detailed discussion of this issue may be found in Calhoun,
Drummond, and Whittington 1987.

4. Even relatively low-level staff of donor agencies demand to conduct
their business with very senior Sudanese officials. USAID project officers
newly arrived for their first posting, for example, felt entitled to bypass all
Sudanese government officials below the rank of under-secretary—even
though the odds were that they could not get an appointment with
someone of that rank in their own government.

5. The Sudan received nearly a billion dollars of foreign aid in 1988
(according to OECD figures; *The Economist*, 10 February, 1990). 1988 was
a relatively good year agriculturally. Nevertheless, the figure might have
been higher had several countries not curtailed their support following the
intensification of civil war. The Sudan ranked ninth in total foreign aid
received in 1988, and on a *per capita* basis, ranked far ahead of such
countries as India which received larger absolute amounts. A particularly

high percentage of this was emergency aid, more difficult in many ways to administer than long-term development assistance.

6. See Adkins 1988 for discussion of similar issues in Tanzania.

7. It should be said that there was much discussion in Sudan during the 1980s of the need for a "proper" system of national accounts. A variety of organizations, including both the IMF and USAID were active proponents of this, and brought several expensive missions of short-term consultants to Sudan to consider possibilities. The idea was of course reasonable in the abstract, and effective national accounts would be an important planning and administrative tool. Concretely, though, it was a bit absurd and its popularity was based on complete inattention to the difficulties of data collection and the need to develop intermediate information systems. Proposals to proceed immediately to the construction of national accounts on the basis of individual returns (for example Morrison 1985) owe more to textbooks in economics or public administration than to concrete considerations of the world's least developed countries.

8. See Whittington, Calhoun, and Drummond 1986 and Whittington and Calhoun 1988 for further description.

9. Lest it be thought that this was purely a matter of Sudanese culture, rather than more specifically bureaucratic style, it should be said that the National Population Committee was more flexible. In fact, the secretarial and administrative staff hold almost all the practical expertise in the organization.

10. The unfortunate, but unavoidable, result of Arabicization was that the operations of the project became less and less accessible to the non-Arabic speaking members of the technical assistance team, and that fewer of the written products generated by the NPC (papers, reports, plans, analyses, graphics presentations) could be read or heard and understood by the project monitors in Washington, the USAID staff in Khartoum, or other interested non-Sudanese. Arabic-speaking OPTIONs team members and NPC staff began to spend a large amount of time simply translating for the sake of the donor.

11. See Naumann and Jenkins 1982 on a "prototyping" approach to systems development. In development planning itself, there recently has been renewed recognition of the need for experimentation and pilot projects for similar reasons (see summary in Rondinelli 1983, Chapter 4). Commenting on a microcomputer implementation in a Portuguese development project, Ingle and Connerly (1984:50) express a similar preference for "a participative, iterative process rather than single-minded, blueprint pursuit of planned products."

3

Microcomputer Adoption in Tanzania and the Rise of a Professional Elite

Suzanne Grant Lewis[1]

In recent years, Tanzania has experienced tremendous increases in computer use and in the numbers of people who earn their livelihood through computers. The Tanzanian computer industry is now a complex matrix of private vendors, computer personnel in government and parastatal service, local private computer consultants, expatriate advisors, educators in public training institutions, data processing clerks, and other less easily categorized elements. The highly trained personnel in the public and private sectors are organizing themselves into a profession, the most notable effort being the 1986 establishment of a national professional computer association. While the emergence of an indigenous computer profession may be seen as a development likely to reduce Tanzania's reliance on foreign experts and expand the knowledge base beyond the small group of private computer vendors, a closer examination finds that it marks the consolidation of an elite which, in pursuing their interests, is restricting both the type of users and uses of microcomputers in the country and doing little to promote the goals of socialist construction. This chapter offers an understanding of the forces behind this professionalization, a look at how technical knowledge is being utilized and suggests the role the possessors of that knowledge play in Tanzania's path toward socialist development.

To set the context for this discussion of the emergence of a professionalizing computer elite and its implications, a brief discussion of the political-economic setting is presented. This is followed by an overview of the microcomputer situation in the country.

The Rise of a Technocratic-Administrative Perspective in Tanzania

A very lively debate has continued for more than two decades on the position of Tanzania in the world economy and its progress towards socialism. Scholars in this debate offer alternative explanations for the inconsistencies in ideology and action of Tanzanian leadership and for the incompatibilities of various policies. For our purposes here, we are interested in recent assessments which note the mid-1980s liberalization measures (including the loosening of import restrictions, support for private education, the reintroduction of school fees, and the divestiture of some previously nationalized sisal plantations) and the 1986 IMF agreement, to the extent that they might assist us in understanding the emergence of a computer elite in Tanzania and its efforts at professionalization.

Analysts draw a wide range of conclusions from recent developments in Tanzania: the abandonment of socialism; the postponement of socialist construction; tactical changes in the continued struggle; and even a renewed opportunity for true socialism. It is striking, however, that observers from a number of perspectives—modernizationist, social democratic, and socialist—suggest that both the party, Chama cha Mapinduzi, and the civil service have become increasingly technocratic and administrative in orientation and that the tension between the technocrats and the politicians has heightened.

> In the struggles among the contenders for power in Tanzania, the experts have displaced the politicians: The

> relative dominance in the late 1960s and mid-1970s of a
> political perspective that regarded development as
> essentially a political process and that emphasized
> politicization, mobilization, and, to some extent, socialism
> was by the early 1980s supplanted by a return to the
> view that development is principally a technical process,
> although, of course, one requiring a supportive political
> environment (Samoff 1990,266).

Samoff sees this as a result of the gradual loss of legitimacy of politicians since the mid-1970s, particularly due to unmet demands for food and consumer goods. The technocratic orientation is gaining ground as policy discussions become apolitical and seemingly neutral in their technocratic-administrative emphasis. As a consequence, "Tanzania's transition is stymied. Its socialist vision is regularly obscured and often overwhelmed by its capitalist practice. . . . Frequently denounced, the modernization orientation is equally frequently reasserted, with both local and foreign support" (Samoff 1990,268).

Lofchie (1985), whom I characterize as a modernizationist, sees the conflict as experts versus socialists. A group of "pragmatic civil servants," including the Minister for Finance, are disillusioned with statism and are pushing for economic reforms such as greater scope for the private sector. Opposition to such reforms, Lofchie says, will be presented as a defense of Tanzanian socialism but it will really be party members fighting to retain their privileged positions in ministries and parastatals.

Biermann (1986) sees the technocracy as a separate entity within the state apparatus. The technocracy, a fraction of the governing strata, has expanded in recent years with the increased need for a technocratic apparatus to manage the complex and extended relationships between the state and different subordinate institutions. Cleavages between political leaders and technocrats appeared following the 1980 IMF negotiations, with the technocracy gaining additional power. A showdown between the two was avoided by the announcement of the National Economic Survival Programme but the new agricultural policies, emphasizing individual cooperative producers, economics of growth, and foreign capital inputs to stimulate economic recovery, featured the technocracy's agenda while still maintaining social achievements as sacrosanct. Technical expertise has become more important than mass mobilization. Biermann interprets both the National Economic Survival Programme and the Structural Adjustment Programme as political victories for the technocracy. The 1984 liberalization of imports is interpreted as an alliance of technocracy with petty bourgeoisie (which is reaping windfall profits) and as a sign of the state's weakening influence in economic affairs. A complete change in the locus of power requires political dismantling of the socialist agenda and the alienation of the leadership from its mass base of support, both of which some observers have suggested are occurring. The technocracy is less interested in private accumulation than power and is national in essence and outlook.

Shivji, one of the strongest radical critics of the Tanzanian state, also cites the preeminence of economics and the displacement of politics evident in the ideology of "developmentalism." Although appearing under different guises, developmentalism—a belief in Tanzania's economic backwardness and the supremacy of economics over politics—has been the dominant ideology since independence, widely accepted by politicians and conservative and radical scholars alike. The contradiction, Shivji argues, is between statism and privatization of the economy. The state bourgeoisie has been put on the defensive by the economic crisis and the inefficiency and corruption of the state bureaucracy. The private comprador bourgeoisie (the private industrial and commercial class) is backed by the IMF, the World Bank, and other funding agencies and is on the offensive. Judging from the concessions it has been able to wring from the state (import liberalization, layoffs, devaluation), the private comprador bourgeoisie seems to be gaining ground. Shivji suggests that these recent policies may undercut economic efforts of the 1960s and 1970s and promote the "narrow interests of the worst kind of compradores, currency smugglers . . . commission agents, local representatives of foreign commercial firms and so on" (1985,13). But Shivji remains hopeful that the politics of the masses will return to center stage as people realize that "no real and sustained economic development has taken place since independence but meanwhile people have lost their political freedom as well" (1985,12).

Jinadu suggests that the move towards a more instrumental view of development and new attention to the private sector is the result of widespread disappointment that Tanzania is more dependent on the international system today than at the time that self-reliance policies were announced (1985,122). He notes that political scientists and sociologists have lost significant ground to economists in policy formulation. The social sciences at the University of Dar es Salaam (UDSM) have been deradicalized, abandoning the progressive reputation of the 1960s and 1970s. Within economics, a more technical, neo-classical approach is being emphasized today and less attention is being given to normative-structural analysis. Jinadu traces this shift indirectly to an increase in overseas staff development programs (Jinadu 1985,124-8). Department of Economics staff receiving training in the US and UK have had trouble with statistics and quantitative analysis. The undergraduate economics program was revised to address this shortcoming, even though the proportion likely to receive further training overseas is quite small. Jinadu refers to this as part of the hegemonic diffusion of US social science into Africa.

As illustrations of the new salience of economics in national fora, Jinadu cites workshops and seminars held in 1983-1984, all focused on economic dimensions of development. I note that in 1985-86, the years of my fieldwork, this preoccupation continued with two more university-sponsored workshops. The first, sponsored by the UDSM Faculty of Commerce and Management on "Liberalization of the Economy in Tanzania," discussed whether the import liberalization policy should continue. The even larger workshop, "Policies and Strategies for Economic Recovery," sponsored by the UDSM Department of Economics and the Economic Research Bureau, was designed as a dialogue between intellectuals and government and party officials. In this forum, the Minister for Finance made no reference to socialism or self-reliance but spoke of regaining Tanzania's competitiveness in world markets; stimulating growth through investment in tourist facilities, game and mining; continuing the search for grants, import support, and investment resources; and encouraging foreign and domestic investment to supplement the people's efforts (Msuya 1986).

Social scientists commenting on Tanzania's political economy have not addressed the question of computer adoption, but analyses of recent developments in Tanzania would suggest that with the resurgence of the modernization approach to development, the expanded application of any Western imported technology would not be surprising. The rapid expansion in the use of foreign computer technology (see appendix to this chapter) is both a reflection of Tanzania's integration into the capitalist world economy and a factor influencing Tanzania's future role in the world economy. What needs exploring is who controls and influences the introduction and application of the technology and which social relations are transformed as part of this process.

Overview of the Microcomputer Situation in Tanzania

The introduction of microcomputers is a recent phenomenon in Tanzania, with most of the importation occurring since 1985. The number of systems is small in absolute terms but high in relative growth terms, having increased by a factor of at least two every year since 1980. (See the Appendix for a more detailed inventory of computers in Tanzania.) The distribution pattern is an urban one, with 73% in Dar es Salaam and another 19% in the next five largest towns. Most of the microcomputers are institutionally owned (89%) rather than owned by individuals. Nearly two thirds of the micro-computers are in the public sector, with 73% of these in parastatals rather than in ministries.

Microcomputers exist in greatest concentration in parastatal organizations in the financial and communications/transport sectors. There are also significant numbers in the agricultural and industrial sectors but in lower institutional densities. The most common application is data analysis, particularly statistical analysis. Record keeping, billing, accounts, stock control, project management and monitoring, word processing, and programming training are other common uses.

Only 55% of the microcomputers present in 1986 were locally serviceable. External aid agencies fund the majority of the systems through a process which has paid little attention to local service and compatibility.

The government has played a prominent role by attempting to restrict the number of computers being introduced. In 1974 an import restriction on computers was established to address three main concerns: the foreign exchange costs of the technology; frustration among end-users of government mainframe computers; and a wider effort by the central government to control all aspects of the economy. In establishing the import restriction, policy makers resisted the advice of Tanzanian and foreign technical experts. In neither its design nor its implementation was the policy linked to broader national goals of socialist construction. The Computer Advisory Committee (CAC), which has reviewed applications for computer imports since 1981, has focused on controlling the distribution pattern rather than promoting effective use. As a result, both private computer vendors and foreign assistance agencies operating in Tanzania have played larger roles than otherwise might have been the case. In regards to foreign assistance agencies, neither the CAC nor the institutions receiving computers have questioned the right of foreign assistance agencies to select computer systems. Both the structure of the foreign assistance agency-recipient relationship and the bureaucratic practices of foreign assistance procurement have constrained Tanzania. In regards to local computer vendors, their control of technical information within the country has made Tanzanian institutions dependent on these commercial firms. Vendors have not shown themselves to be very able, particularly with microcomputers, in supporting and training Tanzanians.

The Professionalization of the Computer Elite

The Tanzanian computer elite is a profession in the sense defined by Eliot Freidson, "an occupation which has assumed a dominant position in a division of labor so that it gains control over the determination of the substance of its own work" (Freidson 1973,xvii). Computer personnel in Tanzania--vendors, computer personnel in public institutions, private consultants, and educators--have gained a dominant role in Tanzania's computer industry, influencing the processes of computer introduction and application. Efforts are now underway to expand that power by determining who enters their profession, with what training, and how their work is done. This process of professionalizing computer personnel represents more than just a collection of interest groups applying pressure on the state and each other. It involves the redefinition of social relations, specifically the relations of local computer vendors to the larger professional community, computer professionals vis-à-vis national policy makers, and in the end, computer professionals and microcomputer users. The establishment of a national professional association and other efforts aimed at ensuring a stronger voice for computer personnel in policy making are evidence of the construction of this profession.

Attention to the ideological and historical aspects indicates the potentially decisive role of the state in regulating the power of professionals. In a context in which individuals and institutions with technological expertise are likely to gain power and prestige, an emerging computer elite has been able to move forward with its efforts to professionalize. Our main concern is in understanding recent efforts to construct a computer profession in Tanzania and the implications for future microcomputer use, education, and training, as well as the broader national goals.

The computer profession in Tanzania is a profession in formation. My comments therefore include both an analysis of enacted events and conjectures of how the situation is likely to proceed. There is sufficient evidence thus far to conclude that rather than presenting a challenge to the state, the construction of this profession is an attempt to find a place for a small technological elite in the ranks of the increasingly technocratic ruling strata.

Impetus to Professionalization: Frustration with Government Policy

The professionalization of computer personnel is being mediated by the role of the Tanzanian state. A major impetus for the construction of a profession is the frustration of computer personnel with government policy efforts, or rather lack of effort. First, despite numerous calls for a national computer policy and a national computer training program, dating as far back as 1969, the government has made no effort to develop a policy beyond an import restriction. The financial leaders have shown great reluctance to heed advice from technical computer personnel. The sole policy mechanism has been the Ad Hoc Computer Advisory Committee (CAC), a group of eleven civil servants, most of them high level computer personnel, which meets regularly to vet applications for computer import licenses and makes recommendations to the Minister for Finance. This committee lost its credibility as a neutral group of experts amid accusations of vendor bias made privately by computer personnel in public sector computer installations, vendors, and top Ministry of Finance officials. Second, frustration has resulted from the repeated battles between public sector computer managers and the CAC over applications to import computers for their institutions. While they concede the need to control foreign exchange expenditures, computer personnel feel that institutions, particularly those with in-house computer expertise, should have autonomy over the choice of technology. Third, few computer installations are represented on the CAC and this lack of voice seems to be another major force behind the formation of the national computer association. Finally, the CAC did not prove to be an effective mechanism for educating managers about computing, a need which was seen as crucial by all sub-groups of the computer community.

As the CAC lost its credibility in the eyes of the wider computer community, attention shifted to the formation of the Computer Association of Tanzania (COMPAT) as a legitimate means of gaining status and policy making influence. CAC members themselves were disillusioned with the CAC--it was only an advisory body and efforts to extend its powers failed to receive the support of the Minister for Finance. By becoming involved in COMPAT, which has wide support in the computer community, the CAC members have attempted to restore their reputations which were damaged by their participation in what has come to be known as a corrupt and biased body. By deferring issues to the COMPAT and by assuming leadership roles in the Interim Committee of COMPAT, the CAC members have been able to reassert themselves as experts who have the interests of the profession and the nation in mind.

Means to Developing the Computer Profession

Six means have been employed in the construction of the computer profession in Tanzania: (1) the establishment of a professional association; (2) expansion of influence over education and training; (3) comparison with other professional bodies; (4) continued alliance with foreign assistance agencies; (5) membership in international organizations; and (6) the development of an ideological rationale.

Establishment of a Professional Association

Trained computer personnel in Tanzania today are, in the words of Jules-Rosette, "technicians of the sacred" (Jules-Rosette 1990,77). They control both the information about computer technology and the information stored and processed by computers. They are interested in maintaining that control and expanding the related rewards. The Computer Association of Tanzania (COMPAT) is in many ways an ideal mechanism for pursuing the interests of computer professionals. Professional associations are an internationally accepted way of promoting group interests while at the same time claiming to serve national interests.

There have been many calls for the establishment of a national professional computer society to consolidate and expand that control. One of the recommendations of the 1972 government report by an ILO advisor was the establishment of a Computer Society of Tanzania, a professional organization of individuals interested in data processing (Smyth 1972). The Society would promote collaboration and cooperation among computer personnel and end-users, provide a forum for the exchange of views on computer issues (possibly publishing a journal), contribute to the morale and competence of professional electronic data processing (EDP) staff, and work for the continuing, professional development of computer personnel in the country. In his 1980 presentation to the UNESCO Regional Meeting of Computer Centre Directors in Africa, a Tanzanian parastatal computer manager called for the establishment of user groups and computer associations (Magambo 1980). Although these organizations would differ in their memberships, they would share two main purposes: to exchange ideas and information and to act as a pressure group on computer manufacturers.

The Computer Association of Tanzania was established through an alliance of four public and private sector factions: vendors; computer professionals in public institutions; consultants; and academics. Such an alliance may appear surprising on the surface but it is quite understandable. There have been cross-overs in public and private sectors of employment in Tanzania's computer industry for a long time. The employment histories of most vendors and full-time consultants include public sector work. While public sector computer professionals do not generally work for vendors, they do work in collaboration with full-time consultants and are called in by the customers of vendors, including foreign assistance agencies, as part-time advisors. All four sub-groups have a common interest: the controlled promotion of computers in Tanzania. Vendors make their living from selling and maintaining hardware and software. Public sector computer personnel and academics obtain their living and professional identity as institutional experts on computers. Consultants offer computer-related services such as feasibility studies, installation and customization of software, and staff training.

Computer professionals in Tanzania view a professional association as a means of becoming major participants in the formulation of a national computer policy. The number of professionals involved in the Ad Hoc Computer Advisory Committee was limited and many of those who previously had no official voice expect to have one in the COMPAT.

A second goal which computer personnel are pursuing through the COMPAT is increased status, both within their own organizations and in the wider society. Calls for management training from computer professionals reflect the desire of this group to have their profession recognized by colleagues in government bureaucracy. Greater awareness is expected to increase the perceived value of the corpus of knowledge over which the computer professionals claim control. Professional privilege is derived from this perceived value. The management courses are not accidentally called computer appreciation seminars. They offer an introduction to EDP terms and a general outline of what EDP can offer managers. The idea is to break down management fears regarding the technology but not to share any "sacred" knowledge. The courses highlight the need for highly skilled technical experts for the implementation of computerized systems and underscore the contribution computer professionals make to contemporary bureaucracies.

Increased status is expected to provide dividends in income as well as other intangible benefits for public sector computer personnel, vendors, and consultants. The vendors, who identify management education as the primary need in Tanzania, hope that foreign assistance agencies, in their preoccupation with management, will lend support to such courses and encourage sales. In addition, increased appreciation is expected to result in more consultancy opportunities for public and private professionals.

The COMPAT constitution was drafted by an interim committee of nine appointed at a general meeting of computer personnel in the country. The document was circulated and then revised at a meeting of more than 30 high level computer personnel in August 1986. The content of the document indicates the drafters' concern with defining a body of knowledge, service ethic, admission rules for new members, and self-regulation--all characteristics of the ideal-type model of a profession (Millerson 1964). The constitution indicates the intention to define the knowledge area and technique through the establishment of educational standards, curricula, and examinations. The constitution also emphasizes service to society and a code of ethics. One of the stated objectives of the association is to give advice on the development and application of computer technology to any interested parties. A code governing the conduct of members is also being developed. With regard to the autonomy of the profession, its intra-professional structure, and its ability to be self-regulating, the association is set up separately from government control but protected by government laws by its registration as an association.

The Multifaceted Role of Education and Training

Education and training is perhaps the most important legitimizing mechanism of professionals. By exercising control over the definition of professional expertise and the process of knowledge acquisition, computer professionals control the reproduction and distribution of knowledge related to their profession.

Selecting Members of the Profession. Education and training is a large part of the definition of the profession. As a selection mechanism, it determines membership in the elite and controls the distribution of privilege. Membership rules of the COMPAT exclude certain individuals who do not hold the required educational credentials, despite extensive computer work experience. The managing director of one of the computer vendors is not accepted as a computer professional because of his training. He is disparagingly referred to as "just a businessman." Computer professionals in Tanzania are large system people who have moved into microcomputer use. Educators who teach microcomputing are not considered computer professionals if they do not have large system training. Provided membership in COMPAT continues to require formal computer science education, it seems likely that the profession will keep its roots in large systems.

About 60% of the computer professionals surveyed have had overseas education, usually for a higher degree. Another 11% have had in-service training overseas. First degrees are usually in a combination of Mathematics, Physics, and Statistics although engineering degrees are also common. Training by vendors is the most common type of in-service training. The high proportion of overseas trained professionals means group exposure to international standards, the valuing of international connections, and the reinforcement of the elite status of the profession.

Education and Training for Reproducing Expertise. The specialized body of knowledge over which a profession claims exclusive authority is socially constructed. It is not universally defined by some objective means but rather through negotiation among factions within the profession as well as in response to external pressures. That body of knowledge can be decreased or expanded, subsections elevated in status or denigrated, from within or outside the profession. In the United States in the 1950s and 1960s, the deskilling of data processing work occurred as a result of the application of management theory and shop-floor practices (Greenbaum 1979). Kraft's study of how programming tasks have been "de-professionalized" through routinization by managers is further evidence of the changing nature of "professional expertise" (Kraft 1977). As a reproductive instrument, training distributes the defined knowledge base composed of two parts: a technical sphere as well as a world view. The technical sphere is not without biases and the Tanzanian profession has a distinct preference for software over hardware skills and for formal computer science training (systems analysis and programming) over end-user knowledge (facility with commercial software). Computer professionals tend to be software people. The Association's expressed interest is in developing standards for high level training, rather than technician level, and on formal academic credentials (degrees and publications), not practical skills.

Training institutions which offer hardware training, such as the Dar es Salaam Technical College and the Posts and Telecommunications Corporation Training School, are not considered "professional" institutions (and their graduates are therefore not members of the profession) because of their hardware bias and the fact that they train personnel at the maintenance technician level. The only commercially licensed training institute which focuses on training programmers and systems analysts has been strongly criticized by professionals rather than praised for its efforts to develop a curriculum. As Jules-Rosette concludes from the Kenyan situation, the motive behind the criticism may be that the institution offers the sacred knowledge to anyone who can afford to pay for it (Jules-Rosette 1990). In Tanzania's public sector-dominated computer world, the state is expected to support such training, with the computer professionals exercising all but financial control. Government-subsidized higher education degrees at the University of Dar es Salaam, graduate programs abroad offered through the government, or on-the-job vendor courses paid for by the public sector employer are the acceptable ways for professionals to be trained in Tanzania. There is also a lack of recognition of computer training efforts in some public institutions, specifically the College of Business Education. Here the criticism is most likely due to the definition of computer knowledge. Business students are taught microcomputer applications relevant to business, rather than programming and systems analysis, the mainstays of "true" computer education.

Structural constraints in the wider work environment hinder any attempt to emphasize practical experience. For example, in the universities, only the director of the University Computer Centre is considered academic staff, with promotion being based on the international academic standard of publications rather than industrial experience and applied research on indigenous engineering problems.[2] Other staff members above the technician level, while promoted on the basis of practical work accomplished, feel they suffer from lack of status as they are considered administrative staff and do not receive a housing allowance. University computer staff continue to move to parastatals and the private sector for better employment terms.

The world view promoted through professional training can be identified through the discourse surrounding the images of computers and their uses. This discourse, both written and oral, borders at times on technological determinism but in the main reflects the ideology of developmentalism, which commentators argue is gaining ground in the ruling class. In a context in which development has become fundamentally a technical and not a political problem, technologies are what are needed. Computer technology is viewed as causally related to development. Its speed and accuracy make management efficient. This modernizing technology will improve Tanzania's competitiveness. Computer professionals are therefore modernizers. The three reference groups of the profession--the state, the foreign assistance agencies, and the international computer manufacturers--further support this discourse.

With computer personnel benefiting greatly from recent developments, particularly from the increased microcomputer use, there is little reason for them to challenge the resurgence of a technocratic and administrative orientation in Tanzania's national politics. In its plans to develop training standards, the COMPAT will attempt to maintain and strengthen the current division of labor to the detriment of alternative efforts to "democratize" computer use among workers.

The role of higher education as the primary reproductive mechanism has been different in the case of Tanzania's computer profession from that in other East African professions such as medicine (Rathgeber 1985). Whereas university medical training has formed the primary background for medical professionals, the education of computer professionals has been accomplished through many channels, increasingly through uncoordinated, foreign assistance-sponsored overseas training. This is due, in part, to the resource troubles of the University of Dar es Salaam Computer Centre and the M.Sc. degree program in Computer Science. Due to a shortage of teaching staff, the Centre has offered the M.Sc. program only three times (in 1972, 1974, and 1981) and has graduated less than 16. Graduates rarely stay on to teach at the university because of more attractive opportunities in the government and private sector.

Professional Legitimation through Education and Training. The legitimation function of training emphasizes the long and specialized training required to perform computer work, thereby justifying claims to power and privilege. The monopoly control which vendors have held over technical knowledge in Tanzania has supported the idea that computer use requires expert knowledge that is available only through high level training. The emerging computer profession's definition of the knowledge base as systems analysis and programming and its emphasis on graduate degrees continue to promote the view that computers require expert knowledge to use, and allow the profession to justify its efforts to control skill assessment and training standards.

To date, efforts to control the type of use and user have been limited to institutions in which computer managers have tried to keep computer resources (especially the high growth area of microcomputing) under the jurisdiction of the computer department and large system computer personnel. The COMPAT is interested in influencing these patterns of use and users nationally.

The manipulation of education and training and its various functions indicates the profession's interest in limiting the secularization of computer technology. Within the profession, the majority of members are also trying to limit the role of the vendors by expanding the distribution of technical knowledge throughout the profession and breaking the monopoly hold of vendors. This expansion of the knowledge base must be executed carefully in order to increase the power of computer professionals, avoid alienating the vendors who provide a vital link with the western computer manufacturers, and at the same time ensure that the knowledge does not enter the public domain. Computer professionals have placed their faith in the COMPAT as the means of orchestrating this sharing of the knowledge base. It remains to be seen whether such faith is well placed.

The computer profession in Tanzania will not have an easy time controlling the educational systems for reproducing expertise. The difficulties of the university's graduate program in Computer Science, the uncertainty of funding for the proposed diploma and certificate courses in data processing, and the vagaries of foreign assistance through which much of the training (particularly in Nairobi and overseas) is provided are factors beyond their direct control. What the professional association will focus on, however, is controlling access to training and influencing the content of that training.

It is too early to comment on the COMPAT's effectiveness in implementing its educational plans, including the delimitation of "expertise" and the design of professional standards for education and COMPAT membership. The Association supports plans to establish diploma and certificate courses at the University of Dar es Salaam in addition to the existing Master of Science (Computer Science) degree program. This calls to mind the situation in Ghana described by Bennell in which the professional association of pharmacists fought government efforts to blur the differences between professional and technician level occupations. The professional groups pushed for clear distinctions and succeeded in devaluing diploma courses (Bennell 1982,601-2). The COMPAT's education plans remain in an early stage of formulation, but the Ghana experience suggests that the profession could be moving towards inflating professional qualifications in order to maintain elite status and power.

Comparison with Other Professional Bodies

Bennell found that comparisons of skills and responsibilities between the emerging pharmacy profession and other professions was one of the tactics used to promote the development of the new profession (Bennell 1982). In Tanzania, the model for the computer profession has been the accountancy and auditing profession. The Tanzanian National Board of Accountants and Auditors (NBAA) is a professional body which sets examinations and runs review courses for professional credentials. The NBAA takes credit for establishing Tanzania's accountancy and auditing profession. With its main focus on training activities, the association supplements the efforts of full-time training institutions.[3] Discussions of education and training needs for computer personnel have frequently made reference to these management and accountancy training programs. The NBAA sees itself as addressing areas of national importance such as the failure of enterprises to produce annual accounts. It designs special semi-professional courses and examinations for certifying government officers (NBAA 1985 and Interviews with NBAA Registrar, September 1986), and stresses "the crucial role played by the NBAA in the economic development of the country" (NBAA 1984). The COMPAT, too, links itself to national development activities by "co-ordinating ideas and performance of computer professionals and the policy making national institutions of Party and Government" (COMPAT 1986,1).

There are important differences between the two professional bodies. The COMPAT is a non-governmental society while the NBAA was set up as a parastatal under the Ministry of Finance, an arrangement which offers autonomy as required for professions but within the limits sanctioned by the government. Until 1984, the NBAA Chair was never an accountant. This recent appointment and the associated change in membership of the Governing Council to 80% accountants have been viewed as evidence of the Government's confidence in the professionals themselves. The COMPAT governing council, on the other hand, is made up entirely of computer professionals. The appointment of high level public sector EDP managers and academics to the Association's interim committee was designed, in my view, to ensure government confidence. The COMPAT started with a good deal more autonomy than the NBAA, which had to struggle for years to expand theirs.

Continued Alliance with Foreign Assistance Agencies

All the professional sub-groups—vendors, public sector computer personnel, private consultants, and academics—are well served by continued, if not increased, foreign assistance for computer acquisition. The positive dispositions of the IMF, World Bank and other funding agencies towards computers ease the proselytizing work of all computer professionals in Tanzania. The bottom line for many of these agencies' recommendations is a push for improved management and, towards that end, the introduction of modern management tools such as computers. In recent years, the Tanzania government has been put on the defensive by the IMF, the World Bank, and other agencies and appears to be succumbing to pressure to accept agency views of the problem. Because of this, there is less of a need for computer professionals to stress their contribution to the national interests on ideological or economic grounds.

With reference to specific sub-groups, vendors benefit from the increased sales which result from foreign assistance projects. Even if they do not make the original sale, vendors generally contract for the maintenance of hardware and software. With support from funding agencies and public sector computer personnel, vendors avoid the problem of customers being refused import permits. There is greater assurance the computers will be allowed into the country if they are funded through foreign assistance than through Tanzania's foreign exchange reserves. To date nearly all microcomputers being introduced through aid projects have been granted import permission.

The enthusiasm of foreign assistance agencies for computers has resulted in increased opportunities for private consultants as well, although these opportunities have been fought for in competition with foreign computer consultants. Increased attention of foreign consultants to the Tanzania market is likely, considering the rapidly expanding Kenya situation and the continued involvement of foreign assistance agencies as long as the government adheres to IMF conditions, but by promoting local expertise through a professional association, computer professionals hope to limit the role of outsiders. An alliance between all professional sub-groups helps consultants inform colleagues of their areas of expertise and presents to the outside world the picture of a responsible self-regulating group interested in serving the needs of the nation.

Public sector computer personnel in the country are interested in gaining access to resources in the form of departmental staff, computer equipment, and training for themselves and their staff. Most of these resources originate in foreign assistance projects and most of the training takes place in Nairobi or overseas. Recent work by Unsicker (1987) argues that the shortages of consumer and capital goods in the 1970s affected the way the government employees viewed foreign assistance. External funding became the only way of gaining access to travel opportunities, scarce commodities, and resources for building a department within the bureaucracy. It is therefore important to maintain the image necessary to secure the foreign assistance, and the development of a profession would serve this need.

In addition to enabling computer professionals to update their knowledge, which increases their value on the home market, training in Nairobi or overseas carries the added advantage of giving computer personnel access to consumer goods and the foreign exchange necessary for their purchase. This is no small perquisite to Tanzanian public sector employees.

Finally, academics who train computer personnel in the classroom and in special courses rely on foreign assistance for the limited equipment that is available in training institutions and for short term regional and overseas training courses for themselves.

While the alliance of vendors, consultants, academics, and public sector computer professionals is served in some ways by foreign assistance agencies, the alliance does not give the agencies limitless influence. Indeed, public sector computer personnel in some instances have managed to manipulate computer-related foreign assistance to ensure that the EDP department maintains institutional control over microcomputers and reaps the benefits of training grants without having to accept expatriate involvement in the daily operations of their organization. The Cooperative Rural Development Bank (CRDB) gained institutional and staff experience with large computer systems and managed to limit foreign involvement in its recent efforts to use microcomputers to serve commercial banking functions (Grant Lewis 1988a,260). More commonly, however, computer professionals do not challenge the right of foreign assistance agencies to determine the problem to be addressed, the selection of hardware and software, or the design and delivery of training.

Membership in International Organizations

A small group of computer professionals worked for years to convince the government to join the Intergovernmental Bureau of Informatics (IBI), a now defunct United Nations organization whose membership was comprised mostly of Third World countries. The original push came from Mr. Amir Jamal, a former Minister for Finance, who requested that a small group advise the government on joining IBI (Informatics Task Force Minutes,February 1986). None of the members of the resultant Task Force[4] sit on the Ad Hoc Computer Advisory Committee. Joining IBI was seen by the group to have many advantages, including obtaining technical assistance in the form of training and advice on the design of an informatics infrastructure. A three day sensitization seminar entitled "Informatics for National Development" was organized by the Task Force and held in August 1987 for high level ministry and parastatal officials (Principal Secretaries and Managing Directors). Sponsored by the Ministry of Finance, University of Dar es Salaam, IBI, and UNESCO, the seminar was seen as a way of encouraging a positive decision regarding Tanzania's membership in IBI by developing a more general appreciation of computers and informatics among top government decision makers.[5]

Ideological Rationale

Computer professionals perceive themselves as promoting national interests. The COMPAT constitution specifies the professionals' recognition and acceptance of "their obligation to bring about rapid Social and Economic Development of our

people through the use of Modern Computer Technologies."
One of the means suggested is the development of national
capacities in computing through COMPAT-directed training
efforts. While such training was proposed as a means of
decreasing dependence on vendors and foreign experts,
present human resource conditions in Tanzania suggest that
foreign influence will remain strong.

It is interesting that the computer professionals defined the
requisite personal qualities of their leaders in a manner
strikingly similar to that used by the country's political party.
The COMPAT constitution contains clauses very similar to
those in the Tanzanian party's 1971 leadership guidelines
known as the Mwongozo, a document officially aimed at
undercutting the influence of the bureaucratic bourgeoisie and
stressing democratic (worker) control of the Party and
parastatals (Hyden 1980,159). The Mwongozo clause states
that a leader "must be forbidden to be arrogant, extravagant,
contemptuous and oppressive. The Tanzanian leader has to be
a person who respects people, scorns ostentation and who is
not a tyrant."[6] The COMPAT constitution states that a
member of the governing council "Must be a person satisfied
with life and not governed by greed." The similarities might
be seen as an effort to identify the professionals with the
ruling party and its standards of conduct and ideology,
hedging their bets in a period of ideological transition.

Although these ideological rationales are in evidence, we
must be careful not to accept them at face value. The service
ethic was "unmasked" by critics of the trait functionalist
approach to professions in the industrialized world as
self-serving ideological commercials rather than objective
definitions (Gerstl and Jacobs 1976,15; Metzger 1987,12). With
reference to the Tanzanian context, Bolton's discussion of
parastatal management points out that giving power to
nationalist elites does not eliminate the class-based nature of
the regime, despite the "claim that the personal interests (i.e.
consolidation of their own class base) become subordinate to
the higher, purer development objectives in the interest of the
nation " (Bolton 1985,12). Computer professionals must pay
lip service to a political ideology which stresses the need to

reduce dependence on the world market, but as Gouldner puts it, "ideological politics can serve to disguise the process of class consolidation" (Gouldner 1976,44).

The professional association itself is elitist in nature. Applicants for membership must pass examinations developed by the association. As these examinations are not yet pre-pared, it is difficult to assess how restrictive they will actually be. They may be mere formalities or they may strengthen the elitist nature of the organization.

The professional association's own organization is rigidly hierarchical. There are three categories of voting members differentiated by professional experience, the passing of successive examinations, and the magnitude of the recognized contribution of the individual to the computer industry. The highest level of membership requires that the individual have a publication record, a criterion reflecting a concern with international academic standards. References from current members are required of all new applicants. This structure does not suggest that democratization will take place within the profession, let alone in the EDP departments and other workplaces of these professionals.

A comment about the gendered nature of the profession is in order here. The profession has been and continues to be predominantly male, a reflection of the gender differentiated participation in mathematics and engineering opportunities in higher education. Female employment in the computer industry has been restricted to clerical data entry levels. Very few high level females are employed in public computer installations or by vendors. There are no female computer consultants or educators. The profession has not indicated recognition of this disparity and therefore no effort has yet been made to understand the problem or effect a solution.

Implications

The Tanzanian computer profession contributes to the diversity of professional forms appearing in varying social contexts in Africa (Johnson 1973; Bennell 1982; Eisemon 1982;

Jinadu 1985; Rathgeber 1985). It exhibits a unique mix of characteristics. It is marked by an alliance of local vendors, private consultants, academics, and high level public computer personnel, including members of the government's Ad Hoc Computer Advisory Committee. The profession aspires to certain academic standards and the strong link to higher education usually associated with professions is being strengthened. While members have received their education from a variety of programs, including vendor courses, post-graduate degrees in computer science are becoming the accepted qualification. Unlike the Ghanaian pharmacy profession of which Bennell wrote, Tanzanian computer professionals have no professional model in the metropole, serving as referent. Rather, the model for the professional association appears to come from within Tanzania in the accounting profession. Foreign assistance agencies, however, are agents of the metropole and the computer profession has a complex, ambiguous relationship with these agencies. In addition, the links with international computer manufacturers offer a reference group for local vendors, but this is a minority within the profession. The lack of an external professional model has the benefit of not marginalizing the local profession to the metropole through the imposition of foreign-defined standards for training and practice, but it remains to be seen if this situation continues. "International standards" of professional computer training exist, and as the COMPAT develops its training plans, a metropolitan model may take hold, made easier by the training of Tanzanian computer professionals in the United States and Europe.

The profession is in formation, still developing its autonomy and the means of reproducing itself. Thus far, it has had no need to take a defensive stance. As noted earlier, computer professionals do not perceive themselves as challenging state authority or even withdrawing their support. Rather, they see themselves as filling a void. They are "co-ordinating" computer professionals and policy-making institutions. Indeed, the profession's emergence has been supported by a recent shift in the state's orientation towards more technical-administrative notions of development. This shift lessens the need for an ideological rationale based on socialist goals and allows a technical/economic rationale to serve as a sufficient basis for the profession's legitimacy.

The importance of the emergence of the computer profession in Tanzania lies in its continuing impact on social relations. This sometimes uneasy alliance of vendors, public sector computer professionals, consultants, and academics reflects the wider tension between statism and privatization of the Tanzanian economy, of which Shivji speaks (1985). We can expect computer professionals to become more supportive of private capital, in part as a compromise required of the alliance with vendors and consultants but more importantly out of frustration with government policy. The professionalization process shows a public-private alliance in the computer profession built out of frustration with the official policy, whose design by the poorly informed ruling class has remained in place despite efforts of individual professionals and the Computer Advisory Committee. The formation of a professional association—another attempt to bring about change—is more likely to succeed, given its allied components, the increasingly "developmentalist" approach of the ruling class, and the increased pressure of international agencies on the state.

Notes

1. The author gratefully acknowledges the financial support of the Fulbright Program to conduct the fieldwork on which this analysis is based.

2. See von Mitschke-Collande in Hinzen and Hundsdörfer (1979) for a broader discussion of the problem of academic certifications and promotion practices for engineers, technicians, and crafts people in Tanzania.

3. It is ironic that the NBAA is playing an increasingly larger role in computer-related training for its professionals. In the compulsory Certified Public Accountants course on systems and data processing, the NBAA is replacing efforts to teach the course in financial training institutes. These institutions are unable to offer the depth of coverage required for the national examination because of a lack of knowledgeable staff and data processing equipment. Concerned about poor examination performance,

the NBAA now offers a mandatory review course which for many students is their first exposure to computing and data processing concepts.

4. The group is called the Informatics Tasks Force and is chaired by a University of Dar es Salaam lecturer in electronics. Other members are the Computer Manager of the Posts and Telecommunications Corporation, a lecturer from Sokoine University of Agriculture who runs that university's computer committee, an official from the Bureau of Statistics, and a University of Dar es Salaam manpower management officer.

5. Informatics Task Force Minutes, February 1986 and personal communication from Dr. Sheya, September 30, 1987

6. For an English translation see Coulson 1979, 36-42.

Appendix:
Survey of Computers in Tanzania

Suzanne Grant Lewis and Mohammed Sheya[1]

An inventory of computers in Tanzania was compiled in 1986 using five sources: interviews and visits to 125 sites where computers are in use;[2] surveys conducted by the University of Dar es Salaam's Department of Electrical Engineering as part of the ongoing research on the state of informatics in Tanzania; an old survey by the Computer Centre at the University of Dar es Salaam; files of the Ad Hoc Computer Advisory Committee; and customer lists from local computer vendors. (See Table 3.1 for the classification of microcomputers, minicomputers, and mainframe computers used in the inventory. This list includes only those systems found in Tanzania.)

Historical Growth in Computer Use in Tanzania

The first computers in Tanzania were ICL mainframes installed in 1968 in the Ministry of Finance and TANESCO. A minicomputer was introduced in Williamson Diamond Mines in Mwadui, Shinyanga Region the following year. This IBM machine is now the oldest computer in Tanzania, the Treasury and TANESCO systems having been replaced by newer mainframes.

When the Imports Control Order restricting computer importation was passed in June 1974, there were six mainframe computers and one minicomputer in the country, all in the public sector. In 1974, the government removed the systems from the State Trading Corporation and the National Provident Fund. No new systems were introduced until 1978. The number of mainframe installations has doubled since 1979 and in 1986 stood at 16, with one unserviceable. Fifty percent of the mainframes in Tanzania arrived within the period 1985-1986. All 37 minicomputers installed in Tanzania are still operating. Forty-three percent of the growth in minicomputers occurred in the 1985-1986 period. The late 1970's and

TABLE 3.1 Classification of Computer Systems in Tanzania

Make	Model	Comments
Mainframes		
ICL	ME29	
	1901	
Wang	VS80	Does not allow Wang Network; max 30 ports
	VS65	
IBM	Sys.34	
Minicomputers		
Hewlett-Packard		
	HP 9845	Engineering workstation; old stand-alones
	HP 9835	
	HP 9825A	
IBM	Sys. 32	
	360/20	
ICL	DRS 8850	Distributed Resources System; max 16 terminals on network
NCR	Tower XP	Super-mini
	Tower 32	UNIX super-mini; 32 users
	9300 IP	Super-mini; 11 workstations
	Tower 1672	Discontinued
	I-9020	
	I-9100	10 workstations
Olivetti		
	M44	Discontinued
	M40	Discontinued
Wang	VS15	
	2200 MVP	Max 13 terminals
	200 LVP	Max 5 terminals
	OIS	Office Information System; max 12 workstations

TABLE 3.1 *(continued)*

Make	Model	Comments
Microcomputers		
Hewlett-Packard		
	HP 125	
	HP 85	
	ICL	Quatro 2 or 4 workstations
	OPD	One Per Desk
NCR	I-9010	Model I single workstations; Model II max of 3; both discontinued
	PC4i	IBM pc/XT compatible
	PC6	IBM pc/XT compatible
	PC8	Multi-user, multi-tasking; max 16 workstations
	DMV	Decision Mate V; MS-DOS and CP/M
Olivetti		
	M24	MS-DOS
	M20	PCOS; discontinued
Wang	APC	Multi-user with Xenix or multi-user MS-DOS
	PC	
Word Processors		
ICL	DRS 8801	CP/M option
	STC	Word processor and telex
Wang	Wang-writer I & II	
Data Capture Equipment		
ICL	CDE 1500	Complex Data Entry. Intelligent data entry on micro-cassettes for transferring to mag. tape
	Key Edit	
HP	2621 A	Data entry terminal
	1945	

early 1980's was a period of slow growth due to foreign exchange constraints and problems getting Treasury permits. Vendors had insufficient spares in stock and some machines were unserviceable for long periods, which heightened end-user frustration.

Computer systems are kept operational in Tanzania long beyond their advertised life and often long after production of spare parts has ceased. The State Trading Corporation mainframe, originally installed in 1970, was moved to TANESCO (and their old system dismantled) in 1974. When TANESCO purchased a new system, the STC computer was moved then to the National Insurance Corporation (NIC). The NIC has only just received a new computer and the 1970 system was finally laid to rest in 1986. The Ministry of Finance's first mainframe served for 17 years. The University of Dar es Salaam Computer Centre's mainframe was in place for 14 years, although it ceased functioning six months before it was removed in 1986. A chronological chart of the installation of large computer systems in Tanzania's public and private sectors for the period 1968 through 1986 appears at the end of this appendix (Table 3.7).

The first microcomputers were installed in Tanzania in 1980. They were an Ohio Scientific Challenger II in the Arusha Regional Planning Office and a Commodore 3032 in the University of Dar es Salaam's Department of Civil Engineering. The Ohio Scientific was introduced by USAID for the compilation and analysis of various regional surveys, for word processing, and for training in BASIC programming. The Commodore was introduced for faculty research work and student projects. Figure 3.1 indicates the growth in microcomputer systems in Tanzania over time. From only two systems in 1980, microcomputers grew to four in 1981, and thirteen in 1982. They then increased by a factor of six in 1983 from the previous year, doubled in 1984 and doubled again in 1985. Although the figures are only through September 1986, it is expected that they doubled again by the end of 1986.

Table 3.2 provides the numbers from which Figure 3.1 was constructed and lists the number of new systems each year, broken down by institutional and individual ownership. As of September 1986, there were 470 microcomputers in Tanzania. It is estimated that 419 or 89% of these are in institutions and only 51 or 11% are owned by individuals.

Geographic Distribution of Computer Systems

Computer technology is concentrated in the capital city. Table 3.3 notes the geographic distribution of all institutional mainframes, minicomputers, and microcomputers in Tanzania. Only two of the sixteen mainframe computers in Tanzania are outside Dar es Salaam and these are both in Arusha. For minicomputers, the distribution is wider with 32% outside of Dar es Salaam, and many of these on rural development project sites in areas such as Mtera, Mufindi, and Oshirombo. Microcomputers are located in 23 towns outside Dar es Salaam but this represents only 27% of the total. Most of these 112 systems (70%) are located in the five large towns of Arusha, Mwanza, Dodoma, Morogoro, and Moshi. Figure 3.2 represents graphically the latest geographic distribution of microcomputers in the country.

FIGURE 3.2   Number of Microcomputers Present in Tanzania, 1980-1986

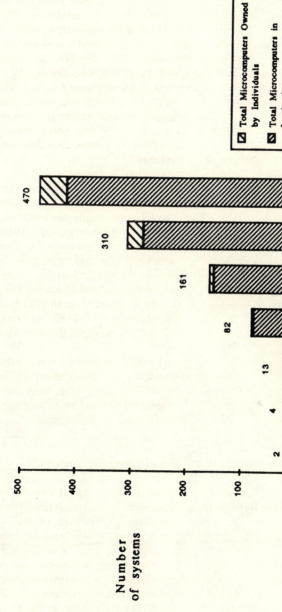

Note: 1986 includes 58 microcomputers with an unknown year of installation. 1986 includes through September only.

TABLE 3.2   Growth of Institutionally and Individually Owned
Microcomputer Systems in Tanzania by Year of
Installation

	In Institutions	Owned Individually	Total Micro-computers	Cumulative Total	% Annual Increase
1980	2	2	2		
1981	2	-	2	4	200
1982	9	-	9	13	325
1983	66	3	69	82	631
1984	72	7	79	161	196
1985	130	19	149	310	193
1986[a]	87	15	102	412	133
Unknown Year	51	7	58		
Total	419	51	470		

a. 1986 includes through September only.

TABLE 3.3   Geographic Distribution of Computer Systems in
             Institutions in Tanzania

Location	Mainframe		Minicomputer		Microcomputer	
Arusha	2		1		28	
Mwanza	-		-		14	
Dodoma	-		-		13	
Morogoro/Ilunga	-		2		13	
Moshi/Lyamungo	-		-		10	
Iringa/Njombe	-		1		5	
Musoma	-		-		4	
Zanzibar	-		1		4	
Mzumbe	-		-		3	
Mbeya/Uyole	-		-		2	
Tabora	-		-		2	
Sumbawanga	-		-		2	
Songea-Makambako	-		-		2	
Mtera	-		3		-	
Mufindi	-		2		1	
Oshirombo	-		1		-	
Mwadui	-		1		-	
Bukoba	-		-		2	
Kyela	-		-		1	
Mtwara	-		-		1	
Karatu	-		-		1	
Muheza	-		-		1	
Kidatu	-		-		1	
Kabulo Ridge	-		-		1	
Bugwema	-		-		1	
Tanga	-		-		1	
Total Outside DSM	2	(12%)	12	(32%)	112	(27%)
Dar es Salaam	14	(88%)	25	(68%)	307	(73%)
Total	16	(100%)	37	(100%)	419	(100%)

FIGURE 3.2   Geographic Distribution of Microcomputers in Tanzania, 1986

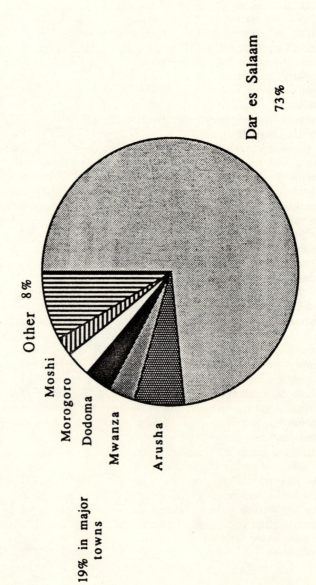

Dar es Salaam

73%

Other 8%

Moshi

Morogoro

Dodoma

Mwanza

Arusha

19% in major
towns

Distribution of Computers Across Economic Sectors

The vast majority of computers in Tanzania are in use in the public sector, that is within government offices or para-statal organizations. Eighty-eight percent of the mainframes, 65% of the minicomputers, and 62% of the microcomputers are in use in Tanzania's public sector. (See Table 3.4 for a breakdown by broad sector with public sector broken down further by source of funding.) Most of the public sector computers are in parastatal corporations rather than in ministries. All but one of the public sector mainframes and three of the public sector minicomputers are in parastatals, a pattern common since the early years of computer use in Tanzania. Approximately 73% of the public sector microcomputers are in parastatal organizations.

Breaking "public sector" down further, the financial and the communications and transport sectors have the greatest concentrations of large systems. The Ministry of Communications and Works has under its charge several large parastatal corporations with mainframe installations: Air Tanzania Corporation; Tanzania Harbours Authority; Tanzania Posts & Telecommunications Corporation; and Tanzania Railways Corporation. The Ministry of Finance, Economic Affairs and Planning has its own mainframe and sizeable installations in other financial institutions: the Bank of Tanzania; the Cooperative and Rural Development Bank; the National Insurance Corporation; and the Tanzania Development Finance Corporation. The energy sector has two mainframe installations (in TANESCO and British Petroleum) and numerous minicomputers in its related parastatal companies.

The greatest concentrations of microcomputers per institution are again in the financial and the communications and transport sectors. Large numbers of microcomputers are located in the Bank of Tanzania, the Cooperative and Rural Development Bank , and the Tanzania Posts and Telecommunications Corporation. These last two parastatals are in the process of getting the systems up and running on multiple sites. The agricultural and industrial sectors also have significant numbers of microcomputers but for these two sectors, microcomputers tend to be distributed across a large number of institutions or programs, averaging between one and two microcomputers per institution. Other areas of noticeable microcomputer activity include health and local government. Eight institutions under the Ministry of Health are using microcomputers. They are in use in six regional governments, usually with only one microcomputer per region. TANESCO is expecting 50 microcomputers in the near future which will make it the largest concentration in a single corporation.

TABLE 3.4   Distribution of Computers in Tanzania by Type of User
                 and Source of Funding

Source of Funding	Number of Mainframes (% of Total)	Number of Minicomputers (% of Total)	Number of Microcomputers (% of Total)
Public Sector Foreign Assistance	8 (50%)	10 (27%)	218 (46%)
Tanzania Government-		3 (8%)	17 (4%)
Unknown	6 (38%)	11 (30%)	58 (12%)
Total Public Sector	14 (88%)	24 (65%)	293 (62%)
Private Sector Organizations	2 (12%)	11 (30%)	105 (22%)
Foreign Assistance Agencies or Embassy Offices	-	2 (5%)	21 (5%)
Individuals[a]	-	-	51 (11%)
Total	16(100%)	37(100%)	470(100%)

a. Figures do not include individuals issued temporary permits.

There is a high concentration of computers in the two universities. The
University of Dar es Salaam has six minicomputers and 33 microcomputers. The Sokoine University of Agriculture has a higher ratio of computers
per department with two minicomputers and 9 microcomputers. Other
training institutions with computers include Muhimbili Medical Centre
(four minicomputers and three microcomputers), the College of Business
Education (with 11 microcomputers between the Dar es Salaam and
Dodoma campuses), and the Tanzania Posts and Telecommunications
Training School (with ten networked microcomputers).

The other training institutions which in the past have received support as centers for computer-related training have very little hardware. The National Institute of Productivity (NIP) has no computers. The Institute of Finance Management (IFM) has only four data entry stations which are used for accounting purposes. The Institute of Development Management (IDM) has two microcomputers, one of which is used exclusively by their printing unit, the other on an irregular basis for class demonstrations.

Computer Applications

The applications for large computer systems in Tanzania fall into the following general categories: storage of records or registers; data analysis involving computations and including statistical analysis; billing preparation; payroll preparation; account keeping including a variety of ledgers; stock control; text processing; training in programming; and as a control device for telephone switching.

Microcomputers have a wider range of applications than the larger systems. Data analysis, including statistical analysis, is the most common application. Other popular uses are record keeping, text processing (including correspondence, report writing, and desktop publishing of textbooks and other training materials), stock control, account keeping, project management and monitoring (a combination of record keeping, accounts, and simple calculations), training, and payroll. Less common uses include budget preparation, costings, production scheduling, development of training materials, engineering design work, and as a control device. Large organizations which had computerized accounting, payroll, and stores on large systems are not now transferring these jobs to microcomputers and small institutions are moving from manual to computerized systems on microcomputers. A significant number of institutions are acquiring microcomputers as replacements for electro-mechanical accounting machines which are no longer manufactured.

A frequently heard complaint from vendors and consultants is that computers are not being used for "management applications" in Tanzania. Some confusion surrounds the use of this term. Some take it to mean accounting, payroll, stock control and billing, all common applications for minicomputers. To others, the term means budget manipulation, forecasting, and costings by the manager him/herself. The difference is that the former means inputs into management level decision making and the latter means a tool for helping managers make decisions once the inputs are received. This latter definition has the manager playing an active role in using the computer, even if he/she is not actually at the keyboard. In Tanzania, it is rare to see a manager (other than the Chief Accountant or EDP Manager) using a computer or directing an assistant on what manipulations to run. Managers rely on information received from subordinates, "reports" which might be computer generated. There is little use of microcomputers as management tools and the computers remain in the hands of computer personnel, not managerial decision makers. One might well ask who is the decision maker, then, the person dealing with output processed by subordinates or the person doing the selection and processing of the information which is passed up to the supervisor?

In regards to software development in Tanzania, three of the computer vendors have software engineers on their staff and offer tailored commercial packages and custom-developed software. A fourth vendor relies on programmers from their Nairobi office. The larger computer installations have software engineers and produce many systems in-house. There are no public or private software houses and a small number of consultants tailor commercial packages for clients.

Financing of Computer Acquisitions

Foreign assistance agencies provide the financing for most computer acquisitions in Tanzania. The following discussion is focused on constraints arising from this practice.

Foreign Assistance Agency Control Over System Choice

Decision making regarding computer technology is often taken out of the hands of Tanzanians with the result that attention to a long-range rationale and such issues as compatibility and local service is not common. Because of the shortage of local computer expertise, foreign assistance agencies often make the needs assessment and decisions regarding hardware and software choice. For small projects, the choice of system, both hardware and software, is often based on an expatriate advisor's familiarity with a limited number of systems. If the proposed installation is large enough that a feasibility study is done, the final choice is usually for systems which are serviced locally, but the majority of institutions acquiring microcomputers will not have large numbers of them. As of 1986, forty-five percent of the microcomputers in Tanzania are systems which cannot be serviced locally. Breakdowns can leave an organization in worse shape than before the microcomputers were introduced, as the manual systems are no longer operating. Foreign assistance agency selection has rarely paid attention to compatibility with systems already present in the organization. It is not uncommon for a consulting firm to "leave behind" a microcomputer or two when their assignment is completed. The consultants bring over a system which suits their needs for completion of their tasks. It is rare that the preference of the recipient is considered, including such issues as repair and maintenance, spare parts, software, and compatibility with existing systems. Such "gifts" become a burden for the recipient by not allowing the development of a rational plan for computerization. They become tools of bargaining as well. The consultants are bargaining for favorable consideration and the recipient is bargaining for equipment they would not otherwise obtain. This practice is divorced from any need or desire to apply the technology. The point here is not only that the decisions resulting from existing practice do not meet the needs of the recipient but that Tanzanians don't develop expertise in analyzing needs and identifying systems to meet those needs.

Bureaucratic Constraints of Foreign Assistance Funding

Foreign assistance agencies operate under bureaucratic constraints which may not allow the recipient to follow the most beneficial course. For example, the US Government's procurement policy (and those of many other bilateral agencies) serves to undercut local computer vendors by requiring purchase in funding countries or through lowest bid price rules, under which local vendors cannot compete.[3] Undercutting local vendors damages long term efforts to develop an indigenous industry. Tying purchases to brands manufactured in funding countries is behind the high proportion of microcomputers with no local service.

The funding process also encourages acquisition first and attention to use later. Microcomputer technology may be part of a larger package or may represent resources not otherwise available or may be the desired end in itself. The relationship between recipient institution and potential funding sources involves negotiation. The recipient's attention is on capturing resources. Foreign assistance agencies are interested in disbursing funds, be they loans or grants. Negotiations do not require, and often do not include, any attention to the actual application, except in the vaguest of terms. The willingness of foreign assistance agencies to fully fund microcomputers with or without planned uses has further encouraged recipient institutions to place major attention on the acquisition of the resources to the detriment of post-acquisition issues such as applications and training.

Because of the nature of the funding agreement, it is not unusual that ordering of equipment, such as computers, be required all at once. This process encourages organizations to order more than they initially need or have plans for in order to have some to "grow into." There is the concern that later there may not be funds to buy more. This practice increases the chances of large and expensive failures. For example, rather than have TANESCO test out its zonal billing system on a few Olivetti microcomputers, all fifty machines were ordered at once through the World Bank, prior to the development of any software, mainframe-microcomputer interface, or staff training plans.

Inability of Recipient to Meet Recurrent Costs

An additional feature of the foreign assistance funding process which causes problems for recipient countries is the handling of recurrent costs. These costs are expected to be met by Tanzania but foreign exchange is required for recurring expenses such as computer disks, ribbons, and even special printer paper. While the project is operating, arrangements are often made to obtain such supplies through the diplomatic pouch. Once a project closes, however, so does the subsidized import channel and many institutions find themselves without such necessary supplies.

It should be noted that computer systems acquired with foreign assistance are not always through grants. The agency playing the largest role, the World Bank, provides loans only, so Tanzania pays for the computer systems along with required pre-investment studies and tender evaluations when the loans are repaid.

Distribution of Computers by
Manufacturer and Local Support

Five computer vendors are operating in Tanzania. These firms represent seven different microcomputer manufacturers: Apple, IBM (personal computers only), ICL, NCR, Osborne, Olivetti and Wang. Five of these are American manufacturers, one British, and another Italian.[4] The British manufacturer, International Computers Ltd. (ICL), opened a Tanzania sales office in 1958.[5] National Cash Register (NCR) followed in 1961 and Business Machines Ltd. (BML) in 1969. As previously mentioned, NCR and BML built their business on the sale and maintenance of electro-mechanical accounting machines and did not market computers until the early 1980's. The other two, Computer Corporation of Tanzania Ltd. (CCTL) and International Communication Systems (ICS) did not arrive until 1981 and 1985 respectively.

BML became the first dealer for microcomputers, securing the Apple dealership in 1982. The company later started selling Olivetti microcomputers and minicomputers and is now selling mostly Olivetti computers, due to problems with the UK Apple supplier. Although BML was originally supplied by the Nairobi Apple distributor, Comprite Ltd., that firm now requires a foreign exchange deposit prior to sale which is unmanageable for most Tanzanian institutions and BML.

Neither ICL nor NCR offered microcomputers until 1985. The latest microcomputer vendor to enter the Tanzania market is ICS with the contract to sell IBM personal computers and Hewlett-Packard printers.

The links between Tanzanian and Kenyan vendors are many, with the Tanzanian companies acting as satellites to the centers in Nairobi. Kenyan vendors generally have a greater volume of business, more staff, and offer more technical support and training services than their Tanzanian counterparts. In addition, some of the manufacturers have established regional support centers in Nairobi to which Tanzanian vendors turn. Use of these services requires payment in foreign exchange.

In Tanzania there exist mainframe and minicomputer systems from eight manufacturers, three of them with local sales and service. Based solely on the number of machines, Wang systems represent the largest proportion of large system installations (26%) for public and private sectors combined. Taking the public sector alone, NCR has the largest number of

TABLE 3.5   Large Computer Systems in Tanzania by Manufacturer
             for Public and Private Sectors

Manufacturer	No. of Mainframes	(%)	No. of Minicomputers	(%)	Total No. of Large Systems	(%)
ICL	6	(38%)	-		6	(11%)
Wang	6	(38%)	8	(22%)	14	(26%)
NCR	-		10	(27%)	10	(19%)
DEC	-		9	(25%)	9	(17%)
Hewlett-Packard	-		4	(11%)	4	(8%)
IBM	2	(12%)	6	(16%)	8	(15%)
Fujitsu	1	(6%)	-		1	(2%)
Apollo	1	(6%)	-		1	(2%)
Total	16	(100%)	37	(101%)	53	(100%)

systems (25%), just ahead of Wang (23%). Table 3.5 shows the breakdown of large systems by manufacturer for public and private sectors combined. ICL, the dominant vendor until 1982, and NCR have all of their business in the public sector whereas Wang customers are in both the public and private sectors.

While 81% of the mainframe computers in Tanzania are serviced locally, only 49% of the minicomputers have authorized servicing available in-country. There are a large number of Digital Equipment Corporation (DEC) minicomputers, mostly in the private sector, but no service is available within Tanzania. None of the larger IBM systems are in extensive use and the General Tyre system has never been operational. IBM service for these systems is not available locally. The Fujitsu mainframe is maintained by Fujitsu trained technicians within the Tanzania Posts and Telecommunications Corporation.

Turning now to the microcomputer situation, 36 brands of microcomputers have been identified in Tanzania. Those with local service available represent only 59% of the microcomputers in institutions and only 24% of the individually owned microcomputers. This means that 210 of the 470 microcomputers in Tanzania (45%) have no manufacturer-supported repair and maintenance service available in-country. Microcomputers manufactured by Apple, ICL, NCR, Osborne, Olivetti, and Wang are sold and serviced locally. The IBM vendor expects to develop servicing capability within Tanzania in the near future.

Apple microcomputers represent the largest proportion of the market with 26% of the small systems in Tanzania. Wang and IBM microcomputers are the next most frequent brands. There are also significant numbers

TABLE 3.6   Microcomputers in Tanzania by Manufacturer

| Manufacturer/Model | No. of Systems | |
	Institutionally Owned	*Individually* Owned[a]
Amstrad	2	3
Apple II/III	98	7
Apple Macintosh	10	5
BBC/Acorn	19	-
Commodore	13	8
Compaq	8	-
Ericsson	7	-
Hewlett-Packard	5	-
IBM pc	23	4
pc/XT	17	1
pc/AT	6	-
ICL	5	-
Jet	5	-
Kaypro	21	6
NCR	25	-
Osborne	14	-
Olivetti	41	-
Sinclair	1	4
Tandy/Radio Shack	4	2
Wang	55	-
Other[b]	30	5
Unknown	10	6
TOTAL	419	51

a. Figures do not include systems imported temporarily.

b. Includes makes with fewer than five in the country: Apricot, Bondwell, Corona, DEC, Epson, Genie, Intertec, Labrus, Microbee, NEC, Ohio Scientific, Phillips, Sanyo, SATT, Sharp, Texas Instrument, Toshiba, Victor, and Zenith.

of Olivetti systems present. Table 3.6 lists the distribution by manufacturer of the institutional and individually owned microcomputers in Tanzania.

Services Offered

All five vendors in Tanzania offer needs assessments, installation, and through separate contracts, repair and maintenance. All but the IBM personal computer vendor also offer customization of off-the-shelf software, the development of custom software, ongoing software support, and training. The experience and capabilities of vendors in providing software-related services vary tremendously. Hardware backup arrangements also vary. The large system vendors rely on the goodwill of other installations to provide processing time when a customer's system is down for any extended period. Only CCTL has an in-house mainframe and a minicomputer which are available to customers for pre-installation work (system conversion), and occasionally for backup, although CCTL's configurations have quite limited memory and therefore may not fit the needs of customers. Most vendors do not assist customers with Treasury permits or foreign exchange allocations, although ICL assists in setting up letters of credit.

All but the IBM personal computer vendor offer in-country training, although experience and capabilities vary for this service as well. For microcomputer training, the four vendors offer demonstrations for the whole organization once the system is up and running, introductory courses on the system, application classes, and management appreciation courses. This last offering is a general introduction to EDP concepts and is becoming increasingly popular prior to purchase. For the most part, vendors place very little attention on training, although offerings have increased in the last two years. One of the main problems is lack of staff to conduct training. Both BML and CCTL's customer bases have grown very rapidly and they have yet to hire sufficient staff to keep up with the training and software development demands. The same people are doing both. Software development takes precedence since the money is in software development and the after-sales training of customers in microcomputer operating systems and applications is not a high status activity among software engineers in vendor firms (although management training is). Another constraint to training is the lack of in-house microcomputers. Vendors no longer stock machines, due to the foreign exchange costs. At most a vendor has one of each model sold which is used for the vendor's own business or software development. Training therefore is usually delayed until after the customer's equipment arrives and is installed.

Staff Sizes and Educational Background

BML has the largest computer staff, with a Director of Systems Division, six systems analysts, four programmers, and twenty technicians.

ICL has the next largest staff with a Managing Director, three software engineers, seven hardware engineers, a secretary who does word processing training, and a technician. Both NCR and CCTL have staffs of eight. ICS is in the process of building its computer staff but has just two regular staff plus access to eight technicians. Many of the vendors previously had sales forces but eliminated them in the early 1980's when business was slow. Managers therefore conduct most of the sales work.

The managers of vendor firms often do not have university degrees, although ICS's new director has a Ph. D. in telecommunications. Managers have usually worked their way up through the firm and have years of experience with computers. It is common for systems analysts and software engineers to have first degrees. There are even a few Master's degrees in this group. Hardware engineers usually have first degrees in electrical engineering or Higher National Diplomas. Technicians or field engineers are usually technical college graduates, although some in NCR have first degrees. Almost half of the vendor personnel above technician level have had experience in the Tanzanian public sector, either in parastatals or the Ministry of Finance's Computer Centre. Experience with a vendor other than the current employer is unusual.

Vendor Monopoly on Technical Information

The vendors play an important role as both "keepers of the hardware" and controllers of technical information regarding hardware and software products. Vendors enjoy a virtual monopoly position regarding computer hardware and software. The five computer vendors in Tanzania are each sole agents for the computers they sell. Once a sale is made, the customer has no alternative source of assistance with system installation, staff orientation and training, or maintenance service. Vendors have been and continue to be the primary source of technical knowledge on microcomputers in the country, in part because the technology is still new and there are few knowledgeable people among the users (although this is certainly changing) and because there is a dearth of journals and trade magazines regarding computers in Tanzania.

Customer reliance on vendors starts at an early stage of the process. Because of the shortage of computer expertise in organizations, vendors are often called upon to conduct needs assessments along with proposing systems. The vendors naturally prescribe the systems which they sell as the solution. These assessments are included in the tender applications and are often evaluated by managers in the customer organization who lack the necessary technical background. Reliance on vendor claims is then the order of the day, sometimes with dire consequences.

Hardware Bias

It is now common advice in the United States that in deciding on a microcomputer, one should pick out the software one wants to do the job and then choose from among the hardware which will run the software. In practice, few individuals or organizations follow this advice. In Tanzania it is the same. Systems are not bought--or sold--on the basis of the software. Computer vendors in Tanzania focus on selling hardware and offer a very limited selection of software. They don't sell "the total solution" or the "system approach." They sell the hardware and offer to develop the software for the customer. The range of off-the-shelf microcomputer packages available is limited to those available from the original manufacturer. BML sells packages which Olivetti frequently "bundles" with its system. ICL sells ICL software for ICL microcomputers. Wang sells Wang software. This arrangement is in part due to habit (these vendors have always sold software for mainframe and minicomputers which required machine-specific programs) and because the vendors have no link to external software distributors. There is no software distributor in Tanzania and setting one up is a difficult task.

When systems are bought outside, i.e. not through Tanzanian vendors, the decision regarding software is made for Tanzanians. A foreign assistance agency does not run demonstrations of various spreadsheet programs and then ask the EDP Manager which he likes best. A choice is made and the program and manuals arrive. Tanzanians therefore only encounter software which has been sold by the vendor (where the selection is machine-specific and usually a product of the computer manufacturer) or brought in by a foreign assistance agency. There is no competing source. Occasionally, when a Tanzanian participates in training overseas, he (and it has always been males who are sent overseas for computer-related training) returns with "borrowed" or demonstration copies.

Custom-designed software for microcomputers is common for large installations such as the financial institutions. Customers have little chance to articulate their needs, given the monopoly hold vendors have on information. Software development is an important fee-earning service for vendors. Most costs are local and the profit margin is large. If ownership of the package is maintained, the vendor can sell it many times over with or without modifications for the new customer. For the Tanzanian buyer, as well, software developed in-country has the important advantage of costing only Tanzanian shillings. Foreign exchange is a very precious commodity and many institutions would prefer to buy additional hardware with the foreign exchange rather than spend it on software, reflecting the widespread emphasis on hardware in system choice.

Summary of the Microcomputer Inventory

The key characteristics of Tanzania's microcomputer situation can be summarized as follows. The introduction is a recent phenomenon, with most of the importation occurring since 1985. The number of microcomputers is small in absolute terms but high in relative growth terms, having increased by a factor of at least two for every year since 1980. The distribution pattern is an urban (73% in the capital and another 19% in the next five largest towns) and an institutional one (89%). Most of the microcomputers are in the public sector and 73% of these are in parastatals rather than in ministries.

The highest concentrations of microcomputers (in terms of number of machines per institution) are in the parastatal organizations of the financial and communications/transport sectors. The agricultural and industrial sectors have lower institutional densities but still significant numbers of microcomputers for the sector as a whole. The most common application is for data analysis, particularly statistical analysis. Record keeping, billing, accounts, stock control, project management and monitoring, word processing, and programming training are other common uses.

While the number of microcomputer vendors have grown in recent years, only 45% of the microcomputers in the country have local service available. This is due in large part to the fact that the vast majority of the microcomputers are funded through foreign assistance and only recently have agencies paid attention to the compatibility and local service issues.

Expectations for the Future

There is every reason to expect continued growth in the number of computer systems in Tanzania. Information from local vendors indicate that orders have been placed for six new mainframes and two minicomputers in the public sector and three minicomputers in the private sector. Orders for 182 microcomputers were identified in September 1986, mostly for public sector institutions. This would mark at least a 158% increase over the September 1986 figures.

In 1987, a number of local area networks (LANs) were planned for installation. To date there are just two LANs in Tanzania, in the Tanzania Posts and Telecommunications Corporation Training School and the International School of Tanganyika. Additional activity with multi-user microcomputers is expected.

There has not been much data communication activity domestically or internationally. The only exceptions are at the airline offices, the United States Information Service, and the Canadian Spare Parts Project which are all involved in data communications with North America or Europe. There has been no data communication within the country or within the region. With the installation of the Tanzania Posts and Telecommunications Corporation's new multiple site configuration, some experimentation with domestic data transmission is expected. Numerous institutions, particularly banks but also private firms, have expressed an interest in this facility. The Corporation's experience can be expected to be monitored by many interested parties.

TABLE 3.7   Large Computer Systems in Tanzania's Public and Private
             Sectors by Year of Installation

Year	Computer System	Location
1968	ICL 1902*	Ministry of Finance
	ICL 1902A*	TANESCO
1969	ICL 1902S*	State Trading Corp.
	IBM 360/20	Williamson Diamond Mine
1971	ICL 1901A*	Tanganyika Farmer's Association
1972	ICL 1901A*	National Provident Fund
	ICL 1902A*	UDSM Computer Centre
	ICL 1902A*	Ministry of Finance
1974	[ICL 1902S	Moved from State Trading Corp. to TANESCO]
	[ICL 1902A	Removed from TANESCO]
1975	[ICL 1901A	Removed from National Provident Fund]
1978	ICL 1902T*	Ministry of Finance
	[ICL 1902	Removed from Ministry of Finance]
	IBM Sys 32	British Petroleum
	DEC Minc	UDSM Dept of Electrical Eng.
1979	ICL 1901T	Tanzania Harbours Authority
1980	DEC PDP 11	Balfour Beatty Construction Co. (private)
1981	Wang 2200MVP	ESAMI
	Wang 2200MVP	Tanganyika Devt. Finance Corp. Ltd.
	DEC PDP 11	UDSM Physics Dept.
	DEC PDP 11	Sokoine Univ of Agriculture
	HP 9845-B	Maji Ubungo, Ministry of Water
1982	Wang VS80	TANESCO
	[ICL 1902S	Moved from TANESCO to Nat'l Insurance Corp.]
	Wang VS80	Computer Corporation of Tz Ltd. (private)
	IBM Sys 34	General Tyre
	Wang OIS 140	U.S. Information Service (private)

TABLE 3.7 *(continued)*

Year	Computer System	Location
1983	ICL ME29	Tanzania Railways Corp.
	Fujitsu FEDEX 100	Tanzania Posts & Telecommunications Extelcom
	Apollo Phoenix 1	Shell Petroleum Development (T) Ltd. (private)
	NCR 9020	Muhimbili Medical Centre
	NCR 9020	Muhimbili Medical Centre
	Wang 2200MVP	Southern Paper Mills
	HP 9835	Ministry of Agriculture
	Wang 2200MVP	Computer Corp of Tz Ltd. (private)
1984	Wang VS80	Cooperative and Rural Development Bank
1985	ICL ME29	British Petroleum
	ICL ME29	Ministry of Finance
	[ICL 1902A and 1902T Removed from Ministry of Finance]	
	ICL ME29	Tanganyika Farmer's Association
	[ICL 1902A	Removed from Tanganyika Farmer's Association]
	IBM Sys 36	Air Tanzania Corp
	NCR Tower1632	Muhimbili Medical Centre
	NCR Tower1632	Muhimbili Medical Centre
	Wang VS 15	Caltex Oil (T) Ltd. (private)
	Wang OIS 60	US Embassy (private)
	DEC VAX	Cogefar (private) 4 systems
1986	Wang VS65	Tanzania Posts and Telecommunications Corp.
	Wang VS65	Tanzania Posts and Telecommunications Corp.
	Wang VS80	National Examinations Council
	ICL ME29	National Insurance Corporation
	[ICL 1902S	Removed from National Insurance Corporation]
	[ICL 1902A	Removed from UDSM]
	NCR Tower	UDSM Computer Centre
	NCR Tower	UDSM Computer Centre
	NCR 9300	UDSM Computer Centre
	NCR Tower XP	Tanzania Petroleum Devt Corp.
	Wang VS15	Bank of Tanzania (renting)
	NCR 9100	Bank of Tanzania
	NCR 9020	Agip (Tanzania) Ltd.
	DEC PDP 11	Sokoine Univ. of Agriculture (built from spares)

TABLE 3.7 *(continued)*

Year	Computer System	Location

Year Unknown

	HP 9825A	UDSM Mechanical Eng
	HP ?	Zanzibar Min. of Water Devt.
	IBM 5110	Cogefar (private) 4 systems

* No longer in operation.
ESAMI - Eastern and Southern African Management Institute
TANESCO - Tanzania Electric Supply Co. Ltd.
UDSM - University of Dar es Salaam

Notes

1. This survey was written in 1987 with data current through September 1986. Suzanne Grant Lewis was supported by the Fulbright Program and Mohammed Sheya by the Faculty of Engineering at the University of Dar es Salaam.

2. It was not possible to visit all of the computer installations in Tanzania. Inaccuracies are therefore inevitable. The most likely source of error lies in the heavy reliance on the files of the Ad Hoc Computer Advisory Committee. The Committee's files record permits issued for the importation of computers but they rarely contain a follow-up. It is probable that some of the institutions issued with permits did not import a computer or imported a different type. In other situations, the computer may have been disposed of. Most if not all of the discrepancies concern microcomputers. We believe that the overestimation from the Committee's records is countered by the number of systems which have not been documented but have made their way into Tanzania through a variety of channels.

3. Calhoun, Drummond, and Whittington (1987:88) make this point in relation to the Sudan.

4. The Italian manufacturer, Olivetti, merged with ATT in early 1987. The implications for Tanzania, if any, are unclear to the authors.

5. In August 1986 ICL (Tanzania) went independent, changing its name to Computers and Telecommunications Systems (T) Ltd. It will remain the sole ICL dealer in Tanzania but will also sell Standard Telephone and Cables equipment from the UK as well as environmental equipment and services. To avoid confusion, we refer to the company throughout as ICL (Tanzania).

TABLE 3.8   Chronology of National Computer Developments in
            Tanzania

1965	Punch card machine arrives in Treasury.
1968	Treasury received ICL 1902. TANESCO received ICL 1902A.
1969	STC received ICL 1902S. Mwadui received IBM 360/20. **Bureau of Census study** "to identify and evaluate the Tanzanian Government's need to improve flow of information for essential government planning and management to avoid proliferation and underutilization of computers in Tanzania with adverse effects on balance of payments and increased requirements for trained computer personnel already in short supply."
1971	Tanganyika Farmer's Association received ICL 1901A.
1972	National Provident Fund received ICL 1901A. UDSM Computer Centre received ICL 1902A. Ministry of Finance received ICL 1902A.
Aug	Deputy Secretary to the Treasury requests UDSM Dean to form UDSM Study Group. Smyth study commissioned by NIP.
Dec	**Smyth report,** "A Comprehensive Survey of Computer Use in Tz & the Urgent Need for a National Computer Training Programme" (ILO expert).
1973 Feb	Bad press on STC computer in Daily News.
Mar	**UDSM Computer Study Group Report,** "Towards a National Policy for Computer Use in Tz."
1974 Jan	STC disbanded - Computer moved to TANESCO during the year.
Feb	Accountant General proposes decomputerization and decentralization of government accounts.

TABLE 3.8 *(continued)*

1974		Economic Committee of the Cabinet charged the Min for Finance to appoint a Task Force to study the rationalization of computer use in Tanzania (EEC Paper No. 12/74).
	June	Imports Control (Electronic Computers and Television Sets) (Prohibition) Order enacted. Computer Task Force appointed.
	Aug	**First report of Computer Task Force** submitted. Rejected by Minister for Finance. Amendment to Imports Control Order allowing for import with the permission of the Minister for Finance.
1975		Computer removed fron NPF.
	April	**Baseley paper,** "Computer Use in Tz: Past, Present, & Future."
	May	**Second report of the Computer Task Force** submitted. "Rationalisation of Computer Use in Tanzania."
1975	June	Second Computer Task Force appointed.
	Oct	**Report of the Second Computer Task Force** submitted. "Rationalisation of Computer Use in Tanzania."
1976	Oct	**Report of the Feasibility of Establishing a Joint Computer Service** (for EAC Corporations) submitted by Chairman Igangas.
1979	May/ June	Bank of Tanzania requests Treasury decision on whether computers studies requiring foreign exchange require Treasury approval.
1980		DCS reviews computer situation and proposes no new review of import restriction until 1984. New Acting Director of Computer Services (DCS) appointed.
	April	**Magambo paper,** "Application of Informatics in Tanzania" at UNESCO Regional Meeting of Computer Centre Directors in Africa.
	Nov/ Dec	Tanzania hosts Computer Managers Conference in Arusha (10 African countries represented).

TABLE 3.8 *(continued)*

1981   July   Acting DCS requests lists of customers using accounting machines from BML & NCR (Audit 5 and NCR 399/499).

1981   Aug   First meeting of the Ad Hoc Computer Advisory Committee (CAC).
Srivastava and Kakuru paper, "A Proposal for the Establishment of National Computer Centre in Tanzania" presented to CAC.

1983   April   **"Computer Usage in Tanzania"** submitted to Presidential Commission on Reduction of Expenditures and Improved Performance. Author unknown.

1983   Sept   Notice in Daily News re: Importation of EDP Equipment.

4

Fragile and Progressive Computer Contracts in Kenya and Ivory Coast: New Social Forms in the Workplace

Bennetta Jules-Rosette

Introduction

A senior programmer at a Kenyan wholesale outlet attempts to manage the transition from a labor-intensive NCR keypunch computer to a new electronic multi-user system, which will increase the number of employees he supervises. That increase may secure him a promotion to data processing manager and double his salary, even though the employees' individual work tasks have diminished. Administrators in Ivory Coast strive to develop a local computer policy that will both limit the activities of multinational computer vendors, such as IBM, BULL, and UNISYS, and at the same time encourage those very companies to invest in Ivory Coast, competing for clientele in a restricted market. The Kenyan government organizes the computerization of the two key ministries, agriculture and finance, and simultaneously proposes an official policy that restricts the widespread use of computers in small enterprises.

These three examples, drawn from actual cases, are not merely management conundrums. They share a common theme. Each case illustrates an effort to use public discourse to control and shape the everyday practices surrounding computer use and new technologies in an African country.

Computer policy is used to project and maintain a specific representation of development and change.

From 1984 through 1987 I conducted in-depth field research on the impact of computers on the African workplace.[1] My research in Kenya and Ivory Coast focused on the ways in which computers alter office interactions, hierarchy, and the aspirations of workers. I have been particularly concerned with the computer as a symbol of opportunity and a sign of the postmodern workplace. The computer is a device for playing with the social "imaginary." Its presence in the overbureaucratized African workplace promises to increase efficiency, reduce processing time, and cut through red tape (de Certeau 1986,207-209). This new vision of the future is firmly rooted in a cognitive utopia based upon the social practices and public discourse that surround and define the computer in an African context. Consequently, my analysis of the impact of computers in Africa is less concerned with *development*, defined in terms of gross national product and narrowing the economic gap between Africa and the West, than it is with representations of development and the imagery of social change associated with new technologies.

Durkheim's classic society under mechanical solidarity is one in which the division of labor is simple and social control is direct and repressive (1949,61-69). By contrast, postmodern culture has been described as "haunted by the . . . representation of a lost 'organic' society" (Lyotard 1984,15). According to this view, automation and electronic technologies eradicate old forms of work specialization and definitions of the labor process and increase the purview of state control. Some argue that new forms of societal analysis must be developed to examine this post-industrial era (Bell 1973; Habermas 1975; Gouldner 1979). Daniel Bell (1973,20) has described theoretical knowledge and the control of technology as key principles motivating policy formation in the new society. The attention of sociologists and cultural critics concerned with this postmodern discourse of knowledge and control has focused almost exclusively on the United States, western Europe, and Japan. African countries have been included in this discussion only to illustrate their losing political and economic position in an increasingly competitive technological contest. My research demonstrates that postmodernity has indeed arrived in Africa in the form of new technologies and new types of public discourse.

The technological environment of small firms provides an incubation ground for government policies about computers. In turn, national policies may restrict the availability of computers to potential users and condition attitudes about the benefits of computerization in the workplace. This conditioning takes place through the medium of what I find it useful to term the *computer contract,* that is, the unstated understandings surrounding the computer's presence nationally and its use in particular work environments. This contract specifies behavior that is played out in terms of social and economic exchanges within firms and between firms and government agencies. These exchanges generate new social forms in the workplace. Drawing on my field research, I have identified two types of computer contract: *fragile* and *progressive.* Initiated at the national level, these contracts affect the attitudes and behaviors that surround the use of computers in the local workplace.

Fragile and Progressive Computer Contracts

By 1981, there were estimated to be 127 mainframe computers officially registered in Kenya and 275 in Ivory Coast.[2] Unfortunately, reliable current microcomputer estimates are not available for either country. By comparison, ten years earlier there were estimated to be over 200 mainframe computer installations at the University of California alone (Mazrui 1978,335). The small number of computers in Kenya and Ivory Coast by 1981, however, represents the beginning, rather than the absence, of a new phenomenon.

Gaining momentum in 1983, the ripples of computer acquisition became a tidal wave in both Kenya and Ivory Coast, though in contrasting ways. Free-standing personal computers began to flood the market in both countries, and computer schools and consulting agencies took advantage of the situation to expand their clientele. The microcomputer invaded private offices and, to a lesser extent, private homes. In Ivory Coast, focused administrative planning for the new technology began in 1980. The Kenyan government initially took a publicly conservative and restrictive approach to these new developments, while the Ivory Coast government opted to encourage the planned growth of high technology as part of an expected economic leap into the post-industrial era. In both cases, as a symbol of postmodernity the new technology stimulated the emergence of innovative discourses and the dream of rapid economic progress (Mudimbe 1988,11-12).

Based on a combination of colonial history and postcolonial decision making, Ivory Coast adopted a *progressive* computer policy. In Ivory Coast's *Plan Informatique National, 1986-1990*, computers are described as the "last train of the twentieth century." The president of the National Commission of Informatics (CNI) warns the country:

> Certain moments of history are periods of reflection. We have arrived today at one of these periods. The old countries are beginning to become aware and to face the situation. The others, those who have recently achieved their independence, must take care this time not to miss the last train of the twentieth century . . . . Ivory Coast now has the possibility to enter fully into the information era and to recover from its economic crisis.[3]

This statement of public policy frames the ways computers are discussed and used in small enterprises in Ivory Coast. I do not mean that policy determines discourse and everyday actions but rather that it influences the horizon of possibilities for interactions with new technologies and affects access to those technologies.

Three conditions of computerization are essential to the progressive computer contract: (1) consistent administrative and economic support of computer adoption from the government; (2) competitive control of sales of goods and services by foreign computer vendors, investors, and expert consultants; and (3) national promotion of computer training programs for administrators, government personnel, and engineers. One consequence of the progressive contract is visible in the initial selection of appropriate computer equipment. With lower import duties and fewer restrictions on equipment purchases than in Kenya, small companies in Ivory Coast can begin with the equipment they need. Anxiety over equipment selection, however, surfaces in other ways. The market for computer sales is small, and the competition is intense. Computer vendors and consulting companies abound. In fact, computer consulting companies are among the primary computer users in Ivory Coast, and their clientele is limited.

Another consequence of the progressive computer contract is internal control of government computerization without depending upon the assistance of donor agencies and outside experts. However, some government computer experts in Ivory Coast criticized the excessive regulations surrounding computerization in their agencies and the government's practice of accepting bids for computers and services from the same "insider" firms regardless of whether their materials were the most appropriate or effective. Computer vendors complained of a closed government bidding system that they feared might drive their companies out of Ivory Coast if government contracts were no longer available to certain firms. Government control of computerization has a trickle-down effect on small businesses by lowering equipment prices and increasing the range of available goods. In some African nations, areas of ambiguity surrounding contractual exchanges between the government and private firms have the potential to generate corruption. Regulation, however, leads to stability in most cases.

In Kenya, prior to 1986, no formal policy concerning computer use had been formulated beyond customs and taxation regulations placing high duties on the importation of computers for nongovernment use. Nevertheless, presidential policy did indirectly affect the computerization of the Ministry of Agriculture, which was one of the first government agencies to adopt microcomputers for fiscal planning. In a speech delivered on September 21, 1982, President Daniel Arap Moi stated that regional districts should become the administrative centers for all rural development projects (Brodman 1985,25). This directive required the Ministry of Agriculture to develop

a new fiscal reporting system to monitor and account for local-
level expenditures as discrete budgetary entries. The process
required the reorganization and compilation of so much data
that computers became the only possible solution. Thus,
government computerization was mandated indirectly and in
an unplanned manner in the Kenyan case (Brodman 1987,117-
142; Pinckney, Cohen, and Leonard 1987,67-93).

The *fragile* computer contract in Kenya reflects the relationship between government policy and computerization.
Computers are feared but not effectively regulated. That is,
official policy is to limit and tax the importation of computers,
but for the most part to impose few regulations on their
distribution and uses. Periodically, however, a government
initiative focused on a particular sector of the economy or
individual firm combines exhortation with administrative
directives. Ambiguous pronouncements, situation-specific rule
making, and onerous bureaucratic procedures all coexist. As
a result, the computer regulatory environment in Kenya is
chaotic and often appears unpredictable to computer vendors
and users.

Three conditions of computerization are essential to the
fragile computer contract: (1) tension between management
and an emerging network of technocrats; (2) an uneasy
relationship between foreign computer experts and local staff;
and (3) limited availability of specific technologies, including
computer hardware and software. One possible outcome of
the fragile contract is the elimination of computers as useless
luxury items. Another outcome is limited participation in
decisions on hardware and software. This is in fact the case
of many donor-sponsored computerizations, in which a firm
or organization uses equipment provided by an external
agency but has little or no voice in determining what is
supplied. In Kenya, the computerization of the combined
Ministry of Agriculture and Livestock Development (MALD)
and of one of the local charge card companies are instances in
which the equipment available was adequate for the initial
stages but lacked potential for adaptation to more sophisticated uses. Although foreign consultants serve as catalysts for
computer adoption, they generally concentrate on short-term

benefits that can be reported within a few months and are less interested in the long-term potential of their experiments. When short-term technological solutions are accepted without the full support of the local administrative staff, the utilization of the technology may last only as long as external advisors are present to monitor the project (Westcott 1987,104-110).

Problems proliferate when technology is selected solely for its accessibility and initial low cost. Data-processing capabilities of the computers may be inadequate for the designated tasks, such as maintaining complex records and managing large numbers of accounts. An agency may be unable to hire or retain sufficient data-entry personnel. These obstacles are characteristic of a fragile computer contract resulting from an ambivalence toward new technologies. The ambiguities and inconsistencies of national computerization policy and regulations create space for misapplication, manipulation, and potential crises. The process of computer distribution and the emphasis on educational credentialing manifest these consequences in Kenya, where limited regulation contrasts with the more centralized planning of technological change in Ivory Coast.[4]

The progressive and fragile computer contracts frame the conditions for national advances in technology. These conditions weave the backdrop for exchanges that constitute the daily business operations of firms that use and market new technologies. Where regulation is well planned, these exchanges permit progress toward a positive attribution and a successful terminal contract. Where there is little national policy or regulation, new technologies appear to be the hidden and unrestrained enemies of the national leadership. In the African setting, where many new technologies have foreign origins, the lack of national planning makes the failure of contractual exchanges more likely, with potentially disastrous and costly consequences. Although the progressive computer contract is not problem-free, it structures a setting in which government and private firms exercise control over the technology and its uses. The fragile contract does not envision regulatory control, leaving the adoption, orientation, and uses of the new technology largely to those able and willing to seize the opportunity. The few successful cases of computer adoption must overcome the impediments inherent in the morass created by conflicting goals and interests, unevenly distributed resources, and spasmodic and inconsistent, though often cumbersome, government efforts to promote a more orderly process.

Contractual Exchanges and New Social Forms in the Workplace

Contractual exchanges encompass interactions that occur between firms and outside agencies as well as within firms. These exchanges introduce computers into the workplace and constitute the springboard for the innovation of new social forms and new ways of relating human behavior to machines. Based upon my research in Ivory Coast and Kenya, I shall specify four types of exchange that occur in the adoption of computers.

The first type of exchange involves the government and firms. In this type, the government sets computer policies and controls access to computer hardware and software. This control operates through import regulations and both direct and indirect monitoring of computer vendors. While firms may sell all their equipment or expertise to the government, they are essentially the recipients of government policy, calls for bids, and other rules and agreements that regulate the distribution of computers.

In the second type of exchange, the firm interacts with a client. This client may be an individual or another agency or firm, or the government. Firms often use the term "contract" explicitly in their references to sales, maintenance, and service agreements.

The third type of exchange occurs within firms. In this type of exchange, the firm's management interacts with its personnel by specifying the use of the computers and the organization of the activities that surround them. Problems with the computerization process within firms often emerge during this exchange.

TABLE 4.1   Typology of Exchanges for Computer Adoption

Type	Sender	Exchange	Recipient
1.	Govern- ment	←———→	Firm
2.	Firm	←———→	Client (including govern- ment)
3.	Firm Manage- ment	←———→	Computer Personnel
4.	Computer Technology	←———→	Firm

In the fourth type of exchange, the computer technology is the acting subject and the firm is the recipient of the messages. That is, the nature of the technology itself requires specific changes in organizational structure, work tasks, and job titles. Over time, the activities of the firm may in turn influence the technology.

Type 1 exchanges are characteristic of the interactions between computer vendors and the government. Since government regulations establish the conditions for computer sales, vendors are particularly concerned with the limitations imposed by these regulations. A crisis resulting from ambiguous or overly stringent regulations generates an outcry in the form of complaints from vendors and computer consulting firms. Type 2 exchanges emerge during the course of normal business transactions. These exchanges include negotiations of sales and service contracts as well as regulation of interactions between firms and their clients. Type 3 exchanges are byproducts of the firm's internal operations. Those exchanges, however, are both frequent and important. Indeed, many of my discussions with enterprise managers in Kenya and Ivory Coast focused on Type 3 exchanges. Type 4 exchanges are

direct products of the strengths and weaknesses of computer
technology. Success and disaster stories describing the initial
impact of computer adoption revolve around Type 4 exchanges. Broken contracts are generally explained and defended in
the terms of Type 4 exchanges: the new equipment is rejected
as inadequate or inappropriate for a particular context.
Overall, Type 2 and Type 3 exchanges were the most common
focus in my interviews with computer   consulting firms in
Ivory Coast, while the principal concerns in my Kenya
research were Type 1 and Type 4 exchanges. More broadly,
while there were many explicit references to the term *contract*
in my interviews in Ivory Coast, the idea of contractual
exchanges remained implicit in most of the Kenya interviews.

A contract (as I am using that term here) is essential to the
computer's presence in the workplace. These contracts may be
either progressive or fragile. Within these contracts several
types of exchange take place. Examples, drawn from my
research in Ivory Coast and Kenya, will clarify the nature and
interactions of contracts and exchanges. Type 1 and Type 2
exchanges are essential to the computerization process.
Depending on the actual situation, all of the exchanges may be
either serial or simultaneous.

Discussion of Type 1 Exchanges

Type 1 exchanges develop in contexts of regulation. One
of the most frequent Type 1 exchanges in Ivory Coast is the
call for bids *(appel d'offres)* in which the government seeks to
purchase computer services. Type 1 exchanges also occur in
cases where firms or individuals have complaints about
national computer policy. The extremes of problematic and
troublesome Type 1 and Type 4 exchanges occur within a
fragile computer contract in which policies toward technology
fluctuate.

Competition and potential conflicts of interest are evident
in some calls for bids. Vendors believe that the government
and large private companies discriminate against certain
smaller firms. Complaints about the bidding system surfaced
repeatedly in my Ivory Coast interviews, while discontent with

government customs regulations was more evident in the Kenyan responses. Both are examples of strained Type 1 exchanges. When complaints become bitter, contracts may be in jeopardy. As the director of a computer vending company in Abidjan[5] put it:

> In general, sixty percent of our sales involve microcomputers. There are very few calls for bids from the government for large, mainframe systems. And when there is a call for a bid, often it specifies a French company, BULL, for example and French computers are required.

The call for bids is the first step in a contractual exchange that entails sales and maintenance contracts and, very often, a long-term financial commitment between the vendor and the contracting agency. The same director described a situation he considered potentially disastrous:

> Well, just this morning I received a call for a bid from a government agency. It's useless to apply. This morning also I, well I, threw other calls for bids in the waste bin because they required French computer equipment, exactly the same obligations . . . . The situation is dramatic. It is a problem.

Calls for bids have six major elements, each of which influences the exchange. (1) The sending party, or contractor, is specified. (2) Financial support conditions are outlined. (3) Terms of participation are presented. (4) Eligibility requirements are described. (5) Bidding procedures are outlined. (6) Deadlines and locations for the receipt of bids are announced. The bid as a contract can be used to include, or more often, exclude potential participants from the exchange. For example, in calling for bids the Ivory Coast government often specifies that local Ivorian or French equipment and capital resources are to be used. That specification effectively eliminates U.S., European, Japanese, and other African firms from the bidding, creating fierce competition among those computer vendors permitted to bid and discontent among those excluded. In addition, as an exchange, the bid affects the social forms of work organization in the bidding agencies, which must not only supply equipment and services but also provide personnel with appropriate skills and the ability to work with all of the parties involved.

This Type 1 contractual exchange, the call for bids, clearly conditions the process of computer adoption. The request for bids sets the terms on which computer companies must establish their credibility. Once accepted, it initiates a sequence of activities, including installing computers, hiring and reskilling computer personnel, and reorganizing work tasks. Without the accepted bid, firms have no mandate for technological adaptation. In this way, the call for bids is fundamental to the implantation and circulation of computers in Ivory Coast. Accordingly, regulating the bidding process is an effective strategy for controlling the presence and uses of computers on a national scale.

Annexe II of Ivory Coast's *Plan Informatique National, 1986-1990* is explicit in delineating Type 1 and Type 2 exchanges between the government and computer consulting firms and between firms and their clients.[6] The plan designates two types of contracts to be scrutinized by the government: (1) contracts that specify outcomes *("contrats avec obligation de résultats")* and (2) contracts that specify the means of support *("contrats avec obligation de moyens")*. Contracts that specify outcomes are used to set tasks to be undertaken by computer consulting firms and to be completed within deadlines accepted by the firms and their clients. These jobs include master plans, audits, accounting schemes, and computer feasibility studies. The client receives work completed with the aid of the firm's computer system in exchange for payment. *Annexe II* of the *Plan Informatique National, 1986-1990* (pp.57-59) suggests that the contractual deadlines and organizational conditions for the completion of work be specified in advance by both parties in the exchange. The plan, however, does not delineate conditions for the enforcement of result contracts. *Annexe II* (p.59) states that "positive or negative sanctions" may be applied to result contracts depending upon the quality of the work received.

The results and means contracts have legal and socioeconomic implications. The informatics plan highlights these contracts as possible areas for regulation, control, and, if violated, legal action. The two contractual exchanges are clearly economic and rely on trust between the contracting parties. It is noteworthy that these contracts *per se* are outlined in the computer planning document. Thus, contractual exchanges are not treated as implicit and problematic concerns in Ivory Coast's computer world. Instead, government planners consider the result and means contracts to be fundamental to the process of regulating computerization in Ivory Coast. By contrast, in the absence of a computer plan, the Kenyan government does not specifically regulate the status of transactions between computer vendors and their clients.

Discussion of Type 2 Exchanges

Profits are the major byproduct of Type 2 exchanges for computer vendors and firms. Vendors attempt to regulate these exchanges in order to assure the stable growth of their firms and their profits. A commercial engineer at IBM Abidjan explained this situation to me.

> Voila. Our growth is not regular. You can grow and receive high profits one year and then have nothing for two or three years. So, since our policy is to offer the same services throughout the world, we install an infrastructure that generates fixed prices and we utilize reliable local personnel. We are very prudent in our local installations in order to assure the longevity of the agency. That is our overall policy. So, in general, when IBM decides to leave a country, it's a question of sales, hein? Or else there is a truly political reason, such as what happened in South Africa, for example.

Hence, the conditions for a violation, that is, a broken contract, in Type 2 exchanges are primarily commercial. The vendor seeks to maximize profits, and where there is little or no profit or other economic benefit to the firm, the contract is eventually abandoned. Failure to fulfill Type 2 exchanges is an endemic feature of the fragile computer contract. For example, major computer vendors withdrew from Kenya in 1985 and 1986 because high duties, taxes, and a restrictive sales arena decreased profits.

Discussion of Type 3 Exchanges

Type 3 exchanges establish the prerequisites for internal interactions within firms, including the social forms and messages that sustain the hierarchy of relationships between the firm's management and its computer personnel. Within a Type 3 exchange, technological mastery makes rapid internal mobility possible. That mastery, however, does not assure advancement and may instead freeze data-entry workers at the bottom of the office hierarchy.

In Ivory Coast, rapid vertical mobility is expected of engineers, but beginning programmers and data-entry workers generally cannot share that aspiration. Nevertheless, the flexibility of internal contractual exchanges encourages workers to believe the dream: progressing to higher levels in the computer profession is within their reach. Computer training uses Type 3 exchanges actualized in the postmodern dream of success as an incentive in recruiting students, especially in the commercial colleges and secretarial schools.

The flexibility and ambiguity of contracts within firms are also sources of workers' complaints. As a firm expands its technological capabilities the management restructures tasks and job titles, hiring new employees who will displace established workers. For computer consulting firms and other small businesses, recoding job titles and tasks often involves engaging temporary employees. As the director of a computer consulting firm in Ivory Coast explained

> In general we hire extra employees for local contracts. These local employees are usually expatriate women whose husbands work in enterprises here in Ivory Coast. Actually, we have three women working in this capacity at [our firm]. They are programmer-analysts with degrees from IUT [the Institut Universitaire de Technologie] in France.

Although hiring women to fill substitute positions is only one strategy for meeting organizational demands, this practice was not universally welcomed. One young female engineer interviewed in Ivory Coast expressed her discontent: "All of the women are at a low level, keypunchers, data-entry people, and computer operations, that sort of thing. The higher one goes, the fewer women one sees." She would have preferred to see more women in the permanent positions of company heads, high-level technicians, and maintenance engineers.

This young woman's response contrasts with the experiences of male research engineers who also have management responsibilities. Many of these engineers and systems analysts have a second role as part-time managers. This division of labor is indicative of a Type 3 exchange. An implicit contract empowers these engineers to manage the firm, even if for short periods. Moreover, it restructures lines of authority, job titles, and perceptions of work. A young engineer in an Abidjan computer consulting firm elaborated on his dual role as research coordinator and part-time manager:

> Well, I do everything and nothing. That is to say, I supervise research and maintenance, and I replace the director while he is away. That's why you are speaking with me today, because the director is away, and I assume those responsibilities in his absence.

While Type 2 and Type 3 exchanges relate to the conduct of "business as usual" in Kenya as they do in Ivory Coast, discussions of these activities in Kenya are often overshadowed by complaints about indirect government regulation and inappropriate technology. Concern about government economic policies dominated my conversation with an administrator in charge of the computer division of Price Waterhouse, which engages in computer consulting as well providing accounting services:

> First of all, high cost is definitely an obstacle. As you've probably gathered, the duties and taxes are very, very high, I think the highest I've come across in any country in the world, considerably higher than other African countries. It means that, for most computers, the cost

has run about 300% of the direct exchange value of most
Western countries when you include taxes, duties, and
import.

In this instance, government policies are described as
obstacles. Although there is no direct reference to contractual
regulations, the taxes, duties, and import costs set by the
government are considered to hinder smooth computer
adoption. This administration also pointed to the consequences of fragile Type 1 and Type 2 exchanges as he explained the
ways in which firms attempt to overcome the government
regulations they see as obstacles to the effective delivery of
services to their clients:[7]

> But I think there's a need for some more explicit policies.
> Tanzania, for example, has some sort of central computer
> committee, I believe, and I think there are a number of
> African countries which have that. I mean, that, I guess,
> is one way where they make some decisions, and then
> that is to me I suppose, one way, but, of course, they get
> bogged down into a sort of unfortunate bureaucracy. I
> don't really favor that approach, but I think there's a
> need for some more explicit policies. A byproduct of
> this situation, is that a very, very large number of micros
> now don't come in through official channels, probably
> more than fifty percent. They come in through people's
> personal effects because the duties are so prohibitive.
> And this must be counterproductive, because rather than
> getting very big duties, they get nothing. So something
> in-between would discourage this alternative path.

Under a fragile computer contract, Type 3 exchanges may
indicate problems with the computer system. The acquisition
of a system deemed inappropriate and the transition from one
system to another may generate frictions and tensions between
computer personnel and other staff. For example, the computer controller at a large trading company in Nairobi regarded
the firm's old NCR system as the principal source of problems
among the staff. At the same time, he considered technology
related problems to be normal in a department whose role and
size were both expanding. Initially, he assumed that the staff
problems could be resolved by employing additional data-

entry personnel. Subsequently, he persuaded his company to change computer systems and restructure the staff. By replacing an old NCR 8400 with a Wang VS/55, he increased both his technological and managerial control. His success made him a prime candidate for promotion. He emphasized:

> We will have *an expansion*. We are looking at getting two new data entry operators in addition to the current ones, one computer operator, whom we are now training, and one programmer who will also develop new systems. . . . I am the computer controller. But when we have all the new changes in, I think that the company will do something about the title.

Discussion of Type 4 Exchanges

Problems in computer adoption also appear in Type 4 exchanges, which treat the new technology itself as a responsible, interacting subject. My research in Kenya involved the experimental installation of a Kaypro 4 microcomputer at the Nairobi Handicraft Cooperative, a local carving and craft production enterprise. The computer was intended to facilitate bookkeeping and inventory control. During the initial stages of integrating the new computer into the cooperative's accounting system, a trainee discovered that carvers were being paid on a sliding scale. That is, notwithstanding the Management Committee's public advocacy of a flat commission of 15% for each carving sold to the cooperative, in practice it paid a larger commission to some carvers than to others.[8] This inconsistency—between public statement and private behavior—was apparently readily managed when records were on paper. The new technology, however, threatened exposure. Although there were sound financial, ethical, and cultural grounds for using a sliding rather than a fixed rate, the Management Committee was unwilling to risk exposing a practice that was known to those involved but that had not been publicly approved or formally documented. The consequence: the computer was devalued (at least in its accounting and record-keeping roles), while the bookkeeper was promoted. Even the proposed maintenance contract was rejected, as a volunteer who supervised the computer experiment described:

> I tried desperately to get them to take out a contract, a service contract, on the computer. It would only have cost them 4,000 shillings [approximately U.S. $25] to have this piece of equipment totally protected for a year, with total service and regular check-ups. They would not do it because they said it would cost too much money. We had the money to do it.

The Management Committee explicitly refused to encourage or support the computer's use for its intended purpose. Instead, the computer remained in the front office of the cooperative as a symbol—to some, of the organization's modernity and technological sophistication, and to others of failed or unrealized technological change.

In this case, the Type 4 exchange was not based solely on payment for services. The interpretation of technology in the cooperative was at issue. The Management Committee regarded the computer as an object of value for its display rather than for its use in accounting and record-keeping. Indeed, actually employing the computer as intended had the potential of destroying the equilibrium of the cooperative's operations. From the perspective of its leadership, the computer was an inappropriate means to accomplish the cooperative's business objectives. The refusal to obtain a maintenance contract was a case of interdiction/violation, or breaking an implicit contract regarding the computer's use.[9] The Management Committee's inaction rendered the computer an impressive and dust-collecting symbolic display of the cooperative's hopes for technological change.

Summary

I have located Type 1 and Type 4 exchanges at polar extremes in my classification because their appearance signals the success or failure of the computerization process, at least in the short term. Type 1 exchanges most often revolve around complaints from vendors, indicating areas of conflict between regulatory agencies and the private sector with particular focus on the government policies and regulations that affect computer imports and sales. In the Kenyan setting, however, Type 1 exchanges are common in small firms as well as among computer vendors. Type 4 exchanges in the Ivorian case focus on computer-related successes and conditions supportive of technological adaptation. In Kenya, Type 4 exchanges include disasters that reflect the underutilization or inappropriate application of computer technology. Type 4 exchanges exhibit broken contracts and gradual or unsuccessful computerization. These problems also surface in complaints about lack of vendor support for computer training (a firm-client relationship, Type 2) and inadequate data-entry staff within the firms (a firm-personnel exchange, Type 3). A broad review of my Kenyan interviews reveals a pattern of sporadic, individual computer-related successes against a backdrop of fragile Type 1 exchanges that limit the access of companies to adequate and appropriate computer facilities. Yet, in spite of these problems, computer training institutions are proliferating and expanding, and their administrators and students appear to be confident about the country's technological future.

Although the progressive computer contract in Ivory Coast involves government regulation of computerization—a process that effectively reduces economic competition—this type of contract is only rarely violated. Difficulties with the progressive computer contract emerge in education, where the aspirations toward new technology are most prominent. In Ivory Coast it is possible that there will develop an oversupply of locally trained engineers and high-level computer experts while computer operators and data-entry personnel remain a scarce resource. This contrast between Kenya and Ivory Coast underscores the conclusion that differences between the fragile and progressive contracts are manifested in the discourse and newly emerging social forms that surround the introduction of computers into the workplace.

TABLE 4.2   Computer Contracts and Exchanges in Ivory Coast and Kenya

Computer Contract	Type 1 Exchanges	Type 2 Exchanges	Type 3 Exchanges	Type 4 Exchanges
Ivory Coast: Progressive Computer Contract	Government regulation of result and means contracts in national plans	Consulting firms' contracts with large companies	Upward mobility of engineers and senior programmers	Accessibility of new computer system
	Calls for bids and indirect government regulation of sales	Competition among computer vendors & consulting firms	Frozen internal mobility of computer operators	Focus on local software development
Kenya: Fragile Computer Contract	Strict government regulation of import duties and taxes on computers	Data bureaus' contracts with large and small firms	Individual computer-related successes	Inappropriate computer systems and high computer costs
	Absence of national computer plan during the 1980s	Problems with after-sales support by vendors	Problems with outmoded computer systems & shortage of computer personnel	Broken sales and maintenance contracts

Table 4.2 compares the progressive and fragile computer contracts in terms of the four types of exchange. Type 1 exchanges determine the extent to which computers are available for sale to firms at reasonable prices. The economic circulation of computers affects the quality of computer-related services. The market, however, does not determine the availability of introductory computer education, which seems to be on the rise in Kenya in spite of the high cost of computers. That expansion emphasizes the importance of computers as a scarce technological resource and the role of education as a symbolic means of access to a scarce commodity. Since a fragile contract is precarious, violation of each type of exchange is threatened. In contrast, the progressive contract is strengthened by the accessibility of new technologies and the government's unequivocal support of their dissemination and use in government, business, education, and research.

Social and Cultural Consequences
of the Computer Contract

The computer contract establishes and reinforces the role of new technologies in business and government. When computers are initially adopted, their potential may appear to be boundless under both the progressive and the fragile computer contracts. Lacking a means-end component, the prospective discourse and symbolism of computer adoption links technology to utopian outcomes. Problems arise, however, at the moment when the obstacles to purchasing and using computers are confronted.

The shortcomings and daily struggles with computers in the world of work are strangely absent from the promising feasibility reports and glowing accounts that glamorize the new technology as a positive ideological force and an instrument of social reform.[10] In contrast to these accounts are the precarious Type 1 and Type 4 exchanges that reflect the effects of inconsistent regulation, ambiguous government policy, and inappropriate computer technology. In his work on Kenyan government computer services during the mid-1980s in

Nairobi, Westcott (1985,2) concludes that "data processing capabilities are lagging far behind the Government's needs." Indeed, outmoded equipment and three- and four-year data backlogs were common at Kenyan government computer installations in 1984 and 1985. Although increased government support for computerization in 1988 and 1989 appears to have remedied some of these problems, the Kenyan situation remains characterized by decentralized and gradual technological planning. Ambivalence associated with the fragile computer contract in Kenya reinforces conditions of scarcity in the computer market. In contrast, the progressive contract in Ivory Coast alters not only the availability of the computers but also the attitudes toward them by firmly linking new technologies to an ideology of economic development and autonomy. In Kenya that ideological linkage remains largely symbolic.

The analysis of the exchanges demonstrates divergent patterns where progressive and fragile computer contracts prevail. The computer's role as a symbol of change and the values associated with the new technology are framed by those exchanges. These patterns range from formal statements of government policy to actual economic transactions and organizational changes. Direct regulation of access to technology leads to a positive evaluation of computers, while ambivalence and indirect regulation result in mixed messages, confusion, and frustration for computer users. There are, of course, exceptions. In Kenya, innovative business strategies in response to government economic regulations have produced numerous individual computer successes. The vitality of syncretism and technological adaptations stimulated by the force of circumstances should not be overlooked. Nevertheless, the importance of the computer contract to the existence and diffusion of new technologies emphasizes the fundamental interplay among government, firms, and individuals in fitting the computer into an organizational structure. A positive response to new technologies does not issue solely from individual acceptance, but is instead the product of the interaction of a number of forces that shape how computers are acquired, regarded, and integrated into the discourse and practices of daily office work.

Conclusions: Terminal Social Practices

The contracts and exchanges analyzed here exhibit patterns of communication and understanding that frame social practices surrounding new technologies. We may term these activities "terminal social practices" because they contain the outcomes of new technological and cultural scenarios. A process of reflexive monitoring (Giddens 1984,5) links every-day practices surrounding computers to public discourse about new technologies. The computer operates as a secondary modeling system in which the program is the macrostructure and the printed text—which is a complex of textual and iconic signs—comprises the infrastructure (Sebeok 1976,23). These signs are embedded in a larger sociocultural context, a web of infinitely extending technological tools, images, and texts that have a direct sensate and controlling force over their users. In the two African countries considered here, the use of comput-ers is limited by policy statements and regulations that constrain their import, dissemination, and applications. The discourse surrounding the computer contract is one of power that refers both to possibilities to be realized through the computer and to the user's perceived goals. These representa-tional and discourse strategies are part of a simulation process in which the computer is valued as a sign of postmodernity as long as it is under the control of the new technicians of the sacred, that is, Africa's rising technological elite.

Terminal social practices are of particular concern to the governments of developing nations. When computers are used as terminals, they provide access to data banks. Prob-lems of transborder data flow emerge. Challenges to govern-ment control and security arise. In sum, terminal social practices go beyond the initial phase of determining the computer's uses in a firm and threaten government authority. In Kenya, anxiety over these terminal practices leads to a restrictive computer policy and a pattern of crisis computerization. High duties and taxes restrict private sector imports of computers in an effort to limit their dissemination and to control access to information. The explanation for this response must be sought by scrutinizing the sociopolitical fabric of Kenya, in which computers function as symbols of external control. In Ivory Coast, potentially threatening practices are tamed in progressive computerization plans and detailed official attention to the development of private sector computer consultancies, to which an entire volume of the *Plan Informatique National, 1986-1990* is devoted. In this case, computers have been harnessed to change the society and improve Ivory Coast's position in the world economy.

Government policy frames the possibilities for actualizing the various strategies described as part of the computer contract. As Lyotard (1984,9) has emphasized, "In the computer age, the question of knowledge is now, more than ever, a question of government." The computer contract does not operate in a vacuum. It links specific social and political actors. One of the major sources of tension in contractual exchanges is the contention for power between the forces of the state and the rising computer elite. This elite is an emerging network of professionals charged with interpreting computers and wielding the informational and cultural capital generated by high technology (Grant Lewis 1988a,268). Their professional and economic standing represents a break with the colonial past. For them, technology provides a source of autonomous empowerment that serves as a potential means of challenging the state and manipulating external economic resources. These computer professionals, however, are also part of the new class structures that have emerged across postcolonial Africa.

Those who have relatively greater access to computers will, in effect, become the new technicians of the sacred who fashion and manipulate the dreams of postmodernity. This social class will be very different from other classes and interest groups molded out of Africa's colonial heritage. As it strives for the benefits of economic development, will this group create a new form of social and political domination? When this group fully masters and indigenizes the computer, it may cease to be dependent on outside sources for credentials, influence, or status.[11] Yet, in marshaling its emerging power against that of the state, this rising information elite risks remaining marginal by splintering into a new white-collar proletariat, dominated and enslaved by the very contracts, social forms, and technological objects that promise to free it.

Notes

1. While my research explored the impacts of computers of all sorts, I am primarily concerned here with microcomputers. Since much of my argument, however, refers to the meanings and behaviors associated with computer technology, I shall retain the term "computer," rather than "microcomputer" in this discussion.

2. Robert J.P. Scott's 1981 survey of computers in Kenya presents estimates of the number of mainframe installations in the country between 1961 and 1981. Although Scott qualifies that exact figures were not available to him, he estimates the number of mainframe installations at 127 as of 1981. A parallel study was commissioned by the Ivorian government in 1979. This study estimated the number of mainframe installations to be 275 as of 1980. Suzanne Grant Lewis and Mohammed Sheya conducted a similar survey of microcomputers installations in Tanzania. They located 500 microcomputers in the country and found that most of them had been imported after 1983 (see the Appendix to Chapter 3). Over 60% of these computers were used in the public sector. Comparable microcomputer estimates are not available for Kenya. According to the *Plan Informatique National, 1986-1990*, the estimate for microcomputers in the public and private sectors in Ivory Coast as of 1985 was 785. The overall estimate for all computer systems in Ivory Coast as of 1985 was 1,225. A more detailed examination of the role of the computer contract in the dissemination of new technologies is contained in Jules-Rosette (1990,283-319). Excerpts from my data analysis have been reprinted with permission of Moutin de Gruyter Publishers. The research was funded by the John Simon Guggenheim Memorial Foundation, the National Science Foundation Grant # Int. 84-07272, and the Wenner-Gren Foundation for Anthropological Research, Grant #4863.

3. This speech by Mathieu Ekra, Minister of State and president of the CNI (Commission Nationale pour l'Informatique) in Ivory Coast, was delivered on December 12, 1983 and reproduced in the *Plan Informatique National, 1986-1990*, p.27. The address outlines the position of African nations in the world economy and offers computers and informatics as solutions to pressing problems of development. In certain respects, the speech resembles a statement by Jean-François Lyotard in which he

describes the position of developing nations in the postmodern era. Lyotard (1984,5) states:

> It is widely accepted that knowledge has become the principle force of production over the last few decades; this has already had noticeable effect on the composition of the work force of the most highly developed countries and constitutes the major bottleneck for the developing countries. In the postindustrial and postmodern age, science will maintain and no doubt strengthen its preeminence in the arsenal of productive capacities of the nation-states. Indeed, this situation is one of the reasons leading to the conclusion that the gap between developed and developing nations will grow ever wider in the future.

4. The projections for computerization in Ivory Coast are outlined in the nation's first and second national informatics plans for 1981 through 1985 and 1986 through 1990. The plans present the use of computers in the public and private sectors as a key feature of national economic development in Ivory Coast.

5. This firm director's complaints about the closed computer bidding system in Ivory Coast are outlined in greater detail in Jules-Rosette (1990,140-150). He expresses the view that limitations on the acceptance of bids from companies without French capital might severely restrict economic competition and the availability of computer hardware and software in Ivory Coast. These regulations threaten the competitive status of his U.S. based company.

6. The importance of contractual exchanges as basis for the dissemination and use of computers is emphasized by the explicit discussion of result and means contracts in *Annexe II* of Ivory Coast's *Plan Informatique National, 1986-1990*. This discussion underscores the government's concern with regulating computer sales, services, and in-house training in the private sector.

7. The case of computerization in Tanzania alluded to here is described at greater length by Grant Lewis (1988a,129-213). In Tanzania, regulation occurs through a government computer commission and through COMPAT, the Computer Association of Tanzania. COMPAT sets national standards for computer professionals.

8. While conducting field research on the Nairobi Handicraft Cooperative in 1981 and 1982, I was informed that all cooperative members receive a 15% commission on the carvings that they turn in to the cooperative for sale (see Jules-Rosette 1984,120-124). When the computer was installed, the bookkeeper confirmed to me that 15% was still the standard commission. The entry of members' payments into the computer revealed that carvers often received payments based on a sliding scale. Although this arrange-

ment was not made public, apparently it was acceptable to the cooperative's Management Committee and to the carvers themselves.

9. At the Nairobi Handicraft Cooperative, the conditions of the computer's use were formalized by a written agreement between the handicraft cooperative and the researcher. The service contract would also have been a written document concerning the computer's maintenance. Thus, in this case, a Type 4 contractual exchange involves both an implicit agreement and a formal written text.

10. Rob Kling and Suzanne Iancono (1988,235-236) discuss the ideological basis of pro-computer movements in the United States. They claim that the proponents of new technologies see computers as a "central medium for creating the world they prefer" (Kling and Iancono 1988,235). In computer movements, the benefits of new technologies are described without reference to the processes by which these technologies are adopted and mastered. This rhetoric of computer adoption may be compared to utopian religious discourse in which an idealized outcome is described without reference to the specific means by which the outcome is achieved.

11. Ali A. Mazrui (1977,297-302) proposes several strategies for "decolonizing" and indigenizing the computer. His examples draw heavily on the Kenyan case. He recommends more systematic training of computer personnel and the nationalization of technical jobs. Mazrui also advocates stricter duties on computers in order to prevent them from being overused as the substitutes for human labor. His ideas are clearly reflected in certain aspects of the Kenyan computer planning process.

5

Foreign Assistance Agencies as Advocates and Innovators

John A. Daly[1]

William F. Buckley recently wrote:

> What would happen if a half-million Kaypros--I speak of the Volkswagen of personal computers--were given away--yes given away--to Eastern Europe and the Soviet Union. The worriers will ask whether we are playing the role of the sorcerer's apprentice, giving away rudimentary instruments that can turn into monsters (with a Kaypro, Stalin might have managed to find and kill even more people). But no: the universalization of the resources of the computer can accelerate that which most needs acceleration: economic relief for 350 million people, East Europeans and Russians, bankrupt by 70 years of socialism (*Washington Post*,February 19,1990,A19).

It is hard to imagine a more political statement about the role of microcomputers in development assistance. Written by a political commentator, appearing on the op-ed page of a Washington newspaper, we have a recommendation for a donation of perhaps $500 million worth of microcomputers to achieve obviously political and economic objectives.

Buckley's statement quoted above lends itself to interpretations of naive political determinism: that donor agencies serve as the effective agents of political elites. I seek to avoid such simplistic models. This chapter starts with the premise that donor assistance has become a complex politico-economic industry in the last half-century. While the behavior of this industry can be predicted by partially deterministic models, such models will necessarily be complex and multifaceted. Effective political action to influence this industry requires mastery of the implications of such complex models. This chapter seeks to make a modest contribution to understanding the behavior of the system of donor agencies in the introduction of microcomputer technology in development assistance. The role of foreign assistance agencies in microcomputer advocacy and innovation is best understood in terms of the political processes to which the agencies themselves are subject. What follows, then, is a discussion of the influence that organizational charters, governance structures, staffing systems and staff characteristics, and bureaucratic organizations and processes play in defining and constraining the roles of donor agencies as advocates and innovators. The discussion draws heavily on my own experience in the U.S. Agency for International Development (USAID) but UNESCO's efforts in informatics and development is also profiled.

Overview of the Development Assistance Agencies

More than thirty countries provide official foreign assistance through government channels (Table 5.1).[2] Ten provided more than $1 billion each in 1986-87. Essentially all of these provide some bilateral assistance--country to country financial assistance implemented by the donor country's institutions. The Organization for Economic Cooperation and Development (OECD) Development Assistance Committee estimates that of a total of $48.1 billion in Official Development Assistance in 1987, $38.1 was bilateral, and $10 billion was disbursed through multilateral channels.

The sources of foreign assistance have changed radically over a period of decades. In 1960 the United States provided 85 percent of bilateral development assistance, but by 1988 the

share was less than 20 percent and the U.S. has been sur-
passed by Japan as the largest single donor (USAID 1989,24).
In the 1970s the Arab nations increased aid significantly, but
those flows (in constant dollars) have significantly decreased
since 1980 (Wheeler 1988,59). While Japanese financial
assistance may continue to increase significantly in the near
future, there appears little reason to believe that overall aid to
developing countries will increase by a comparable percentage.

TABLE 5.1   Official Development Assistance by Classification of Donor
($ millions at 1986 prices)

Source	1970-71	1986-87
United States	7751	9124
European Economic Community[a]	8881	15998
Japan	2302	6016
Other Western[b]	2424	5519
Arab Donors[c]	1259	3689
CMEA Countries[d]	3141	4382
LDC Donors[e]	(1418)	569
Total World	(27176)	45297

[a]   In order of 1986-87 funding: France, Germany, Italy, Netherlands,
United Kingdom, Denmark, Belgium, Ireland.
[b]   Canada, Sweden, Norway, Australia, Switzerland, Finland, Austria,
New Zealand, Spain, Greece, Portugal, Luxembourg, Iceland.
[c]   Including Saudi Arabia, Kuwait, UAE.
[d]   Including USSR, GDR.
[e]   Including China, India, Venezuela, Iran.

Source: Wheeler, Joseph C., *Development Cooperation: 1988 Report* (Paris:
OECD, 1988), Table IV-1, p. 60.

TABLE 5.2   Concessional and Non-concessional Flows from Multilateral Agencies ($ millions)

Source	1970-71		1987	
	Con- cessional	Non-Con- cessional	Con- cessional	Non-Con- cessional
Major Financial Institutions				
IDA	225	-	3530	-
IBRD	-	585	-	4395
IFC	-	62	-	208
IDB	219	104	121	928
AfDF[b]	-	-	374	-
AfDB[a,b]	-	4	-	282
ADF	3	-	514	-
ADB[a]	-	29	-	364
IFAD[a]	-	-	286	-
Subtotal	447	784	4825	6177
United Nations				
WFP	125	-	720	-
UNDP	219	-	786	-
HCR[a]	8	-	386	-
RWA	45	-	207	-
Unicef	47	-	364	-
UNTA	49	-	314	-
UNFPA	-	-	106	-
Other UN	36	-	426	-
Subtotal	529	-	3309	-

[a] Data for 1986.
[b] AfDF: African Development Fund; AfDB: African Development Bank

Source: Wheeler, Joseph C. *Development Cooperation: 1988 Report* (Paris: OECD, 1988), Table 18, p.190.

Bilateral Agencies

Individual countries may have more than one foreign assistance agency, as in the case of Canada which operates both the Canadian International Development Agency and the

International Development Research Center. The United States, while theoretically coordinating bilateral and multilateral foreign economic assistance through the International Development Cooperation Agency, in fact manages economic supporting assistance through the Agency for International Development (USAID), food assistance through the U.S. Department of Agriculture in collaboration with USAID, and provides technical assistance through the volunteer services of the Peace Corps. The Department of State and the Treasury Department oversee U.S. interests in UN agencies and the international financial institutions, respectively. Smaller, decentralized agencies such as the African Development Foundation, the Interamerican Foundation, and the Trade and Development program also exist. Thus bilateral foreign assistance agencies themselves form a complex group even within a single country.

Multilateral Agencies

We may broadly distinguish the multilateral development banks, sometimes called the World Bank family of institutions, from the UN family of institutions. The former are primarily banking institutions, focusing on the provision of concessional and market-rate loans for development projects. The UN agencies include agencies ranging from the UN High Commission for Refugees (UNHCR) and the UN Relief and Works Agency (UNRWA), to the World Health Organization (WHO), the Food and Agricultural Organization (FAO), and the UN Industrial Development Organization (UNIDO). Table 5.2 indicates that these also carry out very substantial programs of foreign assistance.

> The 1970s saw an explosion in multilateral financing of development. Its relatively tranquil, almost somnambulistic, rate of growth till then began to seem like an aberration. . . . Multilateral flows thus accounted for under 9 percent of total developing country receipts in 1970, nearly 13 percent in 1980, and over 20 percent in 1985. . . . Since 1983, growth in almost all sources of multilateral finance has leveled off or has declined substantially (Mistry 1989,117-118).

The number of intergovernmental organizations (IGOs) is significantly underestimated if one only considers the data in Table 5.2. There are some 32 organizations specifically within the UN family. Overall, it has been estimated that the number of intergovernmental organizations was 378 in 1986 and may increase to 450 by the year 2000 (Feld and Jordan 1988,7).

There exist a variety of processes that have the effect, intended or otherwise, of coordinating the activities of the agencies. The OECD Development Assistance Committee serves as a high level interagency forum. In addition, at least 28 sub-Saharan African countries regularly convene Consultative Group meetings organized by the World Bank. Policy, technical, and managerial officials of donor agencies meet to exchange information and coordinate programs. Representatives of bilateral assistance agencies of major donor nations serve on the governing bodies of multinational organizations. Staff members rotate among the bilateral and multilateral organizations, and individuals with experience and knowledge of major bilateral donors are sometimes appointed to senior posts in the multilateral agencies. The Society for International Development and other professional societies provide fora for exchanges among professionals employed in international development, and a significant professional literature exists including specialized journals, in which theory can be promulgated and experience exchanged.

In the foreign assistance industry, the donor organizations and recipient countries interface in an economic market: countries vie for additional resources and donor agencies vie for relative advantage. These interfaces also have strong political aspects, as the transactions are between government and government, or between intergovernmental and governmental organizations. Not only do donor organizations seek to apply bilateral and multilateral political pressure to encourage host countries to make desired policy changes, so too do host countries seek to apply bilateral and multilateral pressure to encourage donor policy changes and exceptions. Several chapters in this volume are case studies offering at least partial views of recipient behavior. This chapter provides an analytic framework for understanding donor agency behavior.

Microcomputer Activities in Foreign Assistance

In the United States in 1988 there were approximately 45 million personal computers (Committee to Study International Development 1988,56). U.S. computer manufactures were estimated at some $52 billion in 1988, up from $6 billion in 1972 (Computer Science and Technology Board 1988). The availability of personal computers is orders of magnitudes less in developing countries, but will surely expand radically in the future. Foreign assistance agencies, mirroring developed country experience in their developing country operations, will be increasingly involved in the introduction of microcomputer technology.

As computer hardware and software become more affordable to the individual user, it appears that total expenditures on computer technology will increase in developing countries (Munasinghe 1989,16). Therefore foreign assistance agencies will probably be asked for more assistance with the foreign currency costs of computer acquisitions. The relative importance of such financial assistance will depend on the situation of the recipient country. For many of the relatively small, low income, and low growth countries of sub-Saharan Africa or Latin America, foreign assistance represents upwards of 20 percent of government revenues. For these countries, donor agencies will be of critical importance in introducing computer technology (USAID 1989,107).

Foreign assistance agencies are involved in the introduction of microcomputer technology in several ways: through example-induced innovation; as project components; through commodity import programs; as the subject of studies and publications; through support for computer research; as an economic sector; and through informatics agencies.[3]

Example-Induced Innovation

The foreign assistance agencies are themselves introducing microcomputer technology in their operations in developing countries. Figure 5.1 shows the number of workstations installed by USAID in its missions outside the United States. The trend to automation of donor agencies is partly due to the very high costs of maintaining staff in foreign countries, which makes increasing employee efficiency through computerization attractive.

The use of microcomputers by the permanent overseas employees of foreign assistance agencies and by their consultants has an obvious demonstration effect, since host country colleagues see the uses of microcomputers in project development and implementation. There is also a process that might be called "induced complementary innovation," in which donor agencies encourage the introduction of compatible computer technology in the host country institutions with which they interact. They do so to be able to transfer data and information between and among compatible systems, and to allow staff members to work easily with donor and recipient hardware and software.

Project Components

Perhaps the most pervasive manner in which foreign assistance agencies are currently introducing microcomputer technology in host countries is as incidental technology within development projects. For example, it has been estimated that the UN Development Program (UNDP) funded some 1500 projects with information technology components between 1975 and 1987, and that World Bank financing for information technology has been growing at 30 percent per year for the last decade (Hanna and Schware 1990,254-5). By 1989, almost 90 percent of all World Bank lending operations had significant information technology components, and "Bank annual lending to the informatics field exceeded $1 billion" (Informal Task Force on Information Technology for Developing Countries 1990,8).

Commodity Import Programs

In some cases foreign assistance is provided as hard currency support for the acquisition of foreign goods and ser-

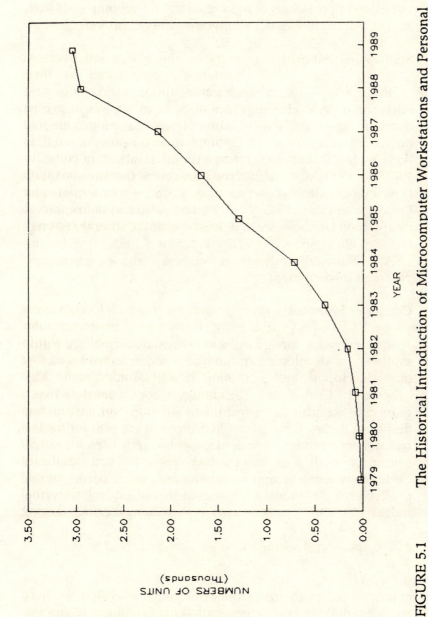

FIGURE 5.1   The Historical Introduction of Microcomputer Workstations and Personal Computers in USAID

vices, including microcomputer hardware, software, and peripheral equipment. In Pakistan, for example, in 1989 there were two importations of more than 100 microcomputers each supported by the USAID commodity import program.

Studies and Publications

Foreign assistance agencies have fostered a literature on microcomputer technology targeted at developing country decision makers. Efforts range from the publication of *Microelectronics Monitor* by UNIDO, to sector-specific publications in health and agriculture (World Health Organization 1988), to non-sector-specific reports such as the Interamerican Development Bank report on microelectronics (Interamerican Development Bank 1988,105-193), the United Nations report on information technologies and development (Center for Science and Technology for Development 1986), and the USAID/National Academy of Sciences series on microcomputers in development.[4]

Computer Research

In a few cases, foreign assistance agencies have made funds available for developing country researchers to participate in the development of hardware or software. The USAID Program in Science and Technology Cooperation has made grants to Mexican investigators to develop computer-aided design software for surface hydrology and to Sri Lankan researchers to develop microcomputer technology for the control of small scale irrigation systems. In its Science and Technology for Development project in Egypt, a portion of the project provides grants to Egyptian investigators to develop industrial control applications for microcomputers.[5]

Microcomputer Technology as an Economic Sector

In at least one project, USAID is seeking to assist the host country, Tunisia, to utilize microcomputers more effectively as the main objective of the project. The effort seeks to use the education system as a vehicle for technological innovation, and is working through a Tunisian national organization dedicated to informatics. The project includes long- and short-term technical assistance, financial assistance for equipment acquisition and training of host country nationals, and funds for projects which will both demonstrate the applicability of computer technology in Tunisia and give Tunisians hands-on experience in major computer innovations.

Informatics Agencies

In at least two cases, agencies have been developed specifically to focus on computer technology. The earlier was the UN Computer Center. Created by an initiative of President Eisenhower at the United Nations, the origins of the Center reflected a view—common in the very early days of computer technology (1940s and early 1950s)—that the computational needs of the world were very limited and that only a few computer centers would be needed for use by all. In this conceptualization, it was perhaps natural to assume that the United Nations could operate one such center and thus make computer power available to developing countries.

As this antiquated idea was abandoned, the organization was renamed the Intergovernmental Bureau for Informatics (IBI), and its leaders sought to find an appropriate role in the foreign assistance community. IBI came to focus on national computer policies, and to try to promote international discussion on policy issues such as transnational data flows. Eventually, however, the major donor agencies withdrew support from IBI. The United States was perhaps the first, and as France, Spain, and finally Italy withdrew in the 1980s, the organization closed its doors and ceased to exist. To some degree it has been replaced by the UNESCO Intergovernmental Program on Informatics.

The World Center for Informatics and Human Resources was created by the Mitterand government of France in accordance with the plans of Servan-Schreiber. Initially the concept of the Center was promoted as one of the national centers in a worldwide network promoting the use of informatics for development. Interest in the concept was international. The U.S. Congress, for example, held hearings on the concept inviting Servan-Schreiber to speak and several very well known U.S. computer experts went to work in the Center in Paris. However, from the United States perspective, the honeymoon was short and the Center soon became perceived as a vehicle to promote French national interests and the dissemination of French technology, especially in Africa. U.S. scientists withdrew in anger, and the influence of the Center was greatly reduced. When I wrote to the Center in 1990 for an update on its activities, the letter was returned stamped "addressee unknown."

Discussion

Most agencies regard information technology innovation as a secondary instrument in achieving their primary purposes. Thus sectoral organizations, such as the World Health Organization and the Food and Agricultural Organization, introduce informatics technology in their efforts to achieve sectoral goals, that is to improve health services and agricultural productivity, respectively. Similarly, multi-sectoral development agencies such as the World Bank, while having reexamined policies in this decade, do not now regard informatics as a lending sector, but regard informatics projects within the context of other sectoral goals. A prototypical statement of this position was contained in USAID Congressional hearings on microcomputers in development in 1982: "We expect our work to be sector focused as we build appropriate microcomputer applications into a package of technical inputs into each sector" (Farrar 1982,118).

Politically, the support for development assistance appears to depend in part on the semantics describing the intervention. One of the major lessons of the 1980s stems from the success of UNICEF in increasing its programs and budgets through emphasis on programs of "child survival," including specific efforts such as the "expanded program of immunization" and "oral rehydration." Simple, visibly effective efforts with strong humanitarian appeal are attractive to both the public and to legislators. Support appears more difficult for programs couched in such jargon as "informatics for development" or "structural adjustment." U.S. public opinion polls suggest that support is strongest for categorical programs such as disaster relief, health care, family planning, and aid to farmers. It is much lower for infrastructure and helping small businesses (Contee 1987,26). Only 54 percent of Americans reported favoring foreign aid as opposed to 39 percent who opposed it in 1986 (Contee 1987,23). The public support in donor countries for building the computer capacity of developing countries is probably minimal.

Having presented an overview of foreign assistance agencies and their activities related to the introduction of microcomputer technology, we turn now to the first of four factors influencing the role agencies play as advocates and innovators.

Charters of the Agencies

Foreign assistance agencies have charters—individual statements of objectives and fields of activity. The chartering of a donor agency is a dynamic political process, changed by modifying the laws and decrees that legitimate its behavior. Chartering is relatively infrequent. U.S. bilateral assistance (dating from Philippine assistance in the Spanish American war, Interamerican cooperation in World War II and the Marshall plan in the late 1940s) is chartered by the Foreign Assistance Act. The current act was written in 1961 and was the subject of major revisions in 1973.[6] Charters of major UN agencies were specified in the aftermath of World War II, and charter disputes such as that which lead to the departure of the United States and Great Britain from UNESCO are relatively infrequent and slow to be resolved.

Typically formal charter revisions reflect political acknowledgement of serious changes of circumstances, as when the UN Computer Center was reorganized into the IBI (reflecting a change in the perceived role of computers in society), or when the Organization of American States program in Science and Technology was rechartered to focus on four areas of cutting-edge technology, including information technology (reflecting major changes in budget levels). The relatively stable charters set a stage in which more rapid processes of change can work—budgetary, personnel, administrative, and the like.

Bilateral Agencies

The charters of bilateral agencies are typically quite complex. The Agency for International Development, for example, has been described as having 33 legislated objectives, while internal documents list 75 priorities (Task Force on Foreign Assistance 1989, 28). Bilateral assistance can be described in terms of a variety of policy objectives: humanitarian, security (e.g. support for military allies), economic (stabilizing debtor countries, contributing to international economic well-being), commercial, and environmental. Bilateral agencies typically are chartered to work in certain classes of countries, and to focus on certain classes of development activities.

International Development Banks

There are, of course, differences among the charters of development banks but consider the World Bank group as illustrating the formal objectives of multilateral banks. Their charters were described in a Bank publication as follows:

> It must lend only for productive purposes and must stimulate economic growth in the developing countries in which it lends. It must pay due regard to the prospects of repayment. Each loan is made to a government or must be guaranteed by the government concerned. The use of loans cannot be restricted to purchases in any particular member country. And the IBRD's decisions to lend must be based on economic conditions alone.
>
> The International Development Association was established in 1960 to provide assistance for the same purposes as the IBRD, but primarily in poorer countries and on terms that would bear less heavily on their balance of payments than would IBRD loans (World Bank 1989d,3).

The multinational development banks have emphasized loan funding of infrastructure (energy, roads, communications, irrigation, etc.) and industrial development projects. However, the interpretation of their charters has changed over the years as development theory has evolved. As human resource investments have been recognized as contributing to economic development, projects in health, education, and population have been added to the list of permissible operations for development banks.

United Nations Agencies

Sectoral UN Agencies, like WHO, UNESCO, FAO, UNEP, UNICEF, ILO, UNIDO, UNFPA, are each specifically chartered to deal with issues in a sector of the economy or society. Their *regular budgets* allow the agencies to deal with issues of international coordination, and provide some technical services for developing countries such as technical assistance and training. In some cases the organizations can provide norms and standards for international collaboration, as the OECD publishes the so called Frascatti manual defining a set of standard categories for reporting of science and technology activities. Small UN agencies like the World Intellectual Property Organization can have large impact on specific computer policy issues such as software copyright and dissemination.

The UN Development Program (UNDP), created in 1966 from elements formed in the early post war years, has a more general charter to manage the *voluntary contributions* of countries for technical cooperation in the UN system. Thus the UNDP channels a significant portion of the funds for the voluntary projects of other UN agencies, as well as managing special programs such as the World Development program. Eighty-five percent of its funds are programmed through country programs, developed in cooperation with the host government, and the remaining fifteen percent are regional and global in nature, focusing on such efforts as research of global impact (United Nations 1985,29-30).

Implications of the Pattern of Agency Charters

Over the last half-century a new industry has developed for transactions between donor agencies and developing countries. On the supply side there are a large number of donor agencies, each with its chartered assistance offering. On the demand side there are a large number of developing country organizations, each with its assistance requirements. One must question the degree to which adequate information exists as to the supply and demand for assistance. The issue is perhaps exacerbated in new and rapidly changing development fields, such as informatics. While donor agency officials may be entrepreneurial in seeking to fill unserved niches, the relative inflexibility of donor agency charters (as well as recipient agency charters) does impose rigidities that result in gaps where no agency is meeting demands or where donor and recipient agencies can not align to create conditions needed for a transaction.

As a group, the charters of the donor agencies change slowly. New major donor agencies have appeared seldom since the formation of the UN and World Bank systems after World War II. While small agencies can be added to the donor community, the creation of a major new entity appears to require very special circumstances. When such conditions do occur, the benefits to one sector or geographic region may be at the cost of another. Thus there is a real possibility that the current global reallocation of development assistance resources will result in a decrease in assistance to Africa.

Alternatively, existing agencies seek to cover new development demands by shifting focus and adding areas of program emphasis. In UNIDO, there has been considerable interest in expansion into informatics industries such as microelectronics, computer hardware, and computer software. In the case of those agencies with a specific charter for science, such as UNESCO and OAS, there has been interest in expanding the work on computer science and moving into more general support of informatics. As new technological areas of informatics are developed from research, such as artificial intelligence and cognitive science, it will be natural for the science agencies to attempt to move into the vacuum of donor assistance for the technology. The World Bank is currently considering changing its policy in order to increase support for the informatics sector, as did the Agency for International Development early in the 1980s.

In terms of the introduction of information technology, the pattern of international agency charters is complex and fragmented. There is no dominant agency with strong staff and financial resources that is specifically charged with information technology. The World Center and the IBI, while chartered for informatics, have not proven capable of providing assistance or leadership comparable to the need. The International Telecommunications Union, while very effective in some areas of informatics technology, has not been chartered to deal with other informatics utilities. Some agencies have defined information science or information technology as sectors of concern, most notably UNESCO, OAS, UNIDO, and International Development Research Center.

Some believe that countries should seek to develop information technology capacity as an economic sector *per se*. The informatics sector is seen as producing goods and services, both as intermediates to be sold to other productive sectors, and as final products to meet direct consumer demands. According to this view, countries should seek integrated policies and institutions to produce informatics professionals, to develop software, to develop support such as maintenance and repair, and perhaps to produce informatics hardware. Seeking to meet the need for computer goods and services by a patchwork of activities in various sectors, in this view, inescapably results in inefficiencies and inadequacies. With the current structure of agency charters, there is no foreign assistance agency likely to provide project or program assistance to the informatics sector as so conceived.

Governance

That governance affects agency behavior appears self-evident. Our principal concern here is with the bodies holding legislative control and the groups appointing senior officials to agencies. What follows is a brief discussion of governance structures and the implications for informatics assistance.

Bilateral Agencies

In the United States, governance of the Agency for International Development is divided between the Congress and the Administration. Congress defines policy and allocates financial and human resources for USAID. The President, with the consent of the Senate, appoints individuals to policy positions both in USAID and in agencies such as the Department of State and the Office of Management and Budget that oversee aspects of the USAID program. Both members of Congress and the Administration face electoral processes, and therefore they must be responsive to a variety of political forces.

Notable among these forces are relatively organized interest groups, such as the environmental, hunger, child survival, and Israel lobbies; the university community, especially the land-grant colleges; the so-called military-industrial complex; the science and technology community; the corporate community including those with interests in the sale of goods and services to the development program and those interested in commerce influenced or potentially influenced by the development assistance program. Not the least effective of the communities that impinge upon and influence the legislative and administrative elite is the cadre of professionals that work within the development assistance program.

In most of the other OECD countries, governmental form is parliamentary, and the party in power in the parliament forms the cabinet and controls the government. Thus there is not the opportunity for the political differences between administration and legislature that have characterized U.S. government for much of the last forty years. There is considerable diversity among the parliamentary systems. For example, it was not until 1979 that Britain created a continuing Foreign Affairs Committee in Parliament while Canada, France, Germany, and Japan have had such committees for many years. There are also differences in the number of parties in the legislature and in the relative strength of the executive (Cassese 1982).

International Development Banks

Again we will take as the prototype of this community the World Bank family. The World Bank's Board of Governors consists of one governor for each member country. The Board of Executive Directors, to whom the Governors have delegated most of their powers, perform the day-to-day governing. These 22 executive directors consist of five appointed by the five members holding the most shares of capital stock and the remaining 17 are elected by the governors (World Bank 1989d,13). The voting power of executive directors is proportional to the contributions of the member states whose votes they cast. The representatives of the United States, Japan, Federal Republic of Germany, United Kingdom, and France in 1989 cast 45 percent of the votes in the International Bank for Reconstruction and Development and 45 percent in the International Development Association (World Bank 1989d, 225). The President of the Bank is elected by the executive directors, and this office has been reserved for U.S. citizens (World Bank 1954,17). Other officers of the bank are in practice selected from a variety of countries—both major donors and developing countries.

Bank operations are constrained by budgets, and there are periodic replenishments of the budget in which member countries, by agreement, contribute to the capital of the bank. Such negotiations may be the occasion of serious challenges to the governance structure. For example, negotiations on the 1987-90 Interamerican Development Bank replenishment broke down when the Reagan administration insisted the Bank give up its right to approve loans with a simple majority of votes.

United Nations Agencies

The general assemblies of UN agencies are typically representative bodies, with each member country entitled to one vote. Simple majority rule is the normal voting process. In UN agency councils, block voting is common. Thus the so called Group of 77 (representatives of developing countries, which have expanded well beyond the original 77 members) often vote together on development issues. While the general assemblies are the top legislative bodies for UN agencies, practical control is often delegated to a smaller governing council, with members elected from the assembly, or in some cases defined in part by the original charter. Table 5.3 shows the distribution of members in some of these bodies for 1987. Note that the OECD countries considerably outvote the centrally planned economies in the governing councils, and can usually outvote African, Asian, or Latin American countries if they vote as continental blocks. Only in the case of united developing country positions can the OECD votes be overridden if the OECD votes as a block. Thus, in the governing councils the balance of power is far more favorable to the donor countries than is the case in the general assemblies.

The chief executive officers typically are elected by the general assemblies. Donor countries are heavily represented at this level, with their nationals directing the majority of the special programs and almost half of the specialized agencies (U.S. Department of State 1988). In practice, the chief executive office in most agencies is rotated among countries, and senior officials are chosen from a variety of different countries.

Informal processes effectively guarantee representation of important donor countries in senior officer positions. The position of Administrator of the UNDP has fallen to U.S. citizens. In some cases, developing country nationals have been elected to the chief executive office, as when Amadou M'Bow from Senegal served as Director General of UNESCO. The election of the chief executive officer of a UN agency can be the occasion of considerable diplomatic maneuvering.

The UN Development Program's governance structure is worthy of special note. The UNDP provides an alternate governance structure for the allocation of funds in the UN, since it collects and allocates a major portion of the UN system

TABLE 5.3   Membership of Governing Councils of U.N. Agencies, 1987

Region	UNICEF	UNDP	FAO	IAEA	ILO[a]	WHO
Sub-Saharan Africa	7	10	11	3	10	10
Asia/Oceana	7	5	7	4	6	4
North Africa/ Middle East	2	3	7	5	4	4
OECD						
USA	1	1	1	1	3	1
Japan	1	1	1	1	3	1
Europe	8	12	7	7	13	3
Other	3	3	3	3	4	-
Latin America/ Caribbean	6	7	9	6	9	4
Centrally Planned Economies						
USSR	1	1	-	1	2	1
China	1	1	1	1	1	1
Other	3	4	2	3	3	1
Total	40	48	49	35	58	30

[a] ILO figures combine government, worker, and employer representatives.

Source: U.S. Department of State, *United States Contributions to International Organizations: 37th Annual Report: Report to the Congress for Fiscal Year 1987* (Washington, DC, 1988).

funds for technical cooperation. In part it represents a superior coordinating body for the decentralized UN agencies, with its Interagency Consulting Board of the directors of agencies, and with UNDP Resident Representatives serving as representatives of many independent UN agencies. The

UNDP Governing Council, with representatives of 48 countries (United Nations 1985,29), increases the voting power of donor countries. The UNDP planning cycle sets indicative figures for voluntary contributions of member countries, as opposed to membership dues established by legislation.

Implications of the Patterns of Governance

The large donor countries have most control over their bilateral agencies, less control over UNDP and the international development banks, and least control over the decentralized UN agencies. Correspondingly, by block voting, even relatively small and poor recipient countries have been very effective at extending influence over some UN family agencies. While recipient countries sometimes complain of the lack of responsiveness of donor country-dominated agencies, donor countries also complain of the fragmentation and lack of programmatic integration of the recipient-dominated agencies.

The influence exerted on multilateral donors by governments is often subtle. Frank confrontation is usually (but not always) avoided. As one observer has written of the IBRD:

> Few, if any, matters of importance are decided by a mere tally of votes. From the very start, the Bank's management has chosen to follow a policy of total avoidance of confrontation (and of divided votes at the level of Directors or Governors) and has adopted instead a decision making process which functions smoothly by means of continuing consultations and informal contacts between Executive Directors and Bank officials at various stages of the lending process and long before a loan is formally submitted for approval. The Directors are thus rarely, if ever, asked to decide issues and problems on which a prior consensus has not been already reached.
>
> This smooth and efficient method of proceeding reaches into the national decision-making structures as well. . . . Informal review consists of personal contacts between officials of the U.S. Government and the Bank staff . . . much of the meaningful review of proposed loans is done before the formal Bank loan documents are distributed (Fatouros 1977,14-15).

The willingness of donor countries to participate in different multilateral foreign assistance agencies may be expected to depend somewhat on the influence the donor has in the governance of the agency. While roughly one-quarter of official development assistance of the countries of the Development Assistance Committee (DAC) of the OECD is channeled through multilateral agencies, the portion ranges from 11.5 percent for France to some 40 percent for Denmark, Finland, and Norway. In the case of the United States, multilateral contributions decreased from 28.6 percent of ODA in 1979-80 to 21.9 percent in 1986-87 (Wheeler 1988,97).

The governance issue is important in the field of informatics assistance. At least one informed observer attributes the demise of IBI largely to the unwillingness of the donor agencies to accept the governance bylaws that were approved by the member countries (Personal communication, Jorge Phillips).

In the field of computers, there is extreme imbalance between the donor and developing countries. Japan and the United States, which are the two largest donor countries, are also competing for domination in the world's informatics industries. European countries, which are individually smaller donors, are also major markets and producers of informatics technology. In those donor agencies in which the governance is dominated by the few countries which are both major donors of funds and major sources of information technology, one will expect foreign assistance to mirror producer country interests in the sector. In those agencies where the governance is dominated by many recipient countries with weak informatics sectors, one will expect foreign assistance to mirror non-producer country interests.

Staffing

In 1981 it was estimated that there were 80,000 to 100,000 international civil servants (Plantey 1981,21). If one were to update that figure and add the employees of the bilateral agencies the number would be considerably higher.

People who work for and with foreign assistance agencies have a powerful influence on the policies and organizational behavior of those agencies. They influence policy level officers and legislative bodies both through formal and informal channels. More fundamentally, the behavior of the participants of the donor agencies' programs is the organizational behavior we seek to understand. Their behavior is influenced by the charters of organizations, and by the policies defined and resources allocated and by the organizational structures and processes discussed in the following section. Their behavior is, however, also influenced by other factors, including their national backgrounds, their areas of expertise, and the ability of agencies to hire the right person for the right job. Such factors can be used as parameters for models of agency behavior.

Professional Discipline

Donor agencies differ in the professional backgrounds of staff members, depending on the organization's focus. In addition, donor agencies differ in the allocation of leadership roles across professional disciplines. In WHO, most high level posts in the organization are held by people originally trained as physicians; in the Agency for International Development, most high level positions are held by people with extensive experience in integrating various sectoral programs, and physicians are most commonly found in subordinated health and population offices.

To the degree that social processes determine the way people construe a technology (Bijker, Hughes, and Pinch 1987), then the process of professionalization should affect the perception of computer technology. Physicians would be likely to construe microcomputers as aids to the practice of medicine, accountants as aids to the practice of accountancy, and agronomists as aids to the practice of agronomy. Such professionally determined construction of the technology should contribute to donor agency sectoral specialization in the introduction of computers. In addition, inequalities in the power of professions within agencies may be reflected in the

degree to which the agencies empower host country professions to have access to and use computers. Physician-domi-
nated WHO may empower host country physicians more than
host country paramedicals simply because influential officials
of WHO may tend to think of computers as empowering
physicians.

In a study of staffing of international agencies, Haas,
Williams, and Babai (1977) confirmed that there are differing
mixes of professionals within the agencies. Their evidence
supported the view that the attitudes toward scientific
information were partially determined by professional
backgrounds of their respondents. People trained in some
disciplines can be expected to value scientifically validated
data more highly than others, and thus to value the application of information technology for the purpose of improving
data quality and availability more highly as well.

Personnel Systems and Staff Quality

In the bilateral and multilateral agencies, personnel systems
have been criticized, leading to questions of quality of staff
services. For example, USAID's personnel system is criticized
as having become less functional over time (Hoben 1989,255).
As USAID personnel systems were reformed in the 1970s and
1980s, the agency probably did lose flexibility in re-staffing to
meet new technological opportunities and developmental
challenges. The agency has become more "managerial" and
less "technical" in its workforce.

In the case of some multilateral agencies, staffing appoint-
ments are through professional services, such as the international civil service of the UN. However, Feld and Jordan
(1988) suggest that "only about 2,700 posts (in the UN with
some 22,600 posts) have been officially subject to the application of all the principles of a truly international civil service"
(Feld and Jordan 1988,101). Moreover, the nature of the
international civil service regulations severely constrain the
nature of the sanctions and rewards that are available to
influence behavior of donor agency employees.

Nationality

The national composition of the multilateral agencies is a matter of some debate among national delegations. Feld and Jordan argue:

> The insistence of the developing countries that more of their nationals be recruited has led to weakening in the U.N. bureaucracy of the principles of impartiality and complete independence and has directly affected task performance. This should not be surprising in an organization that not only is highly political, but that also has a staff that is both multinational and multicultural (Feld and Jordan 1988,101).

Another suggests:

> The most widely known crisis occurred in the 1950s at the United Nations and in certain specialized agencies, when the United States planned to put an end to the employment of certain US nationals for political reasons. A secret agreement was even concluded in 1948 between the Secretary-General of the United Nations and the State Department, making the recruitment and maintenance in employment of United States citizens conditional on prior consultation with their government (Plantey 1981,102).

Surely one of the factors that caused the United States to withdraw from the International Institute for Applied Systems Analysis (IIASA) was the concern caused when a USSR citizen employee of IIASA was accused of espionage and expelled from a client country. While this is surely a pathological example in which a donor country citizen was exploiting the international service for nationalistic ends, the issue of representation is of more generic concern. Haas and his colleagues found in a sample of 120 scientists working in international organizations that the most common answers to the question of who they were representing were: world interests (mankind), 36.7%; the professional discipline, 31.7%; the organization, 30.0%; and the home country, 26.7% (Haas, Williams, and Babai 1977,68).[7] If one-quarter of the multilateral agency personnel see themselves as representing their home country, this must be of concern to host and third countries.

One may characterize the bilateral agencies as dominated by nationals of the donor country. That is not to say that bilateral agencies do not hire host country or third country nationals, but rather that their influence in policy and their role in middle and senior positions is frequently less than that of nationals of the donor country. Bilateral agency personnel are also moved periodically to assure their undivided loyalty to the donor country. Such policies reinforce bilateral agencies' promotion of commercial and economic goals of the donor as well as humanitarian and developmental goals. In contrast, multilateral agencies are staffed by nationals of many countries and strive for (if only partially achieve) freedom from nationalist biases, but suffer from cross cultural differences both with client states and internally.

Computer Expertise

The field of development assistance is itself a field of professional expertise. Thus, foreign assistance agency personnel ideally ought to have an understanding of a number of countries, to have intercultural skills, to have project design, management, and evaluation skills, to understand the process of institution building, to work within established theories of development, to have fluency in two or more languages, as well as have strong professional capabilities in a base discipline such as economics, health sciences, or agriculture.

These factors mitigate against most technicians in foreign assistance agencies also being expert in the cutting-edge aspects of computer technology. In the technical fields, entry into the foreign assistance agencies is frequently open only to older, more senior professionals with distinguished domestic careers. These are felt to have more technical knowledge and skill to offer, and to provide a more acceptable source of technical assistance or advice. However, due to the relative growth of the computer sciences, such professionals often do not have the familiarity or experience with computers of more recently trained professionals. Moreover, training and working in developing countries may also limits the exposure of donor agency officials to advanced computer technology. Thus the professional and managerial cadres of donor agencies tend to be relatively behind their donor country domestic counterparts in computer skills and appreciation.

In the past those with the line responsibilities in foreign assistance agencies were not, and should not have been expected to be, expert in computer technology. Similarly, those in such agencies who were expert in computer technology were not expert in development and were relegated to staff roles in the computer center rather than roles in the management or policy formation for development efforts.

In the case of multilateral agencies, not only does a multinational staff tend to complicate management but drawing senior staff members largely from countries which are themselves developing, and which lag significantly in the availability and application of computer technology, may make computer technology innovation more problematical.

Organization and Process

The three issues discussed under the theme of organization and process are the extent of decentralization, bureaucratic senescence, and the organization's own stage of informatics development.

Extent of Decentralization

All donor agencies are faced with tension between centralization of decision making in the organizational headquarters and decentralization of decision making in the client countries. Some agencies like USAID and the UNDP are considered relatively decentralized, while others like the World Bank are relatively centralized. Similarly, agencies are faced with tension between geographic- and disciplinary-based structures. It is possible to create organizational units which focus on a geographic area, and include all the relevant professional staff disciplines; alternatively, one can organize to focus on disciplines, including all the relevant geographical specialists within the disciplinary or sectoral units.

To some degree these structural decisions will depend on the nature of the organization's charter. It is to be expected that technical assistance agencies will tend to emphasize discipline-based structures rather more than financial assistance agencies. Similarly, it would seem that project-oriented agencies will tend to reflect that emphasis as compared with agencies more involved in non-project lending (for example sector loans and structural adjustment loans).

All other things held equal, one might expect centralized agencies to more quickly organize the transfer of computer technology to developing countries, and to be more uniform in implementing that process and decentralized agencies to be more capable of tailoring the transfer to the host country circumstances. Similarly, one might expect that where disciplinary specialists are subordinated to integrating generalists, the transfer of computer technology will be seen as more generic and less a discipline-specific innovation. Where disciplinary interests dominate, response to the sectoral needs served may be more direct.

Senescence

It is an interesting conceit that aging bureaucracies can experience symptoms of senescence. For example:

> In its early years, USAID was able, to a remarkable extent, to adopt a flexible and error-embracing approach. It was decentralized, with considerable delegation of responsibility to its overseas field missions. Moreover, the missions had more employees in relation to the size of their programs than they had in more recent periods. In addition USAID's Washington based bureaucracy was less complex. Throughout the agency, lines of authority and areas of jurisdiction were blurred, access to superiors was easy, the agency's family-like missions fostered informal working relations . . . and considerable responsibility was assumed by subordinates. These are characteristics of an organization well suited to tasks similar to USAID's. The agency was also less tightly bound by

bureaucratic procedures and contracting regulations. Loans required fewer types of analyses and were subject to fewer restrictions than was later the case. Programming technical assistance required little analysis of documentation, and USAID/Washington review and approval of requests was handled by a small, technically oriented staff. The process was therefore relatively rapid and flexible.

While there may be a nostalgic bias in memories of USAID's halcyon days, it seems clear that the agency was able to capitalize on the comparative advantage of its overseas missions in its early period. Employees had both the time and incentives to devote a greater portion of their energies to working with counterparts, implementing assistance, and thus learning about a country's needs and conditions. They also had more discretionary power to make changes and mid-course corrections (Hoben 1989,254-5).

In general, with the passage of time and replacement of the initial organizational cadre, the enthusiasm for organizational mission can be displaced by a bureaucratic adherence to established procedures. Similarly, the accretion of safeguards to prevent reoccurrence of past mistakes can slow and complicate organizational processes. As has been pointed out above, the major donor agencies date to the post World War II period. To the degree that donor agencies do exhibit such organizational senescence, one must have some concern as to their ability to lead in a social revolution in information technology.

Stages of Informatics Development

To understand the extent to which foreign assistance agencies act as advocates and innovators in microcomputing, one must consider an individual agency's own stage of informatics development. King and Kraemer (1985) have proposed a stage model to explain the influence of factors in computer innovation in local government. The model was developed in conjunction with studies of the introduction of

computer technology in city government in Europe and the
United States. However, it would appear to be relevant both
to the introduction of computer technology in foreign assistance agencies themselves, and to the introduction of computer
technology by foreign assistance agencies within client
countries.

They propose three stages:

- Introduction and conquest
- Experimentation and expansion
- Competition between users and managers for control
  and management efforts at regulation

With the massive introduction of microcomputer systems
in the 1980s, there may well be a fourth stage termed "Widespread Dissemination." In this stage individual computer
workstations would be widely available to staff, and used by
the organization in combination with a variety of mini- and
mainframe computers with specific functions. Area networks
and similar communication systems for computing would be
common.

The OECD bilateral donors are probably all quite advanced
in this four stage process. While developing countries differ
among themselves, they will generally lag behind donor
countries in making innovations in computer usage. To the
degree to which these generalizations are true, computer
innovation in the donor agencies' missions will be in advance
of the host country practice, and thus potentially available as
models for technology innovation. Similarly, we may expect
to see not only gaps in hardware and software between
foreign assistance agency and host government, but also
differences in organizational experience. Most importantly, the
nature of benefits sought from computers in donor agencies
and developed countries may be quite different from those
currently available in developing countries, as would be the
policies and procedures oriented to developing those benefits.

The Donor-Recipient Competition for Control:
The Case of UNESCO

A major factor underlying donor agency behavior is the competition for influence between people from donor countries and those from recipient countries. This is true within agencies at the level of legislative bodies, executive officers, and staff. The distribution of resources among agencies also depends on relative responsiveness to donor or recipient countries. In some organizations, the competition has been relatively non-confrontational; in others, such as UNESCO and the IBI, competition has been radically confrontational. It is no coincidence that those agencies most involved in the "New World Information Order" faced crises in donor support in recent years.

Consider UNESCO's failed effort to develop a new program around the slogan a New World Information Order (NWIO) (Feld and Jordan 1988; Stephenson 1988). The effort began at a time of North-South confrontation around the theme of a New World Economic Order. Developing countries had real concerns about the degree to which their sovereignty failed to extend to information that crossed their borders. Specific concerns included a perception that information resources within developing countries were not optimal for social and economic development and that information on developing countries disseminated abroad was not complete or balanced. As UNESCO developed the theme, under the leadership of Amadou M'Bow, the international press vigorously charged that the program was directed at promoting state control of the press in the developing world. They charged that dictatorial governments saw this as a way to legitimize control of the press.

In 1970 UNESCO announced it was switching attention from information technology to the content of information services. By 1976 the General Conference was asked by the secretariat to address a resolution, supported by the Soviet Union stated that governments should have the power to control the content of the news. In subsequent General Conference meetings, resolutions were advanced for support for the protection of journalists, and eventually for a Commission for the Protection of Journalists. In the 1980 Conference the United States supported the creation of an International Program for the Development of Communications. Major donors apparently saw this as a way to reorient UNESCO to a program of technical assistance, while M'Bow charged that it was an attempt to avoid the more basic political issue and provided evidence that donor financing was not to be available in significant amounts.

The UNESCO position was in part the result of the development of theory by communications scholars, many of whom served as consultants to UNESCO, and a shift in influence from U.S. analysts to more radical Latin and European scholars. Part of the UNESCO secretariat supported the New World Information Order concepts, while other parts opposed M'Bow.

Political pressure in donor countries was rapidly mobilized against the NWIO and UNESCO.

> Overall coverage was extremely negative toward UNESCO—in about 70 percent of agency themes and 76 percent of newspaper themes, for example. Reports, columns, and television spots focused on criticisms of UNESCO, especially some State Department claims of mismanagement, out-of-control spending, politicization, and statism (Jacobson 1990,159-162).

The General Conference was the venue for debates which were to determine the budgetary and personnel priorities for UNESCO, and which saw representatives of Western powers (under pressure from the media and their governments) confront both the Director General and a coalition of representatives led by the African delegations (also under pressure from their governments) and the USSR. This was not the only conflict taking place in the General Conference. The Israel lobby in the United States was particularly incensed by resolutions supporting the PLO and by programs supporting anti-Israeli Arab news agencies. The resulting perception in the West was that M'Bow had politicized UNESCO.

There were also concerns as to the financial and staffing policies under the M'Bow administration. Together these various streams lead to the eventual withdrawal of both the United States and Great Britain from the organization. Of course, the administrations in power in the UK (Thatcher) and the United States (Reagan) were conservative. Other donors countries did not depart. Eventually, in part because of the financial crisis in UNESCO resulting from United States and British withdrawal, M'Bow was forced from office, and has been replaced by a distinguished Spanish scientist and administrator.

In this case of severe conflict, one sees an interplay of the director general, and a coalition of countries backing him, vs. the representatives of the major donor countries. Staff members play a significant role, and in this case the specific issue of information policy was linked inextricably with other policy issues, including those of Middle Eastern politics, national balance of agency staffing, and budgetary efficiency. The conflict was heavily influenced by the media and the scholarly community, which provided the legitimation of the various positions.

Final Comments

Foreign assistance has become an industry since World War II, involving tens of billions of dollars in funds, scores of organizations, hundreds of thousands of employees—perhaps millions—and involving virtually all the countries of the Earth. The development assistance agencies provide a wide range of services and compete among themselves for resources and for clients. The system changes over time, as multilateral agencies have become more or less successful in the competition for resources, or as the emphasis on assistance to Africa has increased or decreased in relative importance. Since this industry will continue to have a significant impact on the introduction of information technology in Africa in the coming years, it is important to understand its operation.

Perhaps the most common models that underlie the literature about the foreign assistance community are "reification" models. Such models allow us to consider World Bank "intentions" for policy reform in Africa, or Unites States "intentions" for the World Bank. A closer look, however, reveals that World Bank actions are the result of complex interplay among many people, as are U.S. governmental positions. The misuse of the reification model is probably responsible for some of the frustrations that are commonly expressed—that the "goals and objectives" of foreign assistance are not clear, that the donor community is not responsive to administration or parliamentary "will." This chapter presents an alternative teleonomic model, in which behavior of the organization is partially determined by a number of parameters—including the natures of charters and the chartering process, governance, staffing, and organizational structure and process. The behavior produced was probably not the intended result when those patterns were created. It should therefore be feasible to make modest changes in the charters, organization, process, and staffing of donor agencies that would significantly improve their performances as advocates and innovators in the application of microcomputers for development.

As advocates and innovators in microcomputer technology, the development assistance agencies lag in terms of the adequacy of services offered. This is particularly true as compared to the developmental opportunities inherent in the revolutionary trends in increasing power and decreasing costs of computers. The donor services in microcomputers are fragmented, there are gaps where no adequate services exist, and those interested in promoting computer innovation (be they developing or developed country citizens) have difficulties understanding and maneuvering among the political processes which define the market and in searching the market for donor agency services or resources.

At issue is how people in developing countries can increasingly use donor agencies to rectify inequitable lack of access to information and information technology while exercising reasonable control over the innovation process and acknowledging the interests of the donors. One alternative is to collaborate with allies within the donor countries: certainly in the computer hardware and software industry, in the university community, and among the humanitarian assistance advocates there are large numbers of potential allies whose interests are generally consistent with increased developing country access to microcomputer technology. A second alternative is to eschew the confrontational style that characterized the NWIO debates of the 1970s and seek a more consultative style that has characterized the more sustainable donor agency efforts.

Notes

1. The author would like to acknowledge his intellectual debts to the N.A.S./BOSTID ad hoc panel on Use of Microcomputers in Developing Countries. Conversations with Drs. Jorge Phillips and Bernard Woods were invaluable in preparing this paper. The editor, Dr. Suzanne Grant Lewis, was of enormous assistance. Any errors are of course the author's responsibility.

2. The discussion is restricted to economic or development assistance, and does not deal with military assistance. It has been suggested that in some developing countries, such as Egypt and Israel, the military sector has been the leader in the introduction of computer and electronics technology. Military assistance has obviously played a key role in innovation in such cases. However, the discussion of military assistance is beyond the scope of this chapter and the author's competence. Private foundations also are not discussed, although they too play an important role, and one with considerable political content.

3. For a general discussion of donor agency policies in microcomputer diffusion see Dow 1989.

4. The series includes: *Microcomputers and Their Applications for Developing Countries. Report of an ad hoc Panel on the Use of Microcomputers for Developing Countries*, 1986; *Microcomputer Applications in Education and Training for Developing Countries. Proceedings of a Meeting on the Applications of Microcomputers for Developing Countries*, 1987; and *Cutting Edge Technologies and Microcomputer Applications for Developing Countries. Report of an ad hoc Panel on the Use of Microcomputers for Developing Countries*, 1988. All three were published by Westview Press in conjunction with the Board on Science and Technology for International Development of the National Research Council.

5. According to the Academy of Scientific Research and Technology journal *Science and Technology Cooperation* 1989,1(1), the Advanced Technology Program in Egypt recently funded projects entitled "Automation of the Textile Industry" for a combination of £.E. 308,000 and $95,000, and "Automation of the Food Industry" for a combined £.E. 250,000 and $120,000.

6. Legislation was introduced in the House of Representatives to rewrite the Foreign Assistance act in 1989 but did not succeed; legislation has been introduced by the administration in 1991, and is still under debate as this is written.

7. One might note that only 5.8% reported representing the interests of society in underdeveloped countries.

6

Issues in Computer-Oriented Innovations in Zimbabwean Education

Kedmon N. Hungwe

Introduction

As we begin the last decade of the twentieth century, educational policy in Zimbabwe is endeavoring ·to come to terms with the advent of computer-related technologies. Initiatives at the primary and secondary school levels have resulted in the introduction of a variety of computer hardware and software in a growing number of the more affluent schools of Zimbabwe. These initiatives have been a bottom-up phenomenon which has appeared in an environment lacking clear official policy guidelines. This is an unprecedented development in a country where education is centrally controlled and historically, the introduction of technology has been centrally directed.[1]

The Ministry of Education and Culture's response was the Computer Education National Panel[2] (CEN Panel). First convened in June 1990, the panel is made up of teachers, representatives from commerce, industry and the University of Zimbabwe; other members are Education Officers and representatives from the Curriculum Development Unit.[3] In opening the first meeting of the panel, the Chief Education Officer indicated that the purpose of the panel was to look into the "urgent" matter of creating a "capacity at the center" for computer education.[4]

This paper examines developments in computer-oriented innovations and raises a number of issues pertinent to the assessment of the new technology in the context of Zimbabwe. In particular the following issues will be considered. First is the historical context in which the new technology is emerging. Zimbabwe has a long history of using technology for educational purposes. In what ways, if any, does computerization represent a historical trend? Second, an assessment of the response of the educational system to the bottom-up emergence of the computer as an educational tool will be made. This report of a school survey will then inform a discussion of how computer-related technologies have challenged the bureaucratic assumptions of the educational system in terms of policy and procedure and how the system is responding to these challenges. Third, the expectations associated with computer technologies will be assessed within the framework of national development goals. The overall analysis will be supported by empirical data derived from a recent study of the emergence of computers in Zimbabwean schools. The discussion now turns to the first of the three issues, namely the historical context of innovation in Zimbabwean education.

Technology in Zimbabwean Schools: A Historical Perspective

Zimbabwe has been at the forefront of experimentation with new media since the 1930s (Hungwe 1991). Schools in Zimbabwe have been involved with radio (since 1943), programmed learning (1962-3), television (1961-1970), and correspondence education (since 1930). Except for correspondence education, none of these innovations have had a long-term impact on education in the country.[5]

The introduction of computers is consistent with a tradition of experimentation with new media established since the

1930s. Furthermore, the ideological framework which motivated technological innovation in colonial Zimbabwe has tended to promote and entrench the advantages enjoyed by socially privileged minority groups. To substantiate this argument it is necessary to backtrack somewhat and present a historical analysis of the assumptions and ideology of the educational system in colonial Zimbabwe.

The origins of the formal education system of Zimbabwe date back to the turn of the twentieth century when European settlers established the country as a British colony. Colonial rule lasted from 1890 to 1980. About four out of every five settlers were of British descent, and the rest were mostly Afrikaners, who had migrated from South Africa.

Colonial government policy discriminated against Africans. A minority white ruling class sought to guarantee its privileged status through, among other things, superior social services such as education. As Tawse Jollie argued in the House of Assembly[6] in 1925, "I think we all agree that we cannot afford to have white children growing up in this country at a lower level of education than some of the natives, or indeed at a low level of education at all."[7]

Tawse Jollie's efforts were to result in the introduction of free and compulsory education for white children, but not for African children. One consequence of the introduction of compulsory education was the inauguration of correspondence education for white children. Correspondence education was intended to enable children from communities living away from main centers to have access to education. Clearly, the correspondence education reflected an ideological commitment to white supremacism. This commitment was also reflected in the large financial support which the state gave to white education. In 1925 for instance, the Colonial Secretary was able to say that "the per pupil cost [on education for white children] in Southern Rhodesia is higher than any other country in the British empire."[8] This is a remarkable statement in a colony which was by no means the richest in the empire and which suffered from a grossly underfunded educational system for Africans.

The generous resources allocated to white education enabled the authorities to closely follow as well as experiment with trends in the use of technology in education as developed in Western Europe and North America. Thus in 1957, a local newspaper argued that:

> Overseas, particularly in Britain and the United States, there is a growing awareness among the people of the value of educational T.V. It is increasingly being recognized that these channels constitute one of the most valuable public resources—the full use of which can bring immeasurable benefit to the nation.[9]

In 1963 the Report on Education was to boast that the colony had established a television production unit "housed in the first entirely educational television studio on the African continent" (Federation of Rhodesia and Nyasaland 1963, 59). In 1962, the main reason advanced for introducing programmed learning was that it was "widely accepted as an approved educational medium by both British and American educational authorities" (Hawkridge undated).

The adoption of technological innovations in schools under the leadership of the industrialized West was therefore clearly established during colonialism. Furthermore, the purposes for which the media were used were not always consistent with democratic principles. The following example of radio illustrates this point from the perspective of white politics of colonial Zimbabwe.

It has been noted that settlers of Anglo-Saxon descent formed approximately eighty percent of the white population, and most of the remaining twenty percent was made up of Afrikaners. This demographic position was to result in conflict as the Afrikaners contested efforts to promote an Anglo-Saxon cultural hegemony. The conflict was mainly over the issue of language policy in schools. A clear instance of the use of technology for cultural purposes was the introduction of radio broadcast to schools in 1943 whose main functions were the promotion of English as the *lingua franca* of the colony and providing what was described as "cultural upliftment."[10]

Attempts to introduce Afrikaans broadcasts to schools were officially rejected for political reasons.[11]

The example cited serves to confirm a historical trend of using technologies of instruction to promote the interests of the ruling elite. Furthermore, there is a clear pattern of the use of technologies of instruction to entrench a dual and unequal education system which operates in favor of white minority interests. In this light, it is useful to assess post-colonial developments in computer-oriented innovations to determine if they are consistent with post-colonial aspirations for more democratic participation in the educational process.[12]

Current Trends in the Adoption and Use of Computers

The data below were collected in a February-March 1989 survey of Zimbabwean schools.[13] A questionnaire was mailed to school heads with the purpose of assessing trends in the adoption of computers by schools.[14] The questionnaire included items which could elicit data needed to answer the following research questions:

- Which schools have acquired computers in Zimbabwe?
- In what ways are the schools which have acquired computers using them?
- What is the distribution of computers between private and government schools as well as between boys', girls' and coeducational schools?
- What are the prospects for the adoption of computers in schools which do not currently have them?
- What are the expectations for the use of computers in schools which do not currently have this technology?

Developing a Population Frame

Zimbabwe has approximately 6,000[15] primary and secondary schools. An estimated 4,500 of these schools are primary and the rest secondary. The majority of schools are poor with no capacity to handle computers.[16] The poor schools were excluded in the survey. Through discussions with education officials as well as an analysis of schools which were known to own computers, a profile of schools which could theoretically sustain computer-oriented innovations was developed. All of the schools in the following categories were included in the survey: (a) all primary and secondary schools designated "European" in colonial Zimbabwe; (b) all secondary schools designated "African Government School" in colonial Zimbabwe; (c) all secondary schools run by missionary bodies in colonial Zimbabwe; and (d) all "high-fee paying" or elite private schools opened in colonial and post-colonial Zimbabwe. These four categories cover the full range of the more privileged schools in Zimbabwe, which could be expected to be able to sustain computer-oriented innovations.[17] In all, the number of schools included came to 213, which is about 3.6% of the Zimbabwean schools. The small number of schools considered eligible for the survey is an indication of the relative poverty of the majority of Zimbabwean schools. All 213 schools were sent the questionnaire. Table 6.1 indicates the breakdown of the schools in the survey by level and responsible authority. The classification used in the study designates "private school" as a school not under central or local government authority, while "government school" refers to a school wholly sponsored by central government. The absence in the population frame of schools under the direction of local government authorities is an indication of their relative poverty. Local schools represent about ninety percent of all schools in Zimbabwe.

Single-sex government schools only exist at the secondary level and were previously for the exclusive use of the white community during colonialism. All single-sex primary schools are denominational while private secondary schools are controlled by denominations or other private groups.[18]

TABLE 6.1   Profile of Surveyed Schools

| | Government | | | Private | | | |
	Coed	Girls'	Boys'	Coed	Girls'	Boys'	Total
Primary	91	0	0	15	5	5	116
Secondary	24	10	14	30	9	10	97
Total	115	10	14	45	14	15	213

In all, 147 (69%) of the schools responded to the questionnaire. These are profiled in Table 6.2. Of these, 41 schools indicated that they had computers, and the rest (106) indicated that they did not.[19] Selected findings are summarized below with the findings from schools with computers discussed separately from those from schools without computers.

TABLE 6.2   Profile of Responding Schools

| | Government | | | Private | | | |
	Coed	Girls'	Boys'	Coed	Girls'	Boys'	Total
Primary	60	0	0	10	4	4	78
Secondary	15	10	10	17	9	8	69
Total	75	10	10	27	13	12	147

TABLE 6.3   Distribution of Computers by Responsible Authority

	Government	*Private*	*Total*
Number of Schools with Computers	12	26	38
Number of Computers	48	291	339
Percentage of Computers	14.2	85.8	100

Missing Cases = 3

Findings from Schools with Computers

Table 6.3 summarizes the findings on the distribution of computing resources in government and private schools. Twelve of the schools with computers were found to be government schools, while 26 were found to be private schools. Private schools therefore appeared to be ahead of government schools as far as adoption of computers was concerned. This trend was further confirmed when the numbers of computers in each of the two school categories was analyzed. Table 6.3 shows that 48 (14.2%) of the computers were found in government schools while 291 (85.8%) were found to be in private schools.

The relative advantage of private schools with respect to access to computer technology is further demonstrated by Table 6.4, which extends the breakdown to the categories of primary and secondary schools.

Table 6.4 indicates that access to computers is more favorable in private schools than in government schools, with private primary schools having the most favorable level of student access to computers—one computer for every 38 pupils. Government secondary schools have the least favorable level of access, 274 students per computer. These schools have small numbers of computers and large enrollments averaging 1,142 pupils. Overall, for both primary and secondary schools, access to computers is much more favorable in private schools. Furthermore, in both government and private

TABLE 6.4   Distribution of Computers by Responsible Authority and School Type

| | Government | | Private | |
	Primary Schools (N=6)	Secondary Schools (N=6)	Primary Schools (N=11)	Secondary Schools (N=15)
Number of Computers	23	25	130	161
Number of Computers per School	3.8	4.2	11.8	10.7
Number of Students	2,722	6,849	4,993	9,541
Students per Computer	118	274	38	59

schools the access appears to be more favorable for primary schools.

Current Use of Existing Computers. The current use of computers in Zimbabwean schools can be divided into three basic categories: classroom-related uses within the framework of subject areas (instructional); administrative uses mainly by the school office; and extracurricular uses for which students are not assessed by the school and which serve a recreational purpose. In many cases, extracurricular uses are organized around clubs within the school. A prominent example of extracurricular use is computer games. Some computer clubs engage in activities like computer programming within the framework of extracurricular activities.

When the 41 schools with computers were asked to indicate the ways in which they used computers, 28 (68.3%) indicated instructional uses, 25 (61.0%) indicated administrative uses, and 26 (63.4%) indicated extracurricular uses. Obviously, many of the schools used the computers in more than one way and instructional, administrative and extracurricular uses appear to be evenly distributed in schools.[20]

Gender Perspectives. Table 6.5 summarizes the data on computers on the basis of gender in primary and secondary schools. The school type is in this instance an indicator of the use by gender groups.

The data indicate that 54% of the schools with computers are coeducational, 27% are girls' schools and 20% are boys' schools. The existence of single-sex schools seems to tilt the balance for computing resources in favor of girls. However, an examination of Table 6.6 indicates that when the number of pupils per computer is computed, the picture changes somewhat.

On average, accessibility to computers appears to be most favorable in boys' schools, with one computer to 60 pupils. In addition, it appears that for both boys and girls, access is most favorable in single-sex schools. This is consistent with the exclusive and privileged status enjoyed by single-sex schools in Zimbabwe.

TABLE 6.5   Schools with Computing Resources by School Gender Type

	Coed Schools	Girls' Schools	Boys' Schools	Total
Number of Primary Schools	11 (61%)	5 (28%)	2 (11%)	18 (44%)
Number of Secondary Schools	11 (48%)	6 (26%)	6 (26%)	23 (56%)
Total	22 (54%)	11 (27%)	8 (20%)	41 (100%)

TABLE 6.6   Accessibility of Computing Resources by Gender

	Coed	Girls' Schools	Boys' Schools	Total Schools
Number of Computers	132 (39%)	113 (33%)	94 (28%)	339 (100%)
Enrollment	14,477 (51%)	8,162 (29%)	5,597 (20%)	28,236 (100%)
Students per Computer	110	72	60	83

Distribution of Teaching Expertise. The distribution of computer-related expertise among teachers is indicated by an analysis of the location of staff using computers. The total number of members of staff indicated as using computers was 150. Of these, 134 (89%) worked in 26 private schools and the remaining 16 (11%) in 12 government schools. Private schools therefore appear to have a clear advantage with respect to teaching expertise.[21]

Prioritizing Computers. Schools with computers were asked if the acquisition of more computers was a current priority. Nearly 93% of the schools indicated that the purchase of more computers was a priority. An increase in the number of computers in schools which currently own computers can therefore be anticipated, making the computer-student ratio more favorable.

The discussion now turns to an analysis of responses from schools which do not own computers.

Findings from Schools Without Computers

The main areas of inquiry with respect to schools without computers were: the need for computers as indicated by school heads; anticipated areas of use of computers in schools which expressed a need for them; alternative priority resources for schools which did not indicate computers as a priority resource; and the proportion of schools which hoped to acquire computers.

In addition, the following three null hypotheses were tested: (1) There is no significant difference in prioritization of the acquisition of computers between primary and secondary schools (see Table 6.8); (2) There is no significant difference in expectations of acquiring computers between primary and secondary schools (see Table 6.10); and (3) There is no significant difference in anticipated uses of computers between administrative, instructional, and extracurricular uses (see Table 6.12).

The Need for Computers. Heads of schools without computers were asked to indicate their assessment of the need for computers in their schools. Table 6.7 summarizes the responses obtained.

Almost 58%, or 59, of the responding schools indicated a need for computers. A much smaller proportion of schools (9%) did not consider computers necessary. One-third or 34 of the responding schools felt that they needed more information to decide either way. The large proportion of schools unable to assess the need for computers because of a lack of information highlights an information gap at the school level.

School Type and Prioritizing of Computers. School heads were asked to consider a hypothetical situation where their school was offered additional and "significant" financial resources to use for purchasing resources needed by the school. In such a situation, would computers be considered a priority resource? The possibility of a difference in the prioritization of computers between primary and secondary schools was also explored. I expected that there would be no significant difference in prioritization of the acquisition of computers between primary and secondary schools. The responses are summarized in Table 6.8.

Almost 58% of the schools considered the acquisition of computers a foremost priority and 42% did not believe that

TABLE 6.7   Assessment of Need for Computers

	Number of Schools	Percentage
Computers Needed	59	57.8
Computers Not Needed	9	8.8
More Information Needed to Decide	34	33.3
TOTAL	102	100.0

Missing Cases = 4

TABLE 6.8   Computers as Priority Within Schools

	Primary Schools	Secondary Schools	Total
Computers as Priority	34 (60%)	23 (40%)	57 (58%)
Computer Not a Priority	27 (64%)	15 (36%)	42 (42%)
Total	61 (62%)	38 (38%)	99 (100%)

Missing Cases = 7
Chi-Square not significant

computers should be accorded the highest priority. Chi
Square analysis found the difference between the two school
types was not significant.

Schools which indicated that computers would not be a
priority resource were asked to indicate alternative priorities.
Table 6.9 summarizes the responses.

The expressed needs for such resources as science teaching
equipment, reading materials, textbooks, chemicals, classrooms, and desks is particularly noteworthy. This finding,
within the context of a survey of the more privileged schools
of Zimbabwe, highlights, albeit indirectly, the crisis of resources facing the poor and majority schools of Zimbabwe, which
were not included in this study.

TABLE 6.9   Alternative Priorities Listed by Schools

Priority	Number of Schools Mentioning Each Priority (n=42)
Media Hardware[a]	21
Supplementary Reading Materials	16
Teaching Equipment[b]	10
Buildings[c]	10
Textbooks	9
Media Software[d]	7
Office Equipment[e]	7
Sports Equipment	7
School Furniture[f]	5
Additional Teaching Staff	3
School Transport	2

a. Overhead projectors, video and audio player/recorders.
b. Science teaching equipment, chemicals, tools, workshop machines.
c. Classrooms, workshops, laboratories, staff housing, and classrooms.
d. Video and audio tapes.
e. Typewriters, photocopiers, and duplicating machines.
f. Desks, chairs, and tables.

Expectation of Acquiring Computers. The 59 schools which indicated a need for computers were asked whether or not they expected to acquire computers. Table 6.10 summarizes the findings. In addition, the possibility of significant difference in expectations of acquiring computers between primary and secondary schools was tested for, with the null hypothesis being that there is no significant difference in expectations of acquiring computers between primary and secondary schools.

TABLE 6.10   Expectation of Acquiring Computers Within Schools

	Primary Schools	Secondary Schools	Total
Hope to Get Computers	16 (52%)	15 (48%)	31 (53%)
Do Not Hope to Get Computers	17 (63%)	10 (37%)	27 (47%)
Total	33 (57%)	25 (43%)	58 (100%)

Missing Cases = 1
Chi-Square not significant

TABLE 6.11   Potential Sources of Computers Indicated

Source	Number of Schools Mentioning Each Source (n=31)
Parent-Teacher Association	15
Fund Raising	10
Zimbabwe Government	4
NGO, Private Firms, and Foreign Assistance Agencies	4
Unclear	4
Fees	1

Almost thirty percent of the schools indicated an expectation of acquiring computers. This is less than the number who felt that computers were a priority resource (57 schools or 53.8%) as indicated in Table 6.8. The gap between expressed needs and expectations of meeting those needs appears to reflect the limitations of financial resources. Chi-Square analysis did not reveal significant difference in expectations between primary and secondary schools.

When the 31 schools which hoped to get computers were asked to indicate the potential source of computers or money to purchase computers, sources summarized in Table 6.11 were indicated. Some schools indicated more than one potential source.

The main sources of support indicated (the PTA and fund raising) are sources operating at the school level. The expectation for financing from these sources is consistent with the experience of schools that have acquired computers. The mention of NGOs as possible sources of support reflects the positive response of a number of non-governmental organizations to requests for computers from educational institutions. Examples of donations publicized in the local press are gifts from foreign governments, private companies and a variety of foreign organizations.[22]

Although some of the respondents (4) were of the opinion that the government could supply them with computing resources, there is no precedent to justify this expectation. The Ministry of Education and Culture has made it clear that it is not in a position to supply computers to schools.

Anticipated Uses of Computers in Schools. The 59 schools which indicated a need for computers were asked to indicate in which of the three areas of teaching, administration, and extracurricular activities they intended to use the technology. Schools were also given the option to indicate if they were unclear about a mode of use. Table 6.12 summarizes the responses. The analysis was extended to test the hypothesis that there is no significant difference in anticipated uses of computers between administrative, instructional, and extracurricular uses. The Chi-Square analysis indicated a significance at the 0.05 level. The null hypothesis was therefore rejected.

TABLE 6.12   Categories of Anticipated Uses

	Use Anticipated	Use Not Anticipated	Unclear on This Use	Total
Administration	51 (86%)	3 (5%)	5 (9%)	59 (100%)
Instructional	46 (80%)	3 (5%)	9 (15%)	58 (100%)
Extracurricular	33 (57%)	7 (12%)	18 (31%)	58 (100%)
Total	130 (74%)	13 (7%)	32 (18%)	175 (99%)

Incomplete Cases = 2
Chi-square = 14.74   df = 4

The use of computers for administrative purposes was indicated the most (86%) and extracurricular uses were indicated the least (57%). Schools which specifically rejected a mode of computer use were relatively few. The least-understood mode of computer use was extracurricular, with 31% of the schools expressing a need for information about it. However, there is evidence that extracurricular uses of computers have grown in importance in schools currently using computers, and as was indicated earlier, an estimated 63% of the schools with computers are using them in this way.

The preceding discussion has highlighted trends in the development of computer-oriented innovations in schools. In summary, the main features arising from the survey of schools are four: (1) private schools have more favorable access to computer technology than government schools; (2) the existence of single-sex schools appears to enhance the equity of access between boys and girls; (3) trends and aspirations for computerization are equivalent in primary and secondary schools; and (4) some of the schools selected on the basis of their relatively privileged status are facing some very basic needs which make it impossible for them to consider purchasing computers. This finding emphasizes the relative affluence enjoyed by a small minority of schools. While government schools have acquired computers, the clear leaders are private schools which have more resources in terms of hardware and staff expertise. In general, the survey points to the persistence of the acute socio-economic inequities which have their origins in colonial Zimbabwe. Another conclusion is that schools are in need of more information about the potential and limitations of computers in a school environment.

The discussion now turns to an analysis of the development of policy on computerization in schools as directed by the state through the Ministry of Education and Culture.

Handling Information Technology:
Toward a Policy Formulation

Zimbabwe has a highly centralized system of primary and secondary education. The system is directed by the Ministry of Education and Culture, which controls examinations, subject areas of instruction, syllabuses, and textbooks. The Examinations Branch of the ministry, which controls examinations, has formal links with the British Cambridge Local Examinations Syndicate (CLES) dating back to the colonial period. Since independence in 1980, the Ministry of Education and Culture has been working with the CLES to gradually localize the control of examinations. In a country where "maintenance of standards"[23] in education is a popular slogan, the CLES has served the role of legitimizing the localization of syllabuses and examinations. That role has at times been a contentious one. For example, in 1989 the Mathematics Education National Panel developed an innovative syllabus for students not wishing to major in mathematics. This syllabus did not meet the "cognitive requirements" of the CLES. The Ministry of Education and Culture did not feel that a syllabus without the stamp of approval of the CLES was viable and so the new syllabus, representing the work of a local panel of experts, was dropped. This resulted in vigorous but fruitless objections from panel members, who felt the Ministry of Education and Culture had belittled their efforts and had given undue weight to the position of the CLES.

The powerful influence of the CLES was again evident when the Chief Education Officer opened the first meeting of the Computer Education National Panel (CEN Panel) in June 1990. The CEN Panel, he stated, should develop a computer education syllabus which must meet the "cognitive requirements"[24] of the CLES.

Two issues arise from these official guidelines: the primacy of central government control and the requirement that Zimbabwe meet the Cambridge standards. The first is not unexpected in the context of Zimbabwean education, but is nevertheless of the greatest significance. The official response to the emergence of computers at the local level has been a move to create a national syllabus. Representations to the first CEN Panel meeting by the different schools using computers indicated that there were varied perspectives about how computers should be used in education. One high school had devised its own syllabus, which all junior students were expected to follow for the purposes of developing habits of "disciplined" use of the computer. Once students had completed the introductory course, they were free to come to the computer laboratory when they liked and to select their own activities. Activities selected by pupils included programming in LOGO and Pascal, playing computer games, and developing easy-to-follow documentation for commonly used software.

Another high school had responded differently, choosing instead to follow an overseas Computer Science syllabus. The use of computers had therefore been limited to those students taking Computer Science as a formal subject.

Initiatives by the Ministry of Education and Culture through the CEN Panel are clearly intended to support the approach adopted by the second high school. This position is confirmed by the statement from the Chief Education Officer, who told the first meeting of the CEN Panel that the Ministry of Education and Culture needed to create the capacity to "regulate and direct computer education" and to create "some order" through a national syllabus.[25]

The response from the center is clearly oriented toward control. The emergence of computers through initiatives at the local level had presented novel circumstances within the context of a centrally directed system of education. Schools had introduced the technology independently and furthermore they had made local decisions on the curriculum. This development posed a challenge to the assumptions of the centrally controlled system, where the curriculum was legitimized through central approval. The move to "restore order" through a national curriculum should be seen as a choice for the status quo. It represents one of a number of possible options which the authorities could have pursued. Computer-oriented innovations had challenged the basic assumptions of the system, and the system has responded by reaffirming its right to direct and control. A potential opportunity for reform in curriculum decision making therefore appears to have been lost. This trend is further confirmed by the insistence that all innovative ideas must be submitted to the test of approval by CLES.

The need for the approval of CLES is the second issue. This requirement appears to have taken some teachers who attended the first CEN Panel by surprise, and one teacher asked "Are our hands tied?" while another queried, "I thought we were moving towards the localization of the curriculum."[26] There was some resentment that a foreign-based certification board had the power to set parameters for the deliberations of a locally constituted panel of experts.

Once the fact that the CLES requirements had to be taken into account was accepted, albeit grudgingly, the next problem was to find out what those requirements were. Three main sources of information were tapped. The first was expatriate members of the panel who had experience in teaching computers in England. The second was members of the local Examinations Branch who had experience in working with the CLES, and the third were syllabuses in current use under the approval of the CLES. Once an "approved" syllabus had been located and distributed, the main task became that of tinkering with it to make it "Zimbabwean." While the outcome may have been bureaucratically satisfactory, it created a clear sense of powerlessness at a local level. As one teacher put it, "if we are going to do what the CLES wants, then this panel looks like a waste of time."[27]

The adoption of a strategy of using computers for the purposes of certification may on the surface appear to represent a triumph for bureaucratic and foreign control of the curriculum. However, another level of analysis indicates that certification serves to legitimize advantage in an environment where employment prospects are bleak. The group which benefits from the advantage of certification is a small proportion of students graduating from the more privileged schools of Zimbabwe. Schools which need certification for the benefit of their clients are willing to compromise with the requirements of the state for central control, and the CEN Panel provides a forum where the nature of the compromise can be worked out.[28]

Computer Education: Reassessing the Promises

Zimbabwe has, by regional standards, a relatively sophisticated computer industry. Computer-oriented technologies are gradually being integrated into the commercial, industrial, and public sectors of the economy.

In education, the press has given prominence to schools which have introduced computers.[29] This has created widespread interest in computers in schools across the country. The commercial sector has also promoted the use of computers in schools through advertising as well as the provision of hardware and software to selected schools. The promotion of computers in schools has also benefitted from the support of school heads and parents, who have been influenced by trends in education in Western Europe and the United States. Many of the parents and teachers associated with the more affluent schools are well-travelled and they are conscious of developments in education in other countries.

One influential view about the role of computer-oriented studies was expressed by the Chief Education Officer in his address to the CEN Panel. In his view, "the computer culture had become part of our civilization." Consequently, the school system must produce graduates "who can perpetuate this culture."[30]   The view that knowledge of computers, or computer literacy, is critical for preparing students for the world of work appears to be widely shared by teachers, parents, and Ministry of Education and Culture officials. This assumption would appear to be problematic for a number of reasons.

First, the main problem confronting Zimbabwe is not lack of employable school graduates, but rather economic stagnation,[31] which makes it impossible for thousands of school graduates to enter the world of work.   As unemployment rises, the criteria for selection for higher education and jobs are becoming arbitrarily high, and school-based achievements are being used more and more as a tool for distributing limited opportunities to an over-supply of eligible candidates.[32] In this context the drive for computer literacy tends to reframe the unemployment crisis in terms of skill shortages rather than economic policies of the state. Consequently, there is a tendency for the public to blame the powerless victim by suggesting that what she or he needs is computer literacy.

A related problem is that the relatively high cost of financing computerization means than the number of students with access to computers is unlikely to be extended significantly beyond the enrollments of a few elite private schools. The scarcity of this knowledge has enhanced its high-status recognition. It would appear that the relatively high scarcity of computer experience in Zimbabwe tends to exaggerate its value, and limited accomplishments assume a much higher value than would be the case in countries like the United States, where the technology is more accessible. The relative advantage of studying computers at the school level is likely to continue for a privileged minority in the foreseeable future. In this sense, computer-related technologies serve to entrench unequal social relations.

The second problem that arises from the drive for computer literacy is the assumption that the introduction of technology in schools will promote the accelerated development of the Zimbabwean economy, a view put forth by government officials as well as representatives of business interests. In this view, the goal of studies in computer-related technologies is to prepare students for competent participation in a computer culture. This analysis grossly oversimplifies the intricate problems of development and technology transfer between the North and the South. The last two decades, which have witnessed declining living standards in many of the poorer countries, should have amply demonstrated that technological gains in the Northern hemisphere cannot, as a matter of course, be expected to be mirrored in the poorer countries. In fact the label "developing country" can be misleading because it connotes some level of material progress when decline is the norm in many poor countries.

Given these bleak prospects for the poorer countries, the computer culture would appear to be beyond the prospects of most of the citizens of these countries. Within the context of Zimbabwe, it can be argued that initiation into the new technologies may for the foreseeable future serve to legitimize existing and unequal social relations.

Finally, advocates of computer literacy tend to treat it as a commodity which can be packaged and delivered with precision. That the assumptions of programs intended to promote computer literacy need to be critically examined and possibly contested, is not considered. In other words, activities are legitimized by the medium and not by an analysis of their intrinsic value and assumptions. This concern is highlighted by emerging evidence of an emphasis on limited functional uses of computers in some schools. One example is the use of computers for certification in secretarial-related studies for females in the non-academic streams.[33] In this context the new technology is being used to initiate young women into a career path which is traditionally female, and the main goal of using computers in this way appears to be to increase efficiency as well as to give the graduating females some advantage in a restricted job market.

A Perspective for the Future

There are prospects for modest increases in the number of schools with computers in Zimbabwe. The preceding discussion has highlighted the point that the number of schools which can sustain computer-oriented innovations is small. The vast majority of schools are poor and cannot be expected to acquire computers. Initiatives to introduce computers have been largely community based. This has tended to entrench the unequal social relations between a small elite group and a majority poor population. It is important to note Robins and Webster's argument in which they "insist that technology . . . will emerge as part of established social relations." They are therefore "sceptical of claims that [because of computers] we are on the edge of a 'new age'" because changes in technology do not transcend "the society in which we find ourselves" (Robins and Webster 1989:31).

The discussion of the adoption of computers by schools has pointed to the persistence of a colonial trend of closely modelling innovative ideas on trends established in Western Europe and the United States. During colonialism, the white schools took a leadership role in following these trends, and in postcolonial Zimbabwe, the elite schools have been able, through community financing, to sustain. As with colonial experiments with radio, programmed learning, and television, current trends may have no long-term impact, but they serve the purpose of legitimizing the high social status enjoyed by private schools.

In conclusion, the problems of narrowing the gap in access to technology between Zimbabwean communities appear to be as intractable as those of bridging the North-South gap. The diminishing economic prospects facing the country, particularly since 1985, make it virtually impossible to anticipate state intervention in favor of the poorer schools.[34] Ultimately the hope for the poor is more rapid economic growth, and indications are that the main constraints to that growth have their origins outside the educational system.

Notes

1. An analysis of the historical use of technology in colonial Zimbabwean Education is developed in Hungwe 1991.

2. The Ministry of Education and Culture has formed similar panels for other subject areas. The formation of the CEN Panel therefore represents a decision to recognize and give direction to initiatives in computer-oriented studies.

3. The Curriculum Development Unit is a section in the Ministry of Education and Culture tasked with the development of syllabuses, and in some cases teaching materials, for a variety of subject areas. Each subject area in the Unit is headed by an Education Officer. It is worth noting that the interim head of the Computer Education subject area is a mathematician.

4. K. N. Hungwe, personal notes on the "Opening Address to the Computer Education National Panel," June 21, 1990.

5. Radio broadcasting to white schools lasted from 1943-1958. The introduction of tape recorders in the late 1950s made radio redundant. In 1962, the facilities established for white schools were redirected for use in African schools. Existing evidence indicates that on the whole, teachers question the value of the radio broadcasts to schools.

6. Africans were excluded from the House of Assembly, the country's legislative body.

7. Debates in the Southern Rhodesia House of Assembly, May 20, 1925, Col. 675.

8. Debates in the Southern Rhodesia House of Assembly, May 20, 1925, Col. 675.

9. "Educational TV," *The Rhodesia Herald*, November 16, 1957.

10. S824/192/2 Correspondence and other papers: Broadcasting to schools: Programme Committee: October 1, 1943 - April 17, 1941 Blakeway to Kinsey March 23, 1945. National Archives of Zimbabwe, Harare.

11. S824/192/1 Correspondence and other papers: Broadcasting to schools: Programme Committee: September 15, 1942 - December 22, 1943: Secretary Announcer to Schools Broadcast Committee, June 11, 1943. National Archives of Zimbabwe, Harare.

12. That post-colonial education in Zimbabwe should promote democratic participation has been advocated in various government statements. In 1990, a cabinet minister declared that the educational system of Zimbabwe should produce graduates who can "participate effectively in the nation's political, social and cultural transformation." See Press Statement, "Education A Right for Every Zimbabwean," 21 March 1990. Speaking in 1981, the state president argued for an educational process that differed in values to the colonial one. In his view "education must at all costs eschew all the tendencies or even appearances of a commitment to the maintenance and reproduction of the unjust social order and undemo-

cratic value system that we sacrificed so much to overthrow." See Press Statement, "Primeminister Opens Education Seminar," 28 August 1981.

13. The research reported here was funded by the Research Board, University of Zimbabwe.

14. A more extensive study of schools which were identified as using computers is currently under way.

15. This figure was complied from the statistical returns indicated in the *Annual Report of the Secretary for Primary and Secondary Education* (1988:35). After rapid growth of the school system in the period 1980-1985, the number of schools has now stabilized.

16. Indicators of the "capacity" to handle computers include the existence of facilities such as electricity as well as teachers competent to use computers. See Hungwe 1988.

17. Government primary schools designated "African" in colonial Zimbabwe are located in urban areas and are generally better off than rural schools, but there are no indications that they are moving towards computerization. The main limitation appears to be teacher expertise. These schools were therefore excluded from the survey.

18. There are eight denominations running schools in Zimbabwe. The Catholic Church and the Church of England run some of the most exclusive single sex schools in the country. The other denominations run coeducational schools only. While these are relatively privileged, they are not as exclusive as the Catholic and Anglican schools.

19. The estimate of 41 schools that own computers represents an increase over a previous estimate of 20 to 30 schools, which had been compiled by Chris Blake of the Curriculum Development Unit.

20. The follow-up study that is now under way will seek to check this apparently even spread of activities through an analysis of, among other things, the time allocated to the different activities.

21. The current follow-up study will probe this finding further.

22. Examples of foreign assistance include grants from USAID, the British Council, and the Palestinian Liberation Organization. A private firm, Computer Processing Group, provided a computer laboratory for a prominent Harare private school. The local press has widely publicized the case of Vainona High School which benefitted from the efforts of a British-based youth project. See for instance "Vainona school scores first in computer education," *The Herald*, July 11, 1990.

23. The colonial system of education for white children has been the dominant influence on standards of excellence in post-colonial Zimbabwe.

24. K. N. Hungwe, personal notes on the "Opening Address to the Computer Education National Panel," June 21, 1990.

25. K. N. Hungwe, personal notes on the "Opening Address to the Computer Education National Panel," June 21, 1990.

26. K.N. Hungwe, personal notes.

27. K.N. Hungwe, personal notes.

28. Schools using computers are not compelled by the state to follow a given course of study. However, the Ministry of Education and Culture only endorses programs of study which it controls. Schools therefore have to negotiate with the authorities over what is to be recognized. That schools are not powerless in the issue of curriculum decision making is reflected by their successful resistance to the Political Economy syllabus, which was particularly opposed by the denominational schools because they alleged that it was atheistic.

29. See for instance "Vainona Sets Up Computer Department," *Financial Gazette*, April 12, 1990.

30. K. N. Hungwe, personal notes on the "Opening Address to the Computer Education National Panel," June 21, 1990.

31. For an analysis of the problems facing the economy see Government of Zimbabwe 1990.

32. Developments in Zimbabwe are consistent with William Johnston's view that "the developing world is producing a rapidly increasing share of the world's skilled human capital." See Johnston 1991, 121.

33. These trends are indicated by the unpublished "Computers-in-Schools Survey" conducted by the Curriculum Development Unit of the Ministry of Education and Culture in 1990, as well as discussions held with teachers whose schools use computers.

34. Economic reversals faced by the poor in Zimbabwe are reflected by the recently announced government decision to reduce its financial commitment to primary education by phasing out tuition and textbook subsidies.

7

The State, Computers, and African Development: The Information Non-Revolution

Bruce J. Berman

Introduction

Many years ago I interviewed a former British district commissioner in Kenya who told me the following story about the 1948 census in the colony. Arriving at a village around mid-day, he retired to a nearby hillside to eat his lunch while his team of census 'counters' carried out their duties. As he watched in amusement, the counters entered one end of the village, while from the other a stream of Africans, mostly women and children, ran and hid in the surrounding fields and bush. "So much for those nice numbers," he remarked.

This anecdote illustrates some of the crucial characteristics of the context in which the relationship between computers and the state must be understood. First, that the bureaucratic apparatus of the state has an insatiable drive to collect statistical data both to reflexively monitor the effectiveness of its own activities and to exercise surveillance over ever wider areas of civil society (Giddens 1985). Second, the collection and analysis of quantitative data are at the heart of the practice of bureaucratic expertise and the basis of the state's understanding of reality. Third, quantification and formalization are components of a technocratic ideology of instrumental rationality that seeks to replace politics with scientific calculation. Fourth, as African peasants quickly understood, such counting was actually a political act and such numbers were instruments of control, usually for the purposes, in Europe as well as colonial Africa, of taxation or conscription. More recently, such data have proliferated as the essential basis for state-managed programs of social welfare and economic development.

Computers as the Magical Solution to Africa's Development Crisis

In its origins and development the electronic computer is a technology rooted in the informational and analytic requirements of the state apparatus, civil and military, in advanced industrial societies (Flamm 1988). While the commercial and industrial applications of computers have spread rapidly and become the principal engine for the reconstruction of contemporary capitalism (Berman 1991; Kaplinsky 1984), the state remains the largest single user of computers of all sizes and, through its research, trade, and purchasing policies, remains the most important influence on the development of computer hardware and software (Flamm 1987). This pattern of the salience of the state in determining national configurations of computer use and development applies *a fortiori* in the African context, where virtually no indigenous computer industry exists and imported technology is an essential component of national development programs.

Awareness in African governments of the importance of computing has grown apace with the deepening economic crisis of the 1980s. The inadequacy of African science and technology has been identified as a crucial part of the crisis (CASTAFRICA II 1988:161-65, 175), and the growing gap between developed and underdeveloped countries in the application of computers and information technology has become an index of backwardness (Rada 1985:582-83, 586-87). While in 1977 there were over 200,000 mainframe computers operating in the United States, in Nigeria there were only 115, and by 1980 the number had increased to only 235 (Kling 1980:63; UNIDO 1989:7). Meanwhile, in Kenya and the Ivory

Coast, frequently regarded as two of Africa's most successfully developing societies, there were 127 and 275 registered main-frame installations respectively in 1981 (Jules-Rosette 1987:7). The sense of relative decline has been intensified by the constant hyperbole of advertising by the computer industry itself and by the portentous pronouncements of the 'computer revolution' by Western media and academia (Roszak 1986 Chapter 2; Winner 1989:82-83). For African governments computers have become a focus of their desperate desire to enter the "post-modern" era and catch up with the developed world, both a threat and an opportunity. As the President of the National Commission of Informatics in the Ivory Coast eloquently put it, computers are "the last train of the twentieth century," and he noted:

> The Ivory Coast now has the possibility to enter fully into the informatics era and to recover from its economic crisis. . . . the countries that will remain in a state of 'crisis' will be those that have failed to understand and to integrate the inevitable character of this evolution (quoted in Jules-Rosette 1987:3,23).

The threat posed by computerization is the emergence of a new concept of development based on information technology in which African societies would not only rapidly fall even further behind the advanced capitalist world, but also lose whatever comparative advantage they may have possessed as cheap labor regions for industrial investment (Rada 1985:571-72, 574-76; Kaplinsky 1984:157-62). This has generated a growing perception of a need for Africa to develop capabilities in information technology and "future oriented" high technology (CASTAFRICA II 1988:190, 214-15).

Computers are viewed as an express train bypassing the way stations of older forms of industrialization to arrive directly at the affluent and ecologically responsible 'information society' of the future. For the state, in particular, computers appear to hold the promise of miraculously solving chronic problems of bureaucratic inertia and incapacity and dramatically improving the speed and quality of decision-making (Jules-Rosette 1987:2,12; Rada 1985:578). This would lead to

spectacular advances in the effectiveness of the state's management of the development process as a whole. Computers can
be the essential guide and monitor of development, and all
areas of national development can benefit from the application
of information technology, including "financial planning and
management, agriculture, transport planning, water resource
management, utilities, primary health care management,
banking, geophysical computing and the design and control of
machinery" (Schware and Choudhury 1989:502).

The role of computers as an essential component of
development has been strongly promoted by international
development agencies which have accepted whole-heartedly
the premise that information technology must be applied and
developed in Third World countries if they are not to be left
behind. The UNDP, for example, between 1975 and 1987
"supported some 1,500 projects with IT components," while
the World Bank supported some 260 projects in 63 countries
between 1966 and 1986 with IT components. "The most
noticeable feature of Bank assistance is the growth of spending
on IT since 1981. During the past six years there has been an
average annual growth of nearly 30 percent, a dramatic
increase from the average 15 percent annual increases in the
previous five years" (Schware and Choudhury 1989:503, 506).
UNIDO, meanwhile, has encouraged the use of computers to
solve the problems of structural adjustment policies and has
started a project for the development of microelectronic and
software industries in developing countries (UNIDO 1989:3;
UNIDO 1988). In individual countries, the number of external
aid organizations promoting computerization can be very
large; in Tanzania, for example, no less than 18 have been
involved in computer acquisition, and their expatriate experts
have played a predominant role in local decisions about
"where, when and for what microcomputers are to be introduced" (Grant Lewis 1988b:4, 11-12). Such enthusiasm reflects
the degree to which these agencies identify the major constraint on development as "poor management skills" and see
computers as "tools for developing analytical skills among
Third World managers and therefore improving decision

making" by making it "a more rational process" (Grant Lewis:3-4).

Whether driven by fear or hope, these visions of computers and development show the effects of the uncritical techno-idolatry that has surrounded this technology from the start. The repeated proclamations of the "computer revolution" share a consistently ahistorical viewpoint which decontextualizes the artifact and the knowledge it represents and focusses narrowly on the technical capabilities of hardware and software. From these proclamations are derived optimistic predictions of the richer and more egalitarian "global village" that is supposed to be the automatic and beneficial outcome of the proliferation of computer technology. The power shifts, institutional changes and class relations that would accompany this "revolution" and the social ideals it is supposed to realize are never clearly specified (Winner 1989:84-89; Grant Lewis 1988b:2-3). What is clearly implied, however, and reflected in the responses of African governments and aid agencies, is that those who do not computerize will be left out of the glorious future. Moreover, the expectations of dramatic changes in bureaucratic performance also reflect the power imagery which saturates computer language, conveys a notion of power as the ability to process limitless amounts of information with absolute correctness, and promises "the power to understand, control and always be right" (Roszak 1986:65-70).

When placed within the historical context of socio-economic, cultural and political factors which shaped its origin and its contemporary development and application, however, the computer is anything but revolutionary. Instead, the computer and the associated components of information technology turn out to be an effort to solve problems rooted in existing institutional structures and practices and intended to preserve rather than transform their fundamental characteristics. We can then understand the probable consequences of the increasing use of computers in the bureaucratic apparatus of the African state, particularly with regard to the management of the development process, in two critical areas: changes in the character of the knowledge and concept of development employed in the bureaucracy and changes in its relations with

the wider society. It is to the analysis of these issues that the
rest of this chapter will be devoted.

Why Computers Are Not a Revolutionary Technology

Computers, as Juan Rada points out, are a consequence
rather than a cause of development (1985:572). More specifically, the computer emerged out of the rapidly expanding
need for the collection, processing and analysis of quantitative
data by state and corporate bureaucracies during World War
Two and the two decades which followed. Wartime national
mobilization, the Cold War, the rapid post-1945 expansion of
the welfare state, and the growth of more interventionist state
policies of economic planning and management in 'mixed'
economies all led to the rapid growth of state bureaucracies,
civil and military, and an increasing burden of 'number
crunching' tabulations.[1] At the same time, the extraordinary
needs for organizational planning and coordination also
generated new developments in management 'science' such as
operations research and systems analysis, as well as econo-
metrics and input-output analysis required for the implementation of Keynesian macro-economic policies, that are based
upon sophisticated calculations involving huge quantities of
statistical data. Both simple tabulation and rational calculation
placed such stress on the bureaucratic apparatus that "American managers and technicians agreed that the computer had
come along just in time to avert catastrophic crises"
(Weizenbaum 1984:27; Berman 1989:24-25).

Rather than being the product of an autonomous process
of invention dictated by an objective technological imperative,
the computer is an artifact developed in a specific social
context and marked by its characteristic structure and distribution of power. Computing is not simply an artifact or device,
but a complex network of social relations (Kling 1980:80;
Winner 1989:124-25). In fact, the essential logical structure of
the modern computer—hierarchy, sequence control, and
iteration—directly reflects the structure of bureaucratic organizations. Organizational authorities (hierarchy) establish a
series of rules determining the order in which a series of

operations is to be carried out (sequence control) and how many times each is to be repeated (iteration) until a predetermined objective is achieved. The instrumental rationality which has increasingly dominated the development of capitalist societies has found its fundamental social expression in the intimately inter-connected development of state and corporate bureaucracy. In this sense "the remaking of the world in the image of the computer started long before there were any electronic computers," and information technology has always been the supreme technical instrument of administration (Weizenbaum 1984:ix; Mowshowitz 1976:18).

The crucial step in the development of the computer was movement from number crunching tabulations toward its use as an instrument of organizational management to improve the effective control over and predictability of both internal bureaucratic processes and the achievement of deliberate objectives in the wider society. This made computers a technology of "command and control" which "perform no work themselves; they direct work" (Bolter 1984:8). From the start, computer development has reflected the distribution of power in organizations and been linked to the interests of management, following the needs for and notions of control, coordination, and efficiency defined by the latter, who alone could pay for the technology. In addition, computer development was also closely tied to military applications, especially in the United States, where the command and control model was an imperative; and that model had proven increasingly attractive to civilian government agencies and corporate managers as well (Noble 1985). Empirical analyses of the impact of computers on bureaucracies suggest that they are frequently introduced as instruments of bureaucratic politics to fit the existing political contours of an organization and usually function to sustain and reinforce the position of existing power-holders, especially top-level administrators. Computer use is intended to favor the interests and augment the effective control of the higher authorities in the organization, usually at the expense of the interests and sometimes the jobs of lower level and middle management personnel (Kling 1980:74-75, 91-92; Winner 1989:88; Danziger 1982). For this reason the introduction of computers is frequently resisted and the technology often becomes the focus of internal political conflicts (Kling 1980:74-75, 86; Kling 1985:5, 9).

Thus, whatever the abstract technical capabilities of computers, the social and political circumstances of their introduction into bureaucracies has been distinctly conservative and non-revolutionary. Computers reinforce the legitimation of bureaucratic authority on the basis of expert scientific knowledge and further extend the continuous drive of organizational authorities to replace what they regard as human fallibility with the predictable and unerring behavior of engineered systems by making "the control of people by other people appear to be the control of people by an automatic mechanism" (Noble 1977:315). The immediate context of their introduction has frequently been to avert a crisis of control due to the rapid expansion of the burden of data processing in a bureaucratic agency.[2] The value of computers as instruments of management is that they concentrate control while they also obfuscate the exercise of power by giving it the appearance of expert decisions based on objective facts and disinterested scientific analysis. Domination is obscured and conflicts elided by treating issues as exercises in technical problem solving processed through an impersonal machine. The new disciplines and management specialties generated by computers, such as cognitive science, artificial intelligence, and management information systems, seek increasingly to automate and depoliticize bureaucratic decision-making (Berman 1989:29-37; Berman 1990a). The instrumental rationality that is the fundamental basis of bureaucratic ideology is thus expressed in the use of the computer to replace "subjective" judgement with "objective" calculation.

What Computers Do to the Character of Knowledge in the State

The fundamental *telos* of modern life, according to Langdon Winner, is the efficient management of information to fill "the need of complex human/machine systems threatened with debilitating uncertainties or even breakdown unless continually replenished with up-to-the-minute electronic information about their internal state and operating environments" (Winner 1989:93). The social process of bureaucratization has been grounded in the reduction of experience to numerical abstractions. Rational calculation has been based on the treatment of the natural and social worlds as discrete and observable elements or characteristics which can be counted and measured, calculated and controlled, and whose relations can be expressed in the behavior of formal systems couched in mathematical symbols. Reality has to be representable as numbers (Mowshowitz 1976:34; Weizenbaum 1984:13-14, 25). Quantification and formalization have been the basis for the professionalization and scientific status of diverse disciplines, including those largely practiced within the context of bureaucracies (Whitley 1977; Berman 1989:15-16; Berman 1990a). They have also become key elements in the internal processes of bureaucratic politics. The control over the generation and interpretation of what is accepted as valid knowledge in an organization becomes a principal power resource in the policy-making process. As Lindblom and Cohen point out, "a tacit agreement comes into play according to which victory goes to the superficial 'winner' of the debate. . . . They in effect follow a tacit rule that *declares the better evidence (especially better numbers) carries the day"* (1979:65, emphasis added).

In apparently resolving the crisis of information processing, computers are thus advancing and reinforcing the historical tendencies in bureaucracy to quantify and formalize experience. African states are no strangers to this general pattern of development. During the last decades of the colonial period after World War Two, colonial states came to rely increasingly on statistical data as a consequence of their rapid growth, increasing reliance on Western technical expertise, and expanding involvement in highly interventionist development programs (Berman 1984; Berman 1990b:319-20). Today, improving the quality of the numbers available to African states, as we noted earlier, is seen as a fundamental way of improving their performance. The World Bank, in particular, is eager to help African states automate their data bases and enhance their managerial capabilities (Schware and Choudhury 1989:506).

The use of computers does more, however, than accentuate the preoccupation of bureaucracies with quantitative data. It also shapes the manner in which such data are employed. First, computers tend to "harden" the data, making the information appear precise, accurate and sophisticated—in short, objective and scientific, regardless of its actual quality or accuracy. This is the classic GIGO (Garbage In, Garbage Out) problem: computer calculation and analysis can only be as good as the data fed into it. Not only can the computer not "improve" the quality of the data, but its use in the social context of an organization can actually obscure and compound errors and biases in the information processed. This is a consideration of particular importance in an African context. Anyone who has conducted research on historical or contemporary Africa knows that official statistics cannot be accepted at face value, being subject to gross errors and distortions due both to technical failures in their collection and to their manipulation for political purposes. Such problems are not readily resolved, and to take existing data bases and subject them to computer analysis can turn distortion into fantasy.

Second, the preoccupation with quantitative data and the illusion of scientific accuracy and neutrality provided by a computer buries the sub-structure of ideas, particularly the underlying assumptions and values, which provides the basis for the collection and analysis of statistical "facts." The implicit biases and limitations of computer programs are difficult to uncover and protected from critical scrutiny, as are the assumptions underlying the notions of "appropriate" computer applications (Kling 1980:74; Roszak 1986:106, 118; Grant Lewis 1988b:5). This is a particular problem in Africa where there is virtually no indigenously produced software and the programs employed, whether mass-produced or custom designed, are products of Western, primarily U.S., companies.

The critical problem with computer programs lies in the linear rationality of the algorithms on which they are based and which require data in standard computational form. In the binary logic of computers valid knowledge is equated with what can be programmed, and qualitative forms of knowledge, especially the structural and cultural features of societies which are not readily quantifiable, tend to be ignored. The type of knowledge deployed in the exercise of bureaucratic expertise thus is significantly impoverished. What is left out is treated as if it doesn't really matter. The loss involved is particularly apparent with regard to an increasing inability to deal with the rich diversity and ambiguity of real social experience, and a tendency instead to focus on readily countable, largely individual, characteristics (Weizenbaum 1984:237-38, 279; Roszak 1986:70-75, 120-26). The tendency to reify quantitative data and confuse a model for reality is particularly dangerous in the simulations that increasingly provide the basis for the use of computers as tools for management decisions. This tendency is also a problem in the effort to develop artificial intelligence programs in the form of expert systems, whose use is particularly tempting in African bureaucracies, where highly trained and experienced individuals are in short supply. Such programs automate a rational calculus by reducing the practice of scientific and technical professions to a series of explicit decision rules. In the process, the knowledge is decontextualized and isolated from the ambiguities of the social world. As Tom Athanasiou has pointed out, "Such isolation is the key. If our sloppy little social universe can be rationalized into piles of predictable little 'microworlds', then it would be amenable to knowledge-based computerization" (1985:16).

Finally, the narrowing scope and increasing contextual isolation of the knowledge employed in bureaucratic organizations that are promoted by computerization also have a critical impact on the understanding of the development process. Computer knowledge elevates the importance of technical means over social ends, fractioning the complex process of social development into a series of discrete 'social problems' of 'poverty, ignorance, and disease' which can be solved by the formulaic application of the right expertise. The problem here is the inability of such 'objective expertise' to deal with the selection of the goals or purposes of development, which remain based on non-empirical, metatheoretical ideas and values, including such unavoidable issues as justice and equity or the fate of ancient cultures. This is precisely the kind of 'metaphysics' that bureaucratic expertise seeks to replace and it is "guilty of a 'radical deafness' towards any non-approved questions" (Ferguson 1984:79). These "great issues" of social structure and culture continue to remain central to the development process. They cannot be dealt with by quantification and mathematical formalization. According to Reuben Davis and Philip Hersh:

> The mathematician knows the method; the method demands a criterion to make it work. The mathematician will be forced, willy-nilly, into the role of the criterion maker. . . . He may be singularly unsuited for this role. He tends to be impatient. He tends to be rigid and authoritarian. He is a true-or-false man, a zero-or-one man, a right-or-wrong man, a yes-or-no man, but the world, we know, is more complex than this. It is full of paradoxes and contradictions, unresolved and unresolvable (1986:85).

Computers thus promote a conception of development singularly unsuited for confronting the most difficult, ambiguous and essentially qualitative questions of social change. Rather than eliminating such questions of ends and values, computerization of bureaucracies hides them, first in the unseen and unacknowledged values and biases of the programmers, and second, in the hidden political agendas of the state authorities who use computers to 'scientifically' legitimate a particular course of development. Computerization thus involves a discourse about power, about the control of human behavior, that is concealed in an apparently apolitical machine.

The Impact of Computers on the
Relation Between the State and Society

The colonial foundation of the bureaucratic apparatus of African states was based on a concept of an authoritarian and paternalistic "guardian" bureaucracy ruling a dependent and backward population. The bureaucratic agents of the state, a carefully recruited European elite, exercised an authority over Africans legitimated by their possession of the *episteme*, or true knowledge, of a superior civilization, in contrast with the *doxa*, or mere opinion, of their supposedly primitive subjects (Berman 1990b:104-15). This apparatus was turned over to a largely Western-educated African cadre of elite bureaucrats in the 'Africanization' programs of the decades preceding and following formal independence. Despite substantial variations in administrative capacity and effectiveness, it has remained the enduring core of African states, while the hastily tacked-on institutions of liberal democracy have been destroyed or reduced to insignificance by military coups and one-party regimes.

African states have been and remain notable examples of the bureaucratic authoritarianism that dominates Third World societies. They continue to be based on the fundamental premise of a wide gulf of knowledge and competence between the state apparatus and the surrounding population; bureaucratic expertise must always prevail over popular ignorance. The mass of the population, particularly the peasantry in the countryside, has been conceived of as something to be controlled and shaped by the benevolent power of the state. In such a context, the general premises of "modernization" theory, involving a unilinear transition towards the model of the secular Western nation-state based on a state-managed capitalist economy, have provided since the waning years of colonial rule a model of development substantially compatible with the interests of the "guardian" bureaucracy. The state is

conceived of as an advanced and modern institution, surrounded by a sea of backwardness, whose role is to lead the
populace to prosperous modernity. This has led to a focus on
"top-down" development strategies, strongly endorsed by
national and international development agencies, including the
World Bank (Stamp 1989:28). Development programs in
practice demonstrate a marked preference for the extension of
bureaucratic controls over a population treated as the passive
recipients of state policies whose essential role is to obey its
directives.[3] Moreover, indigenous forms of knowledge—agricultural, medical and technological—tend to be
dismissed as useless ignorance in contrast with the superior
science of bureaucratic experts and academic specialists (Stamp
1989:30; CASTAFRICA II 1988:208). Both the knowledge and
interests of the local populace tend to be treated as irrational
'obstacles to development', which legitimates the use of
coercion to overcome any resistance to state policies.

The introduction of computers in state agencies in such a
socio-political context can only reinforce the authoritarianism
of the bureaucracy and widen the apparent gulf between it
and the people it seeks to control. Computers, whether they
work effectively or not, become a symbolic display of advanced development and efficiency and enhance the bureaucrats' belief in their own expertise. By narrowing the scope of
knowledge to what can be quantified and programmed,
computers further marginalize indigenous forms of knowledge
at the same time as they make it increasingly difficult for the
state to take account of qualitative variations of social structure
and culture. It becomes increasingly difficult for the urban
poor and rural peasantry, women in particular, to articulate
their interests and grievances because they cannot address the
state in the forms of expert discourse it demands. At the same
time, their activities which do not enter the money economy
are rarely included in the standard statistical indices utilized
by state agencies, rendering them unseen as well as unheard
(CASTAFRICA II 1988:192; Stamp 1989:2-3, 26).

Popular participation, the active involvement of people as
agents in their own development, and democracy as a valued
end of the development process are further discredited, while

the trend to technocratic determinism is strengthened. The failures of development programs can be attributed by the state to the ignorance and lack of cooperation of the local populace, a form of "blame the victim" reaction, and active opposition characterized as deliberate subversion. Computerization also, of course, substantially increases the state's capacity for surveillance and control, blurring the line between the state's treatment of the populace as clients or victims (Winner 1989:93-94; Kling 1980:94-96; Burnham 1984). Rather than promoting reform or revitalizing the development process, computer use will reinforce existing patterns of class and gender relations. As Jules-Rosette found in her study of computer use in Kenya, "the key word 'expert' became synonymous with new forms of bureaucratic control and technological domination" (1987:9).

Conclusions

The expectations of the enthusiasts who proclaim the computer "revolution" are largely idle fantasies that contain little understanding of the social and political factors which shape the character and consequences of computers. Rather than being a solution for Africa's contemporary economic crisis or an engine of a recharged development process, computerization in African states is likely to reinforce existing distributions of power and wealth, create reified images of society based upon quantitative data of dubious value and accuracy, and accentuate the authoritarian relationship between the state and an increasingly marginalized populace.

Computers are the product of particular features of the development of Western capitalism and the nation-state, and constitute the most recent expression of a scientific and technocratic ideology that has sought for more than three centuries to replace the traditional "great issues" of society and politics with a definitive and unambiguous rational calculus (Berman 1990a; Davis and Hersh 1986). Computers, however, are no more capable of resolving such issues than the myriad forms of supposedly "objective" expertise which preceded them.   Instead, such issues are obscured, buried in the underlying assumptions and values built into computer programs and used for "problem-solving," simulations and decision making in bureaucratic organizations.

A planned and "rational" process of development is obviously more than a series of technical "problems" to be solved. It is all too easily forgotten that it necessarily involves crucial decisions for society about what people want to be and how they shall live. Development involves a continuous social debate about the relationship between the choice of means in daily life and their relation to transcendent purposes. The disciplines of instrumental rationality and bureaucratic management which embrace computers both obscure the dimensions of the debate and limit its participants by excluding the "unscientific" discourses of non-experts. In so doing they constitute what David Ricci describes as "small conversations" which "take place in many learned disciplines, when members of a scholarly community speak mainly to one another, in language so specialized and full of jargon that it is largely unintelligible to the public or to their colleagues in other university departments across the campus mall" (1984: 299), or, we might add, to their colleagues in another government department. What the development process requires, however, is a "great conversation" which is:

> larger than any small conversations that members of
> particular social groups, such as professions, or learned
> disciplines, are accustomed to conducting among them
> selves. . . a great conversation relies very heavily on
> timeworn and emotional terms, many suffering from
> imprecise character but still carrying enough moral
> authority, by precedent, habit, experience, and spiritual
> commitment, to be capable of moving many people in
> the right direction much of the time. It is thus an
> extraordinarily wide-ranging affair, touching upon
> knowledge both stored up throughout history and newly
> achieved in manifold realms of learning today (Ricci
> 1984:301).

It is precisely such a "great conversation" that is so rare in African societies today and that the introduction of technocratic solutions, including computers, makes increasingly improbable. Rushing to catch the last train of the twentieth century, prodded and hurried by international experts, the travellers are permitted no time to reflect upon and debate their course and destination. A few isolated voices have been raised in Africa questioning the growth of technological dependence and the appropriateness of computerization in cultural and political terms (*Weekly Review* 1976; Mazrui 1977 and 1978); and the governments of Kenya and Tanzania have pursued restrictive policies limiting the proliferation of micro-computers (Jules-Rosette 1987:24, 31; Grant Lewis 1988b:9-11, 15). Nevertheless, it remains the case that African states generally lack policy and capabilities for controlling, regulating, and adapting computers and other forms of imported technology to indigenous conditions (CASTAFRICA II 1988:183). The development of such critical capabilities, both inside and outside of the state apparatus, is vital if a significant "great conversation" is to take place about development. Such a conversation must also include, if the people of Africa are to be active agents rather than the passive objects of social transformation, the voices of peasants who understand that counting by the state involves politics as well as science.

Notes

1. These trends of rapid growth and increasing structural complexity were also present in African colonial states in the two decades after 1945 when the European metropoles turned to more active promotion of economic development, and established in the process the basic structural characteristics of contemporary African states. For further discussion of these developments see Berman 1984 and 1990b:314-22, 402-05.

2. This appears to be the case in Africa as well. The introduction of computers in the Ministry of Agriculture in Kenya, for example, is described as a response to a 'crisis' in fiscal management and reporting occasioned by a shift in rural development strategy (Jules-Rosette 1987:8).

3. A particularly apt case is that of Tanzania, because of the government's ostensible commitment to 'socialist' development based on popular participation. The program of 'Ujamaa' villages was substantially shaped by the desire of the state authorities to extend bureaucratic controls over the rural population. This replicated and extended colonial policies of villagization going back to the 1920s (Coulson 1982:237-62).

Bibliography

Abu-Lughod, Janet. 1984. "Culture, Modes of Production and the Changing Nature of the Arab World," in J. Agnew, J. Mercer, and D. Sopher, eds., *The City in Cultural Context*. Pp. 94-119. London: Allen and Unwin.

Adkins, Roger. 1988. "Organizational Implications of Information Technology in Third World Countries." *Public Administration and Development* 8:373-389.

Akwule, Raymond U. 1990. "African Communications in an Information Age: What Role for a Joint Soviet-U.S. Development Program?" in Anatoly A. Gromyko and C.S. Whitaker, eds., *Agenda for Action. Africa-Soviet-U.S. Cooperation*. Pp. 129-135. Boulder: Lynne Rienner Publishers.

Athanasiou, Tom. 1985. "Artificial Intelligence: Cleverly Disguised Politics," in Tony Solomonides and Les Levidow, eds., *Compulsive Technology: Computers as Culture*. London: Free Association Books.

Bar, Francois, Michael Borrus, Stephen Cohen and John Zysman. 1989. "The Evolution and Growth Potential of Electronics-Based Technologies." *STI Review* 5:7-58.

Bell. Daniel 1973. *The Coming of Post-Industrial Society. A Venture in Social Forecasting*. New York: Basic Books.

_____. 1979. "Thinking Ahead: An Information Revolution Presents New Opportunities and New Problems for Business and Society." *Harvard Business Review* (May-June):20 ff.

Bender, Gerald J. and Craig A. Johnson. "The Modernizing Link: Cooperation in Telecommunications Development in Africa, " in Anatoly A. Gromyko and C.S. Whitaker, eds., *Agenda for Action. Africa-Soviet-U.S. Cooperation*. Pp.137-147. Boulder: Lynne Rienner Publishers.

Bennell, Paul. 1982. "Professionalisation: The Case of Pharmacy in Ghana." *Social Science Medicine* 16:601-607.

Berge, Noel and Marcus Ingle. 1982. "Analysis of Known Microcomputer Applications Being Used on Development Projects Funded by USAID." Washington DC: USAID. Mimeo.

Berman, Bruce. 1984. "Structure and Process in the Bureaucratic States of Colonial Africa." *Development and Change* 15(2):161-202.

_____. 1987. "Artificial Intelligence and the Ideology of Capitalist Reconstruction." Paper presented at the West Coast Marxist Scholars Conference, University of California, Berkeley, November.

_____. 1989. "The Computer Metaphor: Bureaucratizing the Mind." *Science as Culture* 7:7-42.

_____. 1990a. "Perfecting the Machine: Instrumental Rationality and the Bureaucratic Ideologies of the State." *World Futures* 20:141-161.

_____. 1990b. *Control and Crisis in Colonial Kenya: The Dialectic of Domination.* London: James Currey.

_____. 1991. "Artificial Intelligence and the Ideology of Capitalist Reconstruction." *Artificial Intelligence and Society,* forthcoming.

Biermann, Werner. 1986. "Predictions and Transformation: Tanzanian Politics Under IMF Pressure." Paper presented at Tanzania After Nyerere, An International Conference on the Economic, Political and Social Issues Facing Tanzania, Centre for African Studies, School of Oriental and African Studies, London University, June.

Bijker, Wiebe E., Thomas P. Hughes and Trevor Pinch. 1987. *The Social Construction of Technological Systems: New Directions in the Sociology and History of Technology.* Cambridge: MIT Press.

Bolter, J. David. 1984. *Turing's Man: Western Culture in the Computer Age.* Chapel Hill: University of North Carolina Press.

Bolton, Dianne. 1985. *Nationalization: A Road to Socialism? The Case of Tanzania.* London: Zed Books.

Bowers, C.A. 1990. "How Computers Contribute to the Ecological Crisis." *The CPSR Newsletter* 8(3):1ff.

Brodman, Janice Z. 1985. *Microcomputer Adoption in Developing Countries: Old Management Styles and New Information Systems.* College Park, Maryland: International Development Center, University of Maryland.

_____. 1987. "Key Management Factors Determining the Impact of Microcomputers on Decision-Making in the Government of Developing Countries." In Stephen R. Ruth and Charles K. Mann, eds., *Microcomputers in Public Policy: Applications for Developing Countries.* Pp. 95-116. Boulder, Colorado: Westview Press.

Burnham, David. 1984. *The Rise of the Computer State.* New York: Vintage Books.

Calhoun, Craig. 1981. "The Microcomputer Revolution? Technical Possibilities and Social Choices." *Sociological Methods and Research* 9:397-437.

Calhoun, Craig, William Drummond and Dale Whittington. 1987. "Computerized Information Management in a System-Poor Environment: Lessons from the Design and Implementation of a Computer

System for the Sudanese Planning Ministry." *Third World Planning Review* 9(4):347-365.

Cassese, A., ed. 1982. *Parliamentary Foreign Affairs Committees in a National Setting.* New York: Oceana Publications.

CASTAFRICA II. 1988. *Science, Technology and Endogenous Development in Africa.* Paris: UNESCO.

Center for Science and Technology for Development. 1986. *ATAS Bulletin: New Information Technologies and Development.* New York: United Nations.

Committee to Study International Developments in Computer Science and Technology of the National Academy of Sciences. 1988. *Global Trends in Computer Technology and Their Impact on Export Control.* Washington DC: National Academy Press.

Computer Association of Tanzania. 1986. *Constitution.* Photocopied.

Computer Science and Technology Board of the National Academy of Sciences. 1988. *The National Challenge in Computer Science and Technology* Washington DC: National Academy Press.

Contee, Christine E. 1987. *What Americans Think: Views on Development and U.S.-Third World Relations.* Washington DC: Overseas Development Council.

Coulson, Andrew. ed. 1979. *African Socialism in Practice: The Tanzanian Experience.* Nottingham, England: Spokesman Books.

_____.1982. *Tanzania: a Political Economy.* Oxford: Clarendon Press.

Curry Jensen, Sue. 1989. "Gender and the Information Society: A Socially Structured Silence," in Marsha Siefert, George Gerbner, and Janice Fisher, eds. *Journal of Communication Special Issue, The Information Gap* 39(3):196-215.

Cutting Edge Technologies and Microcomputer Applications for Developing Countries. Report of an ad hoc Panel on the Use of Microcomputers for Developing Countries. 1988. Boulder: Westview Press in conjunction with the Board on Science and Technology for International Development of the National Research Council.

Danziger, James. 1985. "Social Science and the Social Impact of Computer Technology." *Social Science Quarterly* 66:3-21.

Davis, Reuben and Philip Hersh. 1986. *Descartes' Dream: The World According to Mathematics.* Boston: Houghton Mifflin.

de Certeau, Michel. 1986. *Heterologies: Discourse on the Other.* Translated by Brian Massumi. Minneapolis: University of Minnesota Press.

Destler, I. M. 1974. *Presidents, Bureaucrats, and Foreign Policy: The Politics of Organizational Reform.* Princeton: Princeton University Press.

Dow, Michael. 1989. "Review of Selected Donor Agency Policies on Computers and Informatics in Third World Countries," in M. Munasinghe, ed., *Computers and Informatics in Third World Countries.* Pp. 8-40. London: Butterworths.

Durkheim, Emile. 1949. *The Division of Labor in Society.* Translated by George Simpson. New York: The Free Press. (Originally published as *De la Division du Travail Social.* Paris: F. Alcan, 1893.)

Eisemon, Thomas Owen. 1982. *The Science Profession in the Third World: Studies from India and Kenya.* New York: Praeger.

Farrar, Curt. 1982. *Statement in "Measures to Address the Impact of Computer Technology on Lesser Developed Countries," Hearings before the Subcommittee on Investigation and Oversight and the Subcommittee on Science, Research and Technology of the Committttee on Science and Technology of the House of Representatives, 97th Congress, Second Session, No 137.* Washington DC: U.S. Government Printing Office.

Fatouros, A. A. 1977. "The World Bank," in *The Impact of International Organizations on Legal and Institutional Change in the Developing Countries.* New York: The International Legal Center.

Federation of Rhodesia and Nyasaland. 1963. *Report on Education, 1963.* Salisbury: Government Printers.

Feld, Werner J. and Robert S. Jordan with Leon Hurwitz. 1988. *International Organizations: A Comparative Approach.* New York: Praeger. Second Edition.

Ferguson, Cathy. 1984. *The Feminist Case Against Bureaucracy.* Philadelphia: Temple University Press.

Flamm, Kenneth. 1987. *Targeting the Computer: Government Support and International Competition.* Washington DC: Brookings Institution.

_____. 1988. *Creating the Computer: Government, Industry and High Technology.* Washington DC: Brookings Institution.

Freidson, Eliot. 1970. *The Profession of Medicine: A Study of the Sociology of Applied Knowledge.* New York: Dodd, Mead, and Co.

Garrett, John and Geoff Wright. 1981. "Micro is Beautiful," in Tom Forester, ed., *The Microelectronics Revolution: The Complete Guide to the New Technology and Its Impact on Society.* Pp. 488-497. Cambridge, Massachusetts: MIT Press.

Gerstl, Joel and Glenn Jacobs, ed. 1976. *Professions For the People: The Politics of Skill.* New York: Schenken Publishing.

Giddens, Anthony. 1984. *The Constitution of Society: Outline of the Theory of Structuration.* Berkeley: University of California Press.

_____. 1985. *The Nation-State and Violence.* Cambridge: Polity Press.

Gouldner, Alvin W. 1976. *The Dialectic of Ideology and Technology*. New York: The Seabury Press.

_____. 1979. *The Future of Intellectuals and the Rise of the New Class*. New York: Seabury Press.

Government of Zimbabwe. 1988. *Annual Report of the Secretary for Primary and Secondary Education*. Harare: Government Printers.

_____. 1990. *Economic Policy Statement: Macro-economic Adjustment and Trade Liberalization*. Harare: Government Printers.

Government of Zimbabwe, Ministry of Education and Culture, Curriculum Development Unit. 1990. *Computers-in-the-Schools Survey*. Mimeo.

Grant Lewis, Suzanne. 1986. "Training for Public Sector Use of Microcomputers in the Third World: The Experience of Tanzania." Paper presented at the Comparative and International Education Society's Western Regional Conference, University of Hawaii, Honolulu, Hawaii, December.

_____. 1988a. "Microcomputers in Tanzania: A Study of Control and Influence in the Adoption Process." Ph.D. dissertation. Stanford, California: Stanford University.

_____. 1988b. "Microcomputers in Tanzania: A Study of Control and Influence in the Technological Adoption Process," Paper presented at the Conference of the Canadian Association of African Studies, Kingston, Ontario, June.

Grant Lewis, Suzanne and Mohammed S. Sheya. 1987. *Survey of Computers in Tanzania—1986*. Dar es Salaam, Tanzania: University of Dar es Salaam.

Greenbaum, Joan M. 1979. *In the Name of Efficiency*. Philadelphia: Temple University Press.

Guess, George M. 1987. *The Politics of United States Foreign Aid*. London: Croom Helm.

Guttman, William L. 1984. *United States Telecommunications Policy in Sub-Saharan Africa: Determinants and Initiatives*. Washington DC: U.S. Agency for International Development, Bureau for Program and Policy Coordination. Office of Policy Development and Program Review. AID Document PN-AAT-812.

Gyarmati K., Gabriel 1974. "The Doctrine of the Professions: Basis of a Power Structure." *International Social Science Journal* 27(4):629-654.

Haas, Earst B., Mary Pat Williams and Don Babai. 1977. *Scientists and World Order; The Uses of Technical Knowledge in International Organizations*. Berkeley: University of California Press.

Habermas, Jürgen. 1975. *The Legitimation Crisis*. Translated by Thomas McCarthy. Boston: Beacon Press.

Hanna, Nagy and Robert Schware. 1990. "Information Technology in World Bank Financed Projects." *Information Technology for Development* 5(3):253-276.

Hawkridge, D.C. n.d. "Programmed learning in Central Africa contexts." University of Rhodesia Faculty of Education, Occasional Paper, No. 7.

Hinzen, Heribert and V. Harry Hundsdörfer. 1979. *The Tanzanian Experience. Education for Liberation and Development.* London: UNESCO and Evans Bros. Ltd.

Hoben, Allan. 1989. "USAID: Organizational and Institutional Issues and Effectiveness," in Robert. J. Berg and David F. Gordon, eds., *Cooperation for International Development: The United States and the Third World in the 1990s.* Boulder: Lynne Rienner Publishers.

Hungwe, Kedmon. 1988. "Equality of Access to Audio Visual Resources in Zimbabwe." In C. Chikombah, E. Johnston, A. Schneller, and J. Schwille eds., *Education in the New Zimbabwe.* Pp. 68-77. Ann Arbor: Michigan State University, African Studies Center and the Office for International Networks in Education and Development (INET).

_____. 1991. "Educational Development and Media in Southern Rhodesia (1930-1970)." Unpublished manuscript.

Hyden, Goren. 1980. *Beyond Ujamaa in Tanzania: Underdevelopment and an Uncaptured Peasantry.* Berkeley: University of California Press.

Informal Task Force on Information Technology for Developing Countries. 1990. "Development in the Information Age: An Evolving Role for the World Bank." Unpublished World Bank paper.

Ingle, Marcus D. 1983. "Evaluating the Appropriateness of Microcomputers for Management Applications in Developing Countries." Paper presented at the American Society for Public Administration National Conference, New York, April.

Ingle, M. and E. Connerly. 1984. "Application of Microcomputers to Portugal's Agricultural Management," in A. Bhalla, D. James and Y. Stevens, eds., *Blending of New and Traditional Technologies: Case Studies.* Pp. 47-65. Dublin: Tycooly International Publishing for the International Labour Office.

Ingle, Marcus D., Noel Berge and Marcia Teisan. 1986. *Microcomputers in Development: A Manager's Guide.* Hartford: Kumarian Press.

Interamerican Development Bank. 1988. "Information Technology: National Policies and Experiences," in *Economic and Social Progress in Latin America.* PP.105-193. Washington DC: Interamerican Development Bank.

Jacobson, Thomas L. 1990. "A North-South Story: a Review of UNESCO and the Media by C. Anthony Giffard." *Journal of Communication* 40(1)159-162.

James, Gregory A. 1982. "The Information Revolution. Microelectronics and Development." *VITA News* (July):3-6.

Janssens, Allen. 1986. "Usage of Microcomputers in Zimbabwe, Tanzania and Somalia." Stockholm: Statistics Sweden International Consulting Office.

Jaycox, Edward V.K. 1989. "Structural Adjustment in Sub-Saharan Africa: The World Bank's Perspective," *Issue* 18(1):36-40.

Jinadu, L. Adele. 1985. *The Social Sciences and Development in Africa: Ethiopia, Mozambique,Tanzania, and Zimbabwe.* Stockholm: SAREC.

Johnson, Terrence. 1973. "Imperialism and the Professions: Notes on the Development of Professional Occupations in Britain's Colonies and the New States." In Paul Halmos, ed., *Professionalization and Social Change.* The Sociological Review Monograph 20.

Johnston, William B. 1991. "Global Workforce 2000: The New World Labor Market". In *Harvard Business Review* 69(2):115-127.

Jules-Rosette, Bennetta. 1984. *The Messages of Tourist Art: An African Semiotic System in Comparative Perspective.* New York: Plenum Publishing Corporation.

_____. 1987. "New Technologies in Kenya: Domination or Development," Paper presented at the Conference of the African Studies Association, Denver.

_____. 1990. *Terminal Signs: Computers and Social Change in Africa.* Berlin: Mouton de Gruyter Publishers.

Kaplinsky, Raphael. 1984. *Automation: the Technology and the Society.* Harlow: Longman.

_____. 1985. "Electronics-based Automation Technologies and the Onset of Systemofacture: Implications for Third World Industrialization." *World Development* 13(3):423-39.

King, John Leslie and Kenneth L. Kraemer. 1985. *The Dynamics of Computing.* New York: Colombia University Press.

Kling, Rob. 1980. "Social Analyses of Computing." *Computing Surveys.* 12(1): 61-105.

_____. 1985. "Computerization as an Ongoing Social and Political Process." Department of Information and Computer Science, University of California, Irvine.

Kling, Rob and Suzanne Iancono. 1988. "The Mobilization of Support for Computerization: The Role of Computerization Movements." *Social Problems* 35(3):226-243.

Kling, Rob and W. Scacchi. 1982a. "The Web of Computing: Computer Technology as Social Organization." *Advances in Computing* 21:1-90.

_____. 1982b. "Recurrent Dilemmas of Computer Use in Complex Organizations." *AFIPS Conference Proceedings* 48:107-115.

Kraft, Philip. 1977. *Programmers and Managers. The Routinization of Computer Programming in the United States.* New York: Springer-Verlag.

Leonard, David K., David M. Cohen and Thomas C. Pinckney. 1983. "Budgeting and Financial Management in Kenya's Agricultural Ministries." *Agricultural Administration* 14:105-120.

Lindblom, Charles E. and David K Cohen. 1979. *Usable Knowledge: Social Science and Social Problem Solving.* New Haven: Yale University Press.

Lofchie, M.F. 1985. "The Roots of Economic Change in Tanzania." *Current History* 84(501):159-163,184.

Lone, Salim. 1989. "Human-Centered Development." *Africa News* December 5:2-5.

Lyotard, Jean François. 1984. *The Postmodern Condition: A Report on Knowledge.* Translated by Geoff Bennington and Brian Massumi. Minneapolis, Minnesota: University of Minnesota Press.

Magambo, William. 1980. "Application of Informatics in Tanzania," in *Final Report, UNESCO Regional Meeting of Computer Centre Directors in Africa, Arusha, Tanzania, 14-18 April 1980.* Pp. 74-75. Paris: UNESCO, Annex IV.

Mahjoub, Azzam, Editor. 1990. *Adjustment or Delinking? The African Experience.* London: Zed Books for United Nations University Press, Tokyo.

Mann, Charles K. 1983. "Improving the Management of Agriculture in the Third World: A Tale of Two Computers." Paper presented at the United Nations International School Computer Fair, New York City, September.

Mazrui, Ali A. 1978. "The African Computer as an International Agent." In Ali A. Mazrui, ed., *Political Values and the Educated Class in Africa.* Pp. 320-342. London: Heinemann.

Mazrui, Ali. 1977. "Development Equals Modernization Minus Dependency: a Computer Equation," in D.R.F. Taylor and R.A. Obudho, eds., *The Computer in Africa: Applications, Problems, and Potential.* Pp. 279-304. New York: Praeger.

McAnany, Emile G. 1983. "From Modernization and Diffusion to Dependency and Beyond: Theory and Practice in Communication for Social Change in the 1980s." Keynote Address presented at the Conference on International Communication and Agriculture in Urbana, Illinois, April.

Metzger, Walter P. 1987. "A Spectre is Haunting American Scholars: The Spectre of Professionism." *Educational Researcher* 16(6):10-19.

Microcomputer Applications in Education and Training for Developing Countries: Proceedings of a Meeting on the Applications of Microcomputers for Developing Countries. 1987. Boulder: Westview Press in conjunction with the Board on Science and Technology for International Development of the National Research Council.

Microcomputers and Their Applications for Developing Countries. Report of an ad hoc Panel on the Use of Microcomputers for Developing Countries. 1986. Boulder: Westview Press in conjunction with the Board on Science and Technology for International Development of the National Research Council.

Millerson, Geoffrey. 1964. *The Qualifying Associations: A Study in Professionalization.* London: Routledge & Kegan Paul.

Mistry, Percy S. 1989. "Financing Development in the 1990's," in Robert. J. Berg and David F. Gordon, eds., *Cooperation for International Development: The United States and the Third World in the 1990s.* Boulder: Lynne Rienner Publishers.

Moris, J. 1977. "The Transferability of Western Management Concepts and Programs: An East African Perspective," in L. Stifel, J. Coleman and J. Black, eds., *Education and Training for Public Sector Management in Developing Countries.* Pp. 73-83. New York: Rockefeller Foundation.

Morrison, W.I. 1985. "Micro-Data Bases and the Preparation of National Accounts in Developing Countries." *Third World Planning Review* 7:119-129.

Morss, E. R. 1984. "Institutional Destruction Resulting from Donor and Project Proliferation in Sub-Saharan African Countries." *World Development* 12:465-470.

Mowshowitz, Abbe. 1976. *The Conquest of Will: Information Processing in Human Affairs.* Reading, Mass.: Addison-Wesley.

Msuya, C.D. 1986. "Address at the Policies and Strategies for Economic Recovery Workshop," Dar es Salaam, February.

Mudimbe, V.Y. 1988. *The Invention of Africa: Gnosis, Philosophy, and the Order of Knowledge.* Bloomington, Indiana: Indiana University Press.

Munasinghe, Mohan. 1989. "Computer and Informatics Policy and Issues for Third World Development," in M. Munasinghe, ed., *Computers and Informatics in Third World Countries.* Pp. 8-40. London: Butterworths.

National Board of Accountants and Auditors. 1984. *Registrar's Eleventh Anniversary Report to the Annual Conference of Accountants and Auditors.* Dar es Salaam: National Board of Accountants and Auditors.

Naumann, J.D. and A.M. Jenkins. 1982. "Prototyping: The New Paradigm for Systems Development." *MIS Quarterly* 6:29-44.

Noble, David. 1977. *America by Design: Science, Technology and the Rise of Corporate Capitalism.* New York: Oxford University Press.

_____. 1985. "Command Performance: A Perspective on Military Enter-
prise and Technological Change," in Merrit Roe Smith, ed., *Military
Enterprise and Technological Change*. Cambridge, Mass.: MIT Press.

Overseas Development Council. 1989. "The IDB Prepares for the 1990's."
Policy Focus 1.

Peabody, Robert L. and Francis E. Rourke. 1965. "Public Bureaucracies," in
James G. March, ed., *Handbook of Organizations*. Pp. 802-837. Chicago:
Rand McNally.

Perrow, Charles. 1986. *Complex Organizations: A Critical Essay*. New York:
Random House. Third Edition.

Pinckney, Thomas C., John M. Cohen and David K. Leonard. 1983.
"Microcomputers and Financial Management in Development Ministries: Experience from Kenya." *Agricultural Administration* 14:151-167.

_____. 1984. "Kenya's Use of Microcomputers to Improve Budgeting and
Financial Management in an Operating Ministry: An Updated Report."
Cambridge, MA: Harvard Institute for International Development.
Development Discussion Paper No. 169.

_____. 1987. "Kenya's Introduction of Microcomputers to Improve
Budgeting and Financial Management in the Ministry of Agriculture."
In Stephen R. Ruth and Charles K. Mann, eds., *Microcomputers in Public
Policy: Applications for Developing Countries*. Pp. 67-93. Boulder Colorado:
Westview Press.

Plantey, Alain. 1981. *The International Civil Service: Law and Management*.
New York: Mason Publishing.

Press Statement. 1990. "Education a Right for Every Zimbabwean—
Kangai." March 21.

Press Statement. 1981. "Primeminister Opens Education Seminar," August
28.

Price Waterhouse Associates. 1986. *1986 Kenya Computer Buyer's Guide*.
Nairobi: Price Waterhouse Associates.

Rada, Juan. 1985. "Information Technology and the Third World," in Tom
Forester, ed., *The Information Technology Revolution*. Cambridge, Mass.:
MIT Press.

Rathgeber, Eva M. 1985. "Cultural Production in Kenyan Medical Education." *Comparative Education Review* 29:299-316.

République de Côte d'Ivoire. 1981. *Plan Informatique, 1981-1985*. Abidjan:
Commission National pour le Traitement de l'Information.

_____. 1986a. *Plan Informatique National, 1986-1990*. Abidjan: Commission
Nationale pour l'Informatique.

_____. 1986b. *Plan Informatique National, 1986-1990: Annexe II*. Abidjan:
Commission Nationale pour l'Informatique.

Ricci, David. 1984. *The Tragedy of Political Science: Politics Scholarship and Democracy.* New Haven: Yale University Press.

Robertson, A.F. 1984. *The People and the State: An Anthropology of Planned Development.* Cambridge: Cambridge University Press.

Robins, Kevin and Frank Webster. (1989). *The Technical Fix: Education, Computers and Industry.* New York: St Martin's Press.

Rondinelli, D. 1983. *Development Projects as Policy Experiments.* London: Methuen.

Roszak, Theodore. 1986. *The Cult of Information: The Folklore of Computers and the True Art of Thinking.* New York: Pantheon.

Ruth, Stephen R. and Charles K. Mann, eds. 1987. *Microcomputers in Public Policy. Applications for Developing Countries.* Boulder: Westview Press for the American Association for the Advancement of Science.

Samoff, Joel. 1990. "'Modernizing' a Socialist Vision: Education in Tanzania," in Martin Carnoy and Joel Samoff, eds., *Education and Social Transition in the Third World.* Pp.209-273. Princeton: Princeton University Press.

Shivji, Issa, ed.1985. *The State and the Working People in Tanzania.* Dakar: CODESRIA.

Schumacher, E.F. 1973. *Small is Beautiful: Economics as if People Mattered.* New York, Harper & Row.

Schware, Robert. 1987. "Public Domain Software for Development." *Microelectronics Monitor* 24(4):61-64.

_____. 1989. *The World Software Industry and Software Engineering. Opportunities and Constraints for Newly Industrialized Economies.* Washington DC: The World Bank. Technical Paper No. 104.

Schware, Robert and Barry Render. 1987. "The Computerization of Burma." *Information Technology for Development* 2(2):157-165.

Schware, Robert and Alice Trembour. 1980. "Rethinking microcomputer technology transfer to Third World countries." *Science and Public Policy* 12(1):15-20.

Schware, Robert and Ziauddin Choudhury. 1989. "The Role of IT in Third World Development," in Tom Forester, ed., *Computers in the Human Context.* Oxford: Basil Blackwell.

Scott, Robert J.P. 1981. *Computers Kenya: Report on I.D.R.C. Sponsored Project.* Nairobi: Institute of Computer Science, University of Nairobi.

Sebeok, Thomas A. 1976. "Semiotics: A Survey of the State of the Art." In Thomas A. Sebeok, ed., *Contributions to the Doctrine of Signs.* Pp. 1-45. Bloomington: Indiana University Press.

Shear, David. 1989. "U.S. Delivery Systems for International Cooperation and Development to the Year 2000," in Robert. J. Berg and David F.

Gordon, eds., *Cooperation for International Development: The United States and the Third World in the 1990s.* Boulder: Lynne Rienner Publishers.

Siefert, Marsha, George Gerbner, and Janice Fisher. 1989. *Journal of Communication Special Issue, The Information Gap* 39(3).

Simai, Mihaly. 1978. "Some Problems of International Secretariats," in Paul Taylor and A.J.R. Groom, eds., *International Organization.* London: Frances Pinter.

Simon, H.A. 1969. *The Sciences of the Artificial.* Cambridge: MIT Press.

Smith, Kenneth Alan and Barton Sensenig. 1986. "Microcomputers in Development Management: Lessons from Research and Experience." College Park: International Development Management Center, University of Maryland.

Smyth, William. 1972. "A Comprehensive Survey of Computer Use in Tanzania and the Urgent Need for A National Computer Training Programme." Dar es Salaam: National Institute for Productivity.

Stamp, Patricia. 1989. *Technology, Gender and Power in Africa.* Ottawa: International Development Research Centre.

Stephenson, Robert L. 1988. *Communication, Development and the Third World: the Global Politics of Information.* New York: Longman.

Stover, John. 1989. "Social, Economic and Political Trends in the Developing World," in Robert. J. Berg and David F. Gordon, eds., *Cooperation for International Development: The United States and the Third World in the 1990s.* Boulder: Lynne Rienner Publishers.

Task Force on Foreign Assistance of the House Foreign Affairs Committee. 1989. *Presentation, February 1, 1989.* Washington D.C. Mimeo.

U.S. Department of State. 1988. *United States Contributions to International Organizations: 37th Annual Report: Report to the Congress for Fiscal Year 1987.* Washington DC: U.S. Department of State.

United Nations. 1985. *Generation: Portrait of the United Nations Development Program 1950-1985.* New York: United Nations.

United Nations Development Programme. 1990. *Human Development Report.* New York: Oxford University Press for UNDP.

_____. 1991. *Human Development Report.* New York: Oxford University Press for UNDP.

United Nations Economic Commission for Africa. 1989. *African Alternative Framework for Structural Adjustment Programs for Socio-Economic Recovery and Transformation.* Addis Ababa: United Nations Economic Commission for Africa.

UNESCO. 1989. *World Communications Report.* Paris: UNESCO.

UNIDO. 1988. *The Software Industry: Developing Countries and the World Market*. Regional and Country Studies Branch. New York: United Nations.

_____. 1989. *Computers for Industrial Management in Africa: The Case of Nigeria*. Regional and Country Studies Branch. New York: United Nations.

Unsicker, Jeff. 1987. "Adult Education, Socialism and International Aid in Tanzania: The Political Economy of Folk Development Colleges." Ph D dissertation, Stanford University.

USAID. 1989. *Development and the National Interest: U.S. Economic Assistance into the 21st Century; A Report by the Administrator*. Washington DC: United States Agency for International Development.

Weekly Review. 1976. "Computers: Benefit or Detriment." Nairobi, June 7, p. 25.

Weizenbaum, Joseph. 1984. *Computer Power and Human Reason: From Judgement to Calculation*. Harmondsworth: Penguin.

Westcott, Clay G. 1985. *Microcomputers for Improved Budgeting By the Kenya Government*. Nairobi: Ministry of Finance and Planning. Unpublished Report.

_____. 1987. "Microcomputers for Improved Government Budgeting: An African Experience." In Stephen R. Ruth and Charles K. Mann, eds., *Microcomputers in Public Policy: Applications for Developing Countries*. Pp. 96-116. Boulder, Colorado: Westview Press.

Wheeler, Joseph C. 1988. *Development Cooperation: 1988 Report, Organization for Economic Cooperation and Development*. Paris: OECD.

Whitley, Richard. 1977. "Changes in the social and intellectual organization of the sciences: professionalization and the arithmetic ideal," in E. Mendelsohn, et al., eds., *The Social Production of Scientific Knowledge*. Dordrecht: Reidel.

Whittington, D., C. Calhoun, and W. Drummond. 1986. "A Microcomputer- Based Management Information System for Development Planning in the Sudan," Report to the U.S. Agency for International Development. Extract available from the Development Studies Program, Department of City and Regional Planning, University of North Carolina.

Whittington, Dale and Craig Calhoun. 1988. "Who Really Wants Donor Coordination? Reflections on the Development of a Microcomputer-Based Development Project Directory in the Sudan." *Development Policy Review* 6(3)295-309.

Winner, Langdon. 1985. *The Whale and the Reactor: The Question of Limits in an Age of Technology*. Chicago: University of Chicago Press.

_____. 1989. "Mythinformation in the High-tech Era," in Tom Forester, ed., *Computers in the Human Context*. Oxford: Basil Blackwell.

Wolgin, Jerome M. 1990. "Fresh Start in Africa: A.I.D. and Structural Adjustment in Africa." Mimeo.

World Bank. 1954. *The International Bank for Reconstruction and Development 1946-1953*. Baltimore: Johns Hopkins Press.

World Bank. 1986. *Financing Education in Developing Countries: An Exploration of Policy Options*. Washington DC: World Bank.

World Bank. 1989a. *Africa's Adjustment and Growth in the 1980s*. Washington DC: World Bank.

World Bank. 1989b. *Assessment of the Social Dimensions of Structural Adjustment in Sub-Saharan Africa*. Washington DC: World Bank RAF/86/037/A/01/42 [3 volumes].

World Bank. 1989c. *Sub-Saharan Africa. From Crisis to Sustainable Growth*. Washington DC: The World Bank.

World Bank. 1989d. *Annual Report*. Washington DC: World Bank.

World Bank. 1991. *World Development Report. The Challenge of Development*. Washington DC: Oxford University Press for the World Bank.

World Bank, Africa Region, Social Dimensions of Adjustment Project Unit. 1990. *Structural Adjustment and Poverty: A Conceptual, Empirical and Policy Framework*. Washington DC: The World Bank [Report No. 8393-AFR].

World Health Organization. 1988. *Informatics and Telematics in Health: Present and Potential Uses*. Geneva: World Health Organization.

Index